KARLA'S WEB

A Cultural Investigation of the
Mahaffy-French Murders

FRANK DAVEY

VIKING

d by the Penguin Group
Books Canada Ltd, 10 Alcorn Avenue, Toronto, Ontario, Canada
2

Books Ltd, 27 Wrights Lane, London W8 5TZ, England
Viking Penguin, a division of Penguin Books USA Inc., 375 Hudson Street,
New York, New York 10014, U.S.A.
Penguin Books Australia Ltd, Ringwood, Victoria, Australia
Penguin Books (NZ) Ltd, 182–190 Wairau Road, Auckland 10, New
Zealand

Penguin Books Ltd, Registered Offices: Harmondsworth, Middlesex,
England

First published 1994

10 9 8 7 6 5 4 3 2 1

Copyright © Frank Davey, 1994

Printed and bound in Canada on acid free paper ⊛

Canadian Cataloguing in Publication Data

Davey, Frank, 1940–
Karla's web: a cultural investigation of the Mahaffy-French Murders

Includes bibliographical references and index.
ISBN 0-670-86153-7

1. Trials (Murder)—Ontario—Social aspects.
2. Murder—Investigation—Ontario—Social aspects.
3. Criminal justice, Administration of—Ontario.
4. Computer bulletin boards—Ontario.   5. Homolka,
Karla.   6. Bernardo, Paul.   I. Title.

HV6535.C32065 1994   364.1'523   C94-932275-X

George Bowering's poem "At War with the U.S." is reprinted with permission.

for Sara

CONTENTS

INTRODUCTION

At least three young women in their early teens dead. A young married couple arrested and charged with their killing. A large area of Canada's Niagara peninsula—a region of family farms and small industrial cities that fronts on Lake Ontario and the U.S. Niagara Frontier—alternately fearful and angry. Why did this particular murder case, in a North American culture in which both murder and sex-crimes are daily events, become not only notorious throughout Canada and much of the United States but also become a flashpoint for arguments about press freedom, legal rights, North American free trade, and the globalization of information?

The cases began, it is unfortunate to have to say, with vicious incidents that were almost too commonplace to be alarming. In a series of similar assaults, at least seventeen women were violently raped in the Toronto suburb of Scarborough throughout 1987–89. There was much local anxiety, and much long-term psychological trauma inflicted on victims. But no one was killed—at least no killings were linked with these rapes—and when it appeared that this particular rapist had ceased activity, and police investigations seemed to have been in vain, stories about the assaults faded from news coverage. Moreover, these were not the only rapes occurring in the city. In the media, rape appeared virtually a routine crime. As in any North American urban centre, each day's newspaper had small stories of women assaulted, of an alleged rapist being caught or convicted, of women being followed, harassed, or threatened. Many urban women carried with them, as just another normal part of their purse contents, a loud whistle or an alarm device to be sounded in the event of an attack. Then a young woman in Burlington, approximately eighty kilometres away, went missing, and her dismembered body was found two weeks later in a yet more distant lake. Again, this event was distressing but unfortunately not entirely uncommon.

In the same general period other young women in the greater southern Ontario area had disappeared. Some had left behind personal effects, some only bloodstains. Bodies of women had been found in freezers, burned in a rural woodlot, buried in the proverbial "shallow grave," or found slain in their own kitchens or bedrooms. The incidence of these crimes, however, was not significantly greater than elsewhere in Canada, and less than a tenth of their incidence in comparable United States cities. Most of the slayings were resolved in some way by investigators, some with more publicity than others, but none with more than fleeting national attention. There was nothing to suggest that any of these crimes were interconnected, and certainly no reason to believe they were connected to either the Scarborough rapes, as they had come to be called, or to the dismembered teenager from Burlington. They were merely part of a general background of ongoing social violence.

The Burlington teenager's killing was not immediately followed by similar killings, even though the Niagara police expressed some concern over possible "copy-cat" crime. Nor was it connected to the Scarborough attacks. Because of the unusual dismemberment, there was media curiosity about it, but no more than there had been about several other unusual murder cases during the period—a social worker killed in a group home by the boyfriend of an inmate, a boyfriend convicted of a young woman's death even though her body had not been found. Not until more than a year later, when a second young woman was abducted and slain in the same general Niagara area, did the police or press take seriously the possibility that the Burlington teenager's death might not be an isolated crime. With the second young woman's abduction and murder, however, and for a variety of reasons, media attention burgeoned. A police task force was established, joining the investigators of the Burlington and Niagara killings with members of eight other police forces. The lengthy investigation became the major Ontario murder story. When arrests were made in the cases, public curiosity and media attention began to spill across the American border into New York State. Each new development or disclosure increased the case's notoriety. When one of those arrested was brought to trial, and a publication ban of details of her speedy conviction was imposed by the trial judge, public attention doubled and redoubled. In Canada, the ban became the focus of lengthy public discussions that seemed to serve as unconscious substitutes for discussions of the case itself. An underground, amateur publicity industry developed around the case in both countries. In the United States major network television programmes and reputable national magazines and newspapers head-lined details of the case that now could not be legally "known" in Canada. In Britain, a Sunday tabloid published garbled, banned-in-Canada gossip about the case and colourful photos, all alongside its regular photos of semi-nude models and starlets. Each international publication brought a renewed sense of crisis to the judicial system in

Ontario, as well as seizures of magazines and newspapers, interruptions of cable television service, and debates about censorship, constitutional rights, and judicial integrity. A recurrently enlarging web of meaning and issues was spinning from the case, and spinning with it, like E.B. White's famous spider, a strange assortment of words: *fairy tale, globalization, Internet, freedom.*

What had happened to cause such unfortunately ordinary crimes to take on such extraordinary interest and meaning? In fact, a great deal had happened, none of which could have been anticipated by either the unlucky victims or the alleged perpetrators. Some of what had happened had been caused by peculiarities in the police investigation, and in the particular way in which relations between investigators and the media evolved. Some had to do with details that emerged about the suspects, and with how these were interpreted in the media. Some had to do with the unusual and highly competitive situation of the media in southern Ontario, both among Toronto newspapers and southern Ontario and New York and Pennsylvania broadcasters. Some had to do with Canada's long history of ambivalence toward the United States, and its difficulty in viewing violent crime as something which Canadian society could produce. Some also had to do with Canada's own changing position within the global market-place—a market-place in which not only traditional commodities but also the new commodity of information were circulating more freely. A large complication here was Canadians' continuing ambivalence about the North American Free Trade Agreement and about the cultural changes that appeared to be accompanying it. "Free trade" eventually became an implicit metaphor in spirited public arguments over what *Maclean's* journalist George Bain came to call the case's "cross-border journalism."

For a brief period in late 1993 the Scarborough assaults and the murders associated with Paul Bernardo and Karla Homolka became for Canadians one of those rare instances in which a single event or cluster of events is abruptly perceived—much like Russia's 1957 launch of the first Sputnik was perceived by Americans—to represent a whole range of issues which had been troubling a nation. The murders especially had operated to bring into sharp focus cultural changes, and grievances about these changes, that had been festering in the Canadian psyche at least since the 1988 federal election. It was not so much who had been murdered, although the youth and perceived promise of the victims undoubtedly took on symbolic value as public reflection on the case spread. It was not so much who may have committed the crimes, although indeed one important development became the growing horror, continually resisted, that these people weren't as much outside of everyday society as most people would have liked to believe. But it was very much a sense that a country had changed, that perhaps the situations of all nations had changed, and that in some small, extremely unpleasant but important ways the accused—Paul Bernardo, a.k.a. Paul Teale, and Karla Homolka—had forced Canadians to confront those changes.

Yet despite the urgency of the numerous issues arising from the case, very little practical action has yet emerged from it. To the contrary, up to six "true crime" books about the case have been rumoured to be in preparation. With many of their authors reported to be interviewing relatives, friends, and even distant acquaintances of the victims and the accused, and three of the authors being journalists who have already sensationalized similar material, the rumoured books seem more likely to exploit and mystify the national changes that the Bernardo–Homolka case has signalled than to offer useful insight into them. This modest book is offered in the hope of untangling rather than complicating the case's still growing legal, media, and cultural web. It is aimed not only at restoring some dignity to the memory of the young women whose deaths began the case, and some perspective to the portrayals of the accused, but also at stimulating Canadian attention to the urgent sovereignty and democracy issues that the judicial and media developments in the case have raised. These issues are indeed urgent. In the context of the threat of rapidly growing global enterprises that can escape nearly any national authority, almost all of Canada's current difficulties—management of the economy, preservation of social programmes, the recurrent Quebec crisis—can be seen as mere symptoms: symptoms of massive worldwide changes which inexorably transform familiar concepts of nationhood and sovereignty even as some of us grow nostalgic for them.

At the local Canadian level, what has been at stake in the Bernardo–Homolka case has been quite simply our nation's ability to interpret and punish, in its own way, the predatory sex-killing of two of its young female citizens. Judicially, this should have been a relatively straightforward process, undertaken with complex evidentiary matters to be resolved, to be sure, and with the law receiving the close social scrutiny that is essential in maintaining the legal systems of democratic states, but undertaken also without the very structure and effectiveness of the law being called into question. The integrity and effectiveness of a legal system is not simply a matter of national pride—although the inability of a legal system to enforce itself can indeed be a symptom of faltering sovereignty. Legal systems are complex constructions, built through centuries of idiosyncratic cultural process. One cannot thoughtlessly make abrupt changes to aspects as basic as limited pre-trial publicity without risking the collapse of the entire system, or risking years of uncertainty and tinkering to various parts of the system to accommodate that final critical change. Moreover, such changes have cultural meaning; they can help determine the kind of society we have and the kind of people our children become. They should be undertaken only by informed democratic choice—not because a neighbouring country is culturally powerful or because technology "requires" them.

Citizens have a direct interest in ensuring that their nation continues to function as a nation-state. They have a particular interest in ensuring that their state can bring accused killers to justice. The young, who ingenuously trust their elders to have built safe communities and safe nations in which they can walk home in the rain from school without fear, test parental limits in relative safety, and linger securely in a church parking lot or their own back yard, have special expectations that the rest of us will not unnecessarily imperil the cultural structures that protect all of us.

Leslie Mahaffy

THE MARTYRDOM
OF VIRGINS

On the 15th of June, 1991, in Burlington, Ontario, a small city halfway around the west end of Lake Ontario between Toronto and Niagara Falls, fourteen-year-old Leslie Mahaffy failed to return home after she had attended the night before, with many of her schoolmates, a spontaneously organized wake for four friends who had been killed in a high-speed car crash. There was nothing in this disappearance to indicate that within two years it would be a part of international news stories, charges of media exploitation, or of debates about Canadian autonomy. Initially, in fact, the Mahaffy story received much less publicity than had the teenage-thrill fatalities which it had followed. The police released a somewhat indistinct photograph of a slight, smiling teenager with braces and long blond hair, and requested the public to report any information about her. Although the police tended to view the disappearance as a runaway—Mahaffy had twice run away from her home two months earlier, for seven days and ten days, and had been refusing to attend school regularly—her parents suggested that the new circumstances were different, that something might have happened to her, and set about having the "Child Find" organization print and distribute posters. The local newspaper's initial response to the disappearance was to keep it on an inside page as a teenage-problem incident, and seems to have been coloured by the deaths of the young people whose wake she had attended. Reporters at *The*

Burlington Spectator repeated police assurances that she had a lengthy history as a runaway, and that there were no indications of foul play. Two weeks later pieces of a woman's body, dismembered and encased in six large chunks of concrete, came to the surface of Lake Gibson, a popular fishing spot some eighty kilometres away, near the Niagara peninsula city of St. Catharines. On July 11th, after these remains had been, with some difficulty, identified as belonging to Mahaffy, the three Toronto newspapers picked up the story, with the tabloid *Sun* presenting a dramatic two-full-page lead story headlined "How Did Leslie Die?"

Violent crime against young women is unfortunately not uncommon anywhere in North America. In the general southern Ontario region of Mahaffy's killing a number of young women had disappeared or been found murdered in the previous five years. While the investigation of her murder soon seemed to reach a dead-end, regional newspapers published speculations about possible links between it and these other deaths and disappearances. Then college student Nina de Villiers was brutally abducted and killed by a Burlington-area man who shot himself when police attempted to arrest him, and this led to further newspaper speculations and reports that police were attempting to match the cement found encasing Mahaffy's body with bags of cement found at the dead killer's home. Many of these news stories seem to have been attempts to meet reader curiosity about local-interest crime. Some also seem to have constituted attempts by journalists to influence police investigations—to spur the police to consider linkages between killings—or even to work alongside the police as crime investigators. Many were also influenced by the fact that in our culture crime stories about young women take on a sexual ambience directly related to both the youth and gender of the victim and to the implicit or explicit sexual nature of the crime. At the very least, each retelling enables the publication of photographs of female faces that can arouse fears or fantasies among readers.

When fifteen-year-old Kristen French was abducted in broad daylight some ten months later, on 16 April 1992, from a St. Catharines church parking lot while walking home from school in her Catholic school uniform, the response of the media was both more immediate and much more dramatic. The public nature of French's kidnapping, in front of at least seven witnesses, the certainty that she was a crime victim, her long record as an excellent student, her close relationship with her parents, and the possibility that she could still be alive, mobilized both the Niagara Regional Police and the local media to embark on a high-profile rescue campaign. Witnesses were sought out and interviewed. Accounts of French losing one shoe in a struggle beside a car, and being subdued in the back seat while the car sped away, were spread by television and newspaper. Her parents made televised appeals to the kidnapper to release their daughter. *The Toronto Star* and *The Toronto Sun* dispatched both reporters and columnists to the scene, and began printing daily news and special-interest stories. The kidnap car was identified by the police as a 1982 cream or beige Chevrolet Camaro or Pontiac Firebird, and photographs of such a car released to the media. After five days, the police announced the formation of a sixteen-officer task force to investigate the abduction. French's friends helped launch a "green ribbon of hope" campaign to raise public awareness about the crime. Overall, the Kristen French kidnapping was as richly visual and closely followed as the Mahaffy disappearance had been mysterious and disregarded. There was a crime-site, a car, a school uniform, numerous reporters, interviews with police officers, green ribbons worn by citizens, and, above all, the victim's own attractive and cheerful face, in a sharply focused photo, broadcast and printed repetitively.

Although the urgency of the case diminished considerably two weeks after the abduction, when French's nude body was discovered by a Burlington roadside, her long dark-brown hair shorn off, the highly visual public presentation of the case continued. Photos of a 1982 model Camaro similar to the suspect vehicle were republished in Toronto and south-western Ontario newspapers, along with maps of the abduction site and maps showing the proximity of the roadside where French's body had been discovered to the sites both of the fiery accident that had killed Mahaffy's friends and of Mahaffy's grave. The task force members were quickly joined by the nine Halton-region officers investigating the Mahaffy killing. In May the task force received provincial funding and adopted "Green Ribbon" as its official name. Drawings of the possible kidnapper or kidnappers were prepared by police artists on the basis of witness accounts, and eventually published without permission by the press even though the police claimed, somewhat mysteriously, that they were too unreliable to be circulated except to police officers. The drawings showed an unshaven, unsmiling, rather brutal male face. The Toronto papers, for which Burlington is part of a large regional market, continued their regular coverage, with the *Sun* offering a $100,000 reward for information leading to arrest and conviction. A police task force unit went from city to city in the area holding highly publicized inspections of Camaro and Firebird cars, and asking citizens to bring their cars for voluntary inspection so that the list of possible vehicles could be rapidly shortened. Each inspected vehicle was given a decal. An FBI investigator invited to construct a psychological profile of the killer reported that there were probably two killers, the dominant one "a manipulator, a cold-blooded killer with no remorse" who "likely works with his hands in a semi-skilled profession, and uses power tools" and "is likely to have a home workshop." The second killer was "a follower who may now regret his involvement and is suffering some kind of guilt" (*The Hamilton Spectator*, 22 July 1992). In an attempt to encourage further public participation in solving the crimes, the task force arranged with a local television station for a ninety-minute French–Mahaffy "special," *The Abduction of Kristen French*. Broadcast to more than one million viewers throughout Toronto and south-western Ontario on 21 July 1992, the show featured the first release of the FBI report, the first announcement that the police believed French to have been taken by two abductors, additional maps, a partial re-enactment of the crime, and an actual example of a rusty, early 1980s, cream-coloured Camaro. Forming a backdrop to interviews and commentary were large blow-ups of the now familiar photos of French and Mahaffy.

All these various visual images gave the French slaying much more media appeal than the Mahaffy case had possessed. Mahaffy's killing had been associated with a fluid world of school drop-outs and runaways, with a late-night wake organized by teenagers in the woods behind a super-market. Newspaper reproductions of her school photo had been blurred and grainy. The site of her abduction had been unknown. Her body had been found in pieces, mixed with cement, and after some days in a lake. In contrast, the French case was almost excessively described and visualized. Reports of suspicious Camaro cars came in from across Ontario. Accounts were published of French's figure skating, her participation on her school's rowing team, her generosity toward her friends, and her enthusiastic participation in her school's events. There were photos of the Lutheran church to which she may have been going to plan a meeting of her youth group, and from the parking lot of which she had been abducted, photos of her rowing with her rowing club, photos of the school at which she'd been a straight-A student, photos of searchers forlornly looking for clues. A television clip showed police officers standing over her body and bending to inspect one arm.

Although numerous news articles on the Green Ribbon investigations emphasized an increasing level of distrust between the Niagara Regional Police and the media, few if any noticed how much like one another the police and media were becoming. From the beginning of the Kristen French abduction case, the police had sought to "media-tize" their investigation—to make the news media a police instrument, using them to publicize selected details, to attempt to communicate with the abductor and potential witnesses, and to advertise their Camaro screening pro-gramme—ultimately converting the investigation into a much-anticipated television special. At the same time, the

14

media were becoming more investigative, second-guessing the police, complaining about police withholding information, and suggesting lines of inquiry the police should follow. In part, this merging of police and media occurred because the general crime site, St. Catharines, was a small city in which the solving of the crime could easily be perceived as a kind of collective duty. Nevertheless, the blurring of police and media roles very early in the case, and the immediate and intrusive presence in St. Catharines of Toronto newspaper and television reporters, imparted entertainment values to it far beyond those usually found in crime, fire, and accident reporting. While high levels of publicity might help the police solve the crimes, they also could sell newspapers and boost television ratings far beyond the reaches of the crime scene. Moreover, the growing conflict between police and press became itself part of the entertainment. With the police releasing insufficient information to give direction to news reports, journalists felt free to seek their own information, to write columns about police–press conflict, to publish speculative stories, and even to attempt to bluff rivals into publishing unverified stories which could later be refuted.

The ninety-minute television special became a matter of particular controversy for the media. The print media felt angry and slighted that television had been given preferential treatment. Both print and television were angry also that the Niagara police had apparently withheld information for a week or more in order to give the television special greater impact. They accused the police of having jeopardized public safety and damaging their own investigation through this withholding. "Public safety hurt by secrecy," announced *Toronto Sun* reporter Alan Cairns (23

July 1992). The *Sun* declared editorially that the police had taken a "deadly gamble" in not alerting the public that it was endangered by a pair of killers, and that they had even been careless with Kristen French's life in not having asked potential witnesses to recall and report "suspicious pairs of individuals." *The Toronto Star* complained that the police had at first denied and then confirmed a *Star* story that French's captors had kept her alive for almost two weeks, and quoted a criminology professor as saying that police withholding of information "jeopardizes public safety" (23 July 1993). *The Hamilton Spectator*, in an article titled "Police, media battle over coverage," approvingly quoted a Canadian Police College expert as saying that "when reporters are alienated by police, it hurts investigations," and a Toronto lawyer as suggesting that the Niagara force had been anti-democratic: "In totalitarian regimes, information is released on a selective basis" (25 July 1992). The next day *The Spectator*'s lead headline was "Police let tip-off slip through cracks." By July 30, a police task force that had a week earlier been enjoying the success of its television show—the show had prompted more than 5,000 phoned-in tips in the first twenty-four hours—was announcing that it had a new public-relations officer.

Exacerbating this police–media relationship was the extraordinarily competitive media situation in southern Ontario. Toronto is one of very few North American cities to have three competing daily newspapers, each with different ownership. While *The Globe and Mail* had responded strategically to this situation by positioning itself as both the Canadian business paper and the national paper of record, and by publishing simultaneous editions in all major Canadian cities, the *Toronto Star* and the *Toronto Sun* had been left competing for the lower- and lower-middle-class Toronto regional news market. Although the *Sun* had focused since its inception in the early 1970s on a readership that preferred short, heavily interpreted news articles on sensational local subjects and an equal proportion of photographs to type, and *The Star* had attempted to retain the appearance of delivering objectively reported local and international news, their potential readerships overlapped considerably in the area of local-interest stories. In response, *The Star* had been steadily increasing its number of colour photographs, introducing a more folksy tone to its columns, and reducing the density of its type. By 1993 it would even begin reducing its page size in order to be easier to hold, to compete with the tabloid format *Sun*. Moreover, outside Toronto both papers competed with local dailies like *The Hamilton Spectator* and *The St. Catharines Standard*.

In television, the southern Ontario market is equally saturated—one of the most heavily serviced in the world. A typical southern Ontario television guide may list more than fifty channels available on cable, including seventeen Canadian, twenty American, and fifteen specialty channels. The competition here is not merely among Canadian networks, or between Canadian and American networks, but also among American border stations for Canadian viewers and Canada-targeted advertising. In the areas of news broadcasting and print news reporting, a major trend had been to make news more entertaining: to transform reporters into news personalities, to increase the proportion of incident news—fires, accidents, and crimes—over political or economic news, or to insert dramatic sounds into news broadcasts. The *Sun* had begun inserting photographs of reporters into their news stories. Crime news dominated its front page, which because of photographs rarely had room for more than three news stories.

A darker aspect of the media's coverage, however, was their repeated slipping past the mere reporting of information, or investigation of purported leads, to the reporting of non-events in emotional terms that seemed designed far more to stir the feelings of readers than to convey information. This tendency was particularly evident in the fiercely competitive *Toronto Star* and *Toronto Sun*. On the day after Kristen French's body was found *The Star* ran these three headlines on a single page: "Victim's family, friends share grief"; "Man haunted by sight of body beside rural road"; "Girl's death stirs feelings of other dad." All three, with their vocabulary of emotional affect, appeared aimed to stir feelings in the readers—to create a sense of empathy with the family and its grief, the man haunted by the body, or the other father moved to recall his loss. Meanwhile, the *Sun* was running headlines like "Ordeal of death?" (2 May 1992); "For Kristen with love..." (4 May 1992); "Tears for Kristen" (5 May 1992); and "She lived 13 days" (6 May 1992). As it had since the third day of her disappearance, the *Sun* continued to personalize its relationship with the French girl, addressing her familiarly as "Kristen," and presenting itself not as a newspaper but as a deeply caring friend, one that sent Kristen its love, and shed tears for her at her funeral.

On May 2 it appallingly emblazoned a story with the 24-point headline "Let us mourn in peace"—the story recounted the French family's plea to the media that they respect the family's "desire to grieve in private." In reporting the plea, the *Sun* also explicitly ignored it, adding ten more column-inches and a nearly half-page colour photograph of Mr. and Mrs. French, boldly titled "Grief," to its invasion of the family's privacy. The plea became merely one more melodramatic invitation for the public to purchase the newspaper and thereby "grieve."

There is, of course, no fixed line between civic duty and entertainment: citizens may follow an election campaign in order to decide who they will support while also being entertained by how the campaign unfolds. They may follow a legal case in order to assure themselves that "justice is done," or that their community is being "protected," while also finding the events of the case surprising or fascinating. In the early months of the French investigation, there was a considerable and reasonable fear in the St. Catharines-Niagara area that the killer or killers could strike again. Despite Mahaffy's troubled past, her death, like that of Kristen French, was now perceived, both by local residents and by the media, not as the result of keeping "bad company," as so many young women's deaths are dismissively perceived, or of family or courtship conflicts, but as the result of a criminal aggression that could strike other local families at any moment. "Mahaffy neighbours living in fear," *The Hamilton Spectator* began an article shortly after her body was discovered, noting that Burlington residents were locking doors and driving their children to school (18 July 1991). "Disappearances alarm north end residents," *The St. Catharines Standard* titled a similar article after French's disappearance (20 April 1992). "Kidnappings spark terror in St. Kitts," *The Toronto Star* proclaimed with visibly

19

added melodrama (23 April 1992). The two young women were both quickly perceived as "good" girls—in Mahaffy's case troubled but good—and thus served psychologically as images of "everyone's girls." Area journalists had thus begun with not only an interested and curious audience but also substantial community support in their efforts to keep the police investigation in public view—particularly because of the strongly felt need to keep other potential young victims vigilant. To a considerable extent, these journalists felt entitled to most of the information they suspected police had, felt obstructed by the police in their attempts to keep a strong story alive, while the police saw them as an investigative tool they could use at their will, yet also as demanding too much police time, as encouraging individual officers to leak information, and as ultimately constituting a danger to the investigation. And indeed the police were continuing to withhold information, including information about the physical evidence that had allowed them to link the French and Mahaffy cases.

This clash between journalists eager both to sustain a story and to help solve two slayings which had horrified a small city, and a police department similarly eager to keep a highly public investigation public, yet also determined to keep details secret which might help authenticate or discredit future sources of information, continued during half a year of unfruitful investigation. It was a clash between two cultures determined to do their very different jobs, and held the seeds of a conflict between "freedom of the press" and "due legal process" that would erupt once arrests were made and court proceedings begun. Because of its public nature, this clash eventually began to involve the people of St. Catharines, some of whom—at least when asked by Toronto journalists—claimed a "right to know" similar to that claimed by the media, and others who, increasingly alienated by the rumours being packaged as "news" by information-starved reporters, began to mistrust both police and the Toronto media and to resent what they saw as the latter's callousness toward the feelings of the victims' families. Little of this mistrust of the police, however, filtered into the city's own newspaper, *The St. Catharines Standard*. It seldom criticized the police investigation, and rarely published a letter critical of it, but instead reported the complaints of the Toronto newspapers without comment.

Ironically, when arrests were eventually made in the killings, they had little to do with either police diligence or media investigation. Moreover, these arrests did not mark the end of the emerging story, but both its mystification and the beginning of a new story. St. Catharines, a city which through historical accident bears the name of the tutelary saint of nuns and virgins, went from being the site of fear of the sexual assault and murder of its girl children to the site of whispered rumours of betrayal, perversion, torture, ██████████████████████████████████ ███████. Three more young, blond-haired, and conventionally attractive faces were added to the news photos of Mahaffy and French. The possible site of the murders—an upscale, Cape-Cod–style bungalow in the St. Catharines suburb of Port Dalhousie—was added to the case's accumulating images. But in terms of available detail the new images remained one-dimensional. The gap between police knowledge and public information widened.

Imagination and suspicion, assisted by the rich tradition of murder story and legend, grew with it, as did the commercial potential of the cases, particularly if a public could be persuaded that the crimes were still mysterious, perhaps even that they were being wilfully made obscure and one-dimensional by powerful bureaucratic interests.

On the face of things, the new events which led to arrests and trial appeared straightforward. A twenty-three-year-old woman went to Niagara police early in January 1993 complaining of having been severely beaten with a flashlight by her husband, and on January 6 he was charged with her assault and released on bail. On the same day that the husband was charged the young woman moved to Brampton, in suburban Toronto, to stay with relatives. Meanwhile, a report based on DNA evidence that had been given voluntarily by a suspect in a series of sexual assaults in the Metropolitan Toronto borough of Scarborough was completing a leisurely twenty-six-month journey to police offices. (Metro Toronto police would later admit that while understaffing at police laboratories and the low priority assigned to the sample had delayed the tests, such a long delay was nevertheless unexplainable.) On the basis of the DNA evidence, Toronto police began surveillance in mid-January of the young woman's husband in St. Catharines, apparently continuing for two weeks before informing the Niagara Regional Police. At that time a computer check by the Niagara force revealed that they had spoken with him about the French slaying in May 1992, after receiving a tip from one of his acquaintances, and reminded them of the recent wife-assault charge. Toronto police began interviewing the young woman in Brampton in the first week of February. On

February 17 the suspect, Paul Bernardo, was arrested by Metro Toronto police on forty-three charges arising from the sexual assaults in Scarborough, and Niagara police announced that they expected to charge him with the murders of French and Mahaffy. Rather than immediately charging him (although both *The Toronto Star* and *The Toronto Sun* reported in their February 19 editions that murder charges had been laid), the Niagara force began preparing the 900-page search warrant that would launch a ten-week forensic examination of the couple's rented Port Dalhousie house. On May 18 the young woman, Karla Homolka Bernardo, a veterinarian's assistant, was charged with manslaughter in the deaths of Mahaffy and French. On May 19, Bernardo, an unemployed accountant who was in the process of legally changing his name to "Paul Teale" (most likely in hope of using Ontario's privacy laws to throw the Toronto police investigation of his DNA sample off his trail—several months later he would decide to return to being called "Bernardo") was charged with their murder.

But the day-to-day reporting of the investigation during this period, by both the police forces and the media, was anything but straightforward. The facts announced by the police often tended more to encourage public speculation than to discourage it. Many of the announcements had fairly obvious implications that the police refused to confirm, and which they could have foreseen would baffle or annoy the press. Continuing to be refused information by the police, journalists covering the case began acting even more than before as crime investigators. Several turned, or purported to turn, to underground or unofficial sources for their information—to so-called friends of the accused, or to people said to be connected with investigating police departments or with defending lawyers—filling news columns with undocumented "facts," off-the-record disclosures, and rumours. Rival Mahaffy–French "experts" Nick Pron of *The Toronto Star* and Scott Burnside and Alan Cairns of *The Toronto Sun* alternately made much of their access to such allegedly knowledgeable but unnameable sources and complained about how police reticence was impairing the public's ability to know.

Overall, gaps and puzzles among the known facts of the murder investigations acted like the gaps and vaguenesses in a child's educational toy: a marvellous stimulus to the imagination. Why had the DNA test results taken so long to return to the Scarborough assault investigators? How had Homolka and the Toronto police come to make contact? Why had the Niagara force announced on the day of Paul Bernardo's arrest on the Scarborough charges that it was charging him in the Mahaffy–French slayings, and announced the day after that, although he had not yet been charged, he would be arraigned within five days on such charges? Why did it then take the force more than three months to lay those charges? What were the implications of the February announcement by the Niagara coroner that he was reopening the investigation into the death of Karla Homolka's fourteen-year-old sister Tammy, purportedly asphyxiated by her own vomit in a drinking accident on Christmas Eve, 1990, and his April announcement that he had exhumed her body? Why was Homolka being charged with manslaughter rather than with murder? Why had she been released on bail? Had the Crown accepted a plea-bargain from her in exchange for information about, or even her testimony against, her husband? What was her degree of involvement in crimes whose victims so closely resembled herself? Was she in any way herself one of Paul Bernardo's victims? In a sense both journalists and members of the public were invited by this fractured web of fascinating detail to participate in an elaborate and real-life game of Clue. Obviously the Niagara police had been confused about how to go about charging Bernardo with the murders. Obviously that force had discovered much less decisive physical evidence in the Bernardo–Homolka house than they had anticipated. Obviously Tammy was another Bernardo–Homolka victim. Obviously the Crown had accepted a plea-bargain from Homolka, and she was obviously damn lucky it had needed to. For the public, part of the pleasure of playing this game was the hope of having one's guesses confirmed by the innuendo and unattributed quotations offered in the media. For some of the media, one of the imperatives was to prolong the game by never letting the public be sure it had guessed right.

And yet, to a great extent the answers to these questions were obvious, and not at all the mysteries which several of the journalists on the cases pretended they were. Tammy Homolka's body would not have been exhumed had there not been suspicion that her death was wrongful; the fact that this exhumation was ordered shortly after Paul Bernardo's arrest on the Scarborough charges, and shortly before he and Karla Homolka were charged in the Mahaffy–French slayings, reasonably implied that it was connected to those events. Homolka's being charged with manslaughter indeed implied a plea bargain. Manslaughter is not a charge "usually laid in accidental deaths," as Nick Pron and John Duncanson of *The Toronto Star* were complaining as late as 7 April 1994, but is an included charge within a murder charge; moreover, it is often a plea allowed both for unpremeditated wrongful killing and for wrongful killings done within mitigating circumstances. The three-month delay between the Niagara police announcement that Bernardo would be charged and the actual laying of charges is similarly not mysterious. In such a high-profile case, it would be important to draft the charges with the utmost precision, so that there could be no error of detail that could give the defence a pretext to call for dismissal. It would also be desirable to include all possible charges in the Mahaffy–French killings in the same indictment, both to avoid having to hold separate trials on these charges and to allow all evidence on each charge to be heard by the same jury. To know what charges could be laid, the authorities would reasonably have to know both what evidence Homolka would agree to give them and what forensic evidence the examination of the Bernardo–Homolka house would provide. When Bernardo finally was charged, the indictment included, in addition to two counts of first-degree murder, charges of kidnapping, forcible confinement, and aggravated assault in the cases of both young women, and a charge of committing an indignity to Mahaffy's body. The delay may also have been caused in part by the need to establish beyond a doubt the precise locations of some of the crimes, particularly the places of the murders. Moreover, as the media themselves reported, there had apparently been poor communication between the Metro Toronto and Niagara police forces: the Metro police had been slow to alert Niagara police about their investigation, and had been unwilling to delay their arrest of Paul Bernardo in order to give Niagara authorities time to draw up a detailed search warrant for the Bernardo house.

However, instead of reassuring the public that there were reasonable assumptions to be made about the unfolding of the case, the main Ontario journalists covering it not only continued to act as if there were mysteries about it but also began hinting that there may have been outrageous "deals" made behind the public's back. Frequently writing about "unanswered questions," and about their own professional difficulties in getting information, they undermined the public's confidence in its own ability to interpret events, and encouraged it to be hostile and skeptical toward the entire police and Crown performance. In the process, they created the illusion that the media were in the same state of mystery and uncertainty as the public—as if media and public were buddies in bad times being cavalierly ignored by an élitist legal system. "Questions need answers: but will an anxious public get them?" the *Sun*'s Cairns and Burnside titled an article, published on the eve of Homolka's trial, in which they listed their own quite answerable "questions" and implied that these were ones which "most reporters and citizens" wanted resolved. "A *Sun* poll across the city [St. Catharines] found an overwhelming number of people in agreement—the questions need answers," the article concluded. This strategy of pretending that the case was even more mysterious than it was, of hinting to both readers and "poll" subjects that there might be some conspiracy of silence that was interfering with a public "right to know," operated in the short term to keep the story alive and controversial, and to keep the public believing that it needed journalists to discuss it. In the longer term it also helped create a "need" for books about the case. While this media strategy of convincing the public that it was badly informed about the case was unfolding, no fewer than three books were being planned by *Toronto Star* and *Toronto Sun* reporters: Christie Blatchford and the Cairns/Burnside team of the *Sun*, and Nick Pron of *The Star*. Not coincidentally, an earlier book by Pron and fellow reporter Kevin Donovan, *Crime Story*, had created a docudrama narrative of the investigation into another dismemberment slaying of a young woman. Writing of themselves in the third person, Pron and Donovan had depicted themselves as outrageously resourceful journalist-investigators who felt—as Pron and others seemed to feel during the Mahaffy–French case—stifled by Canadian law and police practice in their efforts to get the story out to "fascinated" readers. While their self-characterizations in this narrative did not directly compete with the police in investigating the crime, they did seem to see themselves as justified in acting somewhat like TV cops—as justified in invading the privacy of potential witnesses and in out-jockeying unmarked police cars in their pursuit of information.

By the time Karla Homolka came to trial on 28 June 1993, the media had firmly established the now well-known faces of Leslie Mahaffy, Kristen French, Tammy Homolka, Karla Homolka, and Paul Teale as sites of fascination, speculation, mystery, and imagination. The seemingly innocent smiles of the young victims presided over news stories they appeared incapable in their lifetimes of ever conceiving. The *Sun* alone had run at least twenty front pages that featured Kristen French's name or picture in combination with words like "autopsy," "murder," "serial killer," "cops," and "abductor." This strange juxtaposition between junior-high-school photos once meant for relatives and friends and the sensational vocabulary of crime reporters created peculiar spaces behind the photos. The photos were one-dimensional because this space behind was both there and was unseeable. What had the young women experienced between these smiles and the moment of the deaths? What undeclared desires had been crushed? What illusions, hopes, and trusts had been betrayed and shattered? Even the sparsely known details of the crimes they had suffered tended to accentuate the contrast between picture and story, operating to idealize the young women in the pictures, and brutalize the world of crime and law of the accompanying story. Apparently betrayed by young people only half a generation older than themselves, they were now starkly contrasted with images of deal-making lawyers, indignant citizens, and self-righteous reporters. Yet in a sense all three victims were becoming creations of the readers and viewers who gazed day after day at their faces, imagining them not only in terms of the awful fates they had suffered but also in opposition to these fates. The victims were rapidly ceasing to be the actual young women they had been and were becoming as innocent as their attackers had been depraved. Their lives were becoming as saintlike as their killers' lives had been evil. Mr. Justice Francis Kovacs, in sentencing Homolka, described Mahaffy and French as "two young girls who lived beyond reproach."

If there is one thing which has characterized our time, it has been underestimation of and disdain for imagination. In a century that has seen nationalist imaginings twice

plunge us into world war, mutual political fantasies maintain thirty years of "cold war," economic fantasies plunge
us into depressions and recessions, and rival imaginings of
Canada keep our country in a long-term constitutional
deadlock, one would imagine that we might be wary of
imagination's power. Psychoanalysts may theorize that
human beings imagine themselves into being as
"individuals," or that our political ideals are the imaginary
re-casting of actual economic relationships. But most of us
continue resolutely to believe that imagination is for poets
and that our own lives are solid and actual. Few of us
reflect that it is the absence of the actual—of actual
accomplishment or actual information—that most encourages fantasy, or that we deploy our imaginative skills to
give interpretation and meaning even to the most infor-
mation-rich parts of our lives.

Consider, for example, what happened to the image of
Leslie Mahaffy in her brief month of fame in the Hamilton
and Toronto media. The first *Hamilton Spectator* story presented her as the child who had twice run away, who wandered extemporaneously with friends at two in the
morning. The third story led off with the police assurance
that foul play was not suspected, and emphasized the
police characterization of her as someone with "a history
of running away." Immediately after identification of her
body, *The Spectator* ran a factual summary of the case but
accompanied it with a story entitled "'If they ever find the
killer I'll kill him' boyfriend says," in which the boyfriend
is described as last seeing her at "a teenage hangout"
where they got into a fight and she "took off." He is
quoted as saying she was wearing "very explicit" clothing
and that on her last running away he was with her, at a

Burlington motel: "She was just out to have a good time" (11 July 1991). On an inside page, another story, "Police efforts blasted in search for teen girl," attacked the police for seeming "less committed in cases that could involve runaways," and a third, entitled "Leslie's friends live 'runaway' lifestyle," narrated that Leslie and a friend had run away on a third occasion, the previous February, "to escape punishment from their parents after being caught for shoplifting." A story in *The St. Catharines Standard* persisted in this runaway theory, quoting Child Find Ontario's Judy McDonald as having called her killing "a message to runaways...that life out there is not all the fun and glamour that you think it is" (11 July 1991). The weight of these stories was to suggest that Mahaffy had been to some extent responsible for her own death, courting danger, living on the margins of criminality, and making it difficult for parents or police to protect her.

On the same inside page as the *Spectator* story about Mahaffy's "'runaway' lifestyle," however, was a much different imagining of her: "Flower child's dreams won't come to pass," an article which described an "attractive blonde" who "followed the code of Woodstock, a peace movement that found euphoric beginnings in a massive rock concert," who "favoured 60s...hand-picked second-hand clothes" and "daisies" in her hair. Rather than shoplifting, this girl "loved suntanning and shopping, hitting Toronto for a little excitement." Even when running away, "she always let her parents know where she was." This article seemed to constitute a kind a turning point in Mahaffy's image, and a turning also from an adult-world perspective on her as a difficult child to one that was sympathetic, appreciated her energy, and associated her with idealism. The next day's edition offered a brief article headed, "Leslie recalled as 'polite' and 'bright,'" quoting kind words from her high-school and public-school principals. The July 15th edition offered a somewhat longer story about a group of Leslie's friends, from the same teenage "hangout" that she had attended on her last night, constructing a large wooden memorial plaque with a red peace symbol in its centre, and presenting it, with "their last respects," to her family. The article concluded with one of the youths saying that his dad now says "I love you" to him every night, and another denouncing Leslie's death as "a moral outrage."

Presented now from the teenagers' own perspective and through their self-perceived values, it is this latter image of Leslie—showing her as part of a group that may have conflict with its parents but which nevertheless has moral reflections, and values peace and love—that Toronto readers were given in the *Sun*'s first story. "'Shy' teen mourned," was the headline of this page-two article—the first time that "shyness" had been presented as her main attribute. Her boyfriend who had threatened the murderer with death in a *Spectator* article was pictured above but not quoted. "She was a shy, quiet and really nice girl to talk to. She was really popular," eighteen-year-old Eric Drage was quoted as saying. "Leslie was a really popular and typical, pretty teenage girl," Nick Kelly, sixteen, was cited as adding. For the *Sun* this attractive image was part of the larger "horror" image it was building by juxtaposing on page one a full-page colour blow-up of a smiling Mahaffy with the words "Dismembered body found in cement."

Mahaffy's transformation from suspected runaway and shoplifter to Judge Kovacs's girl "who lived beyond reproach" was sharply accelerated by the Kristen French abduction. From almost the very first news stories, television stations juxtaposed photos of French with archive photos of Mahaffy, and newspapers in the Toronto, Hamilton-Burlington, and St. Catharines areas published speculations about links between the two cases. The initial public image of French, however, was almost the reverse of the public image of Mahaffy. Whereas the Burlington police had discounted the significance of her disappearance because of her history as a runaway, the Niagara police announced at once that they were "taking this very seriously because her disappearance is totally out of character" (*The Toronto Star*, 18 April 1992). While Mahaffy had been presented as having experienced difficulty with institutional and adult-organized activities, and as preferring a casual teen world of spontaneous, group-organized events, French was pictured as eagerly participating in volunteer activities at her church, her school, and her skating club. A sense that her allegiances lay more with the adult than the teen world was hinted at in the opening sentence of one of *The Star*'s first sidebars on the case: "To her schoolmates she is affectionately known as 'Browner.'"

The public transformations of Kristen French were less dramatic but equally substantial—partly because her name and face remained in the news for so long. Here are some examples. On the third day of her disappearance, *Star* columnist Rosie DiManno arrives at the French home hoping for an interview, and is, she reports, politely turned away by a man in a "sombre suit." Through the door, DiManno reports, she can see a woman whose "face is raw with anxiety." She nevertheless manages to report that the house is "a modest bungalow," with "lace curtains," and

33

"an enclosed area" in which "an almost white dog trots back and forth.... The dog's name is Sacha and he is waiting for his mistress to return." She goes on to interview several of French's schoolmates and concludes with a direct address to her: "Be well, Kristen. Be safe. Be alive" (20 April 1992). The overall effect of the column has been to make the family of French more familiar. In its modesty and careful touches—the lace curtains, the enclosed yard, the sombre attire, the small and faithful dog—the family here resembles, if not our family, at least some rose-covered-cottage family we have wished was ours. French, repeatedly called by her first name, is well on her way to becoming our child, our daughter.

Around the same time, *Toronto Sun* columnist Christie Blatchford makes a similar journey. She goes to French's high school, Holy Cross Secondary, and speaks with students there. In her resulting column, "The monsters prey on youth," she presents herself as overwhelmed not by what the students say but by what they are: *"Bright, friendly, beautiful*. Good Lord, Holy Cross is filled with students like this; it is not to diminish Kristen's uniqueness to say this...a beautiful girl in a school of beautiful kids. It is their youth, I think, the monsters want" (21 April 1992). She is looking at teenage students, who, like Kristen French, are having to deal with the workloads, conflicting demands of sport, academics, and family, and the uncertainties of future employment that are the lot of most North American teenagers, and she is seeing idealized figures in some macabre version of *Beauty and the Beast*.

With Kristen French's death, a further transformation occurred, possibly facilitated by the Roman Catholic faith in which she had lived and been buried. On 22 July 1992,

The Spectator reported that her mother, "when she is having trouble coping...goes into Kristen's room which has not changed since the day she was abducted, and talks to her daughter. She feels her daughter's presence, as though she sends messages." This theme of Kristen French as having, in her death, become a helper of others was repeated the following February by Christie Blatchford of the *Sun*:

> What a beautiful young woman Kristen French must have been, that even now, in the dust of memory, she is a light in the blackness....
>
> There is a room at a nearby hospital, Hotel Dieu, dedicated to Kristen's memory.
> It's called the Green Room, and it is as serene as Kristen herself.... (18 February 1993)

Two months later, Nick Pron and John Duncanson of *The Star* reported that Kristen French's grave

> remained loaded with gifts and messages of love—including a blue teddy bear, a stuffed yellow duck and bunches of hand-picked wild flowers.
> One tribute stated, "Whenever I need someone, I feel you all around me. Thank you for everything. You have touched my soul. Love, Angela." (26 May 1993)

When a memorial to French, inscribed "in memory to Kristen French and all missing children," was dedicated in

St. Catharines in July, *The Toronto Star* headlined its report "Shrine unveiled as tribute to slain teen." The article quoted her father as having told the crowd "I know that Kristen will be looking down in awe that so much has been done in her memory.... May God watch over you and bless you," he continued, "Kristen's spirit will live with each of us." It concluded by reporting that Inspector K.R. Davidson of the Niagara Regional Police had said that "the memorial will be visited by police officers for decades to come" (18 July 1993). Some seven months later, *Chatelaine* magazine wrote that one of French's friends sometimes "feels Kristen is hovering close by, a benign spirit come to endorse her choice of clothes or the way she's done her hair" (February 1994). In these various remarks Kristen French was becoming a martyr, a holy person who could be prayed to, given offerings, and whose gravesite and "shrine" could become a place of pilgrimage. One understands and identifies with the parents' personal reconciliations with the loss of a clearly loved and remarkable daughter—many of us have comforted ourselves in a time of grief by "talking" to a dead beloved. What is more curious is the general social veneration of Kristen French—the gifts and note at the gravesite and the journalists' willingness to participate in the process.

In a sense we are returned here to a medieval understanding of the abuse of women in which a woman becomes sanctified by the violence a man has done to her body. It is this understanding that gave us most of the early female saints, including St. Catherine. The story of the martyrdom serves as both a sanctioned narrative of violence and as a lesson that the woman's body, an invitation to violence, was of less value than her soul. Rather than causing us to seek solutions to this violence by changing society, her death moves us to imagine assistance from outside society.

Whoever Leslie Mahaffy and Kristen French actually were—to their friends, parents, or to themselves—is, after all the transformations, most likely unknowable. The one special thing about the two young women that the early stories indicated, their earnest engagement in their own very different teen communities, was quickly lost in the various new versions of them manufactured to meet the conflicting needs of the adult world.

The addition of Tammy Homolka, Karla Homolka, and Paul Bernardo to these evolving imaginary narratives, through the arrests of spring 1993, not only filled in missing character roles but drastically complicated and enriched the imagery. Bernardo's addition as a suspect was the easiest to absorb: he was merely to be the "monster" that Blatchford and others had anticipated. "He"—the monster was universally assumed to be male—had been spoken about on numerous occasions since Mahaffy's disappearance. The 15 July 1991 *Sun* had reported that the police were seeking a "scruffy man" in the Mahaffy case. On 18 April 1992, it had quoted the father of another missing teen as saying "It makes you wonder if there is some kind of loony in the neighbourhood." *The Star* had quoted the same man as having said "it makes you wonder just what kind of sick person is out there." "Serial killer feared loose" an April 19 *Sun* article had announced, and reported that one of the "local people" had said "I think we have some kind of crazy person roaming around here." In May, Alan Cairns of the *Sun* had quoted a fellow student of French's as saying "there's some kind of psycho running around out there" (10 May 1992). Media speculation about the abductor's car had focused on whether there were one or two *men* in it. The sketches by police artists had produced an extremely surly looking male face, in need of a shave. The FBI profile, with its suggestion that the murderer would be a remorseless working-class man, and be knowledgeable about tools, had implied a killer who would be muscular, crude, and inarticulate. The fact that the suspect who was arrested and charged turned out to be arguably attractive rather than "scruffy," and of white-collar rather than blue-collar background, enriched the mystery about him even as the earlier mystery of what face could be attached to the crime was resolved. If anything, this figure's monstrousness was accentuated by the fact that he had been able to pretend to be quite civilized; moreover there was mythological resonance in such deceptive monstrousness: the wolf in sheep's clothing, Red Riding Hood's wolf in her grandmother's shawl, or even the legendary Bluebeard who could charm eight wives.

Karla Homolka's addition to the narrative was much more complicated. A character like her—a person who in age and gender resembled the victims, but who in actions had been on the side of the monsters—was totally unexpected. Almost at once, she had replaced Kristen French as the primary focus of media attention in the case; her photos displaced those of French as the most frequently published. The reason for these changes was relatively clear. There were many more unknowns attached to her than there were to even Mahaffy and French for a public to consider, hypothesize, and reconcile. They had been passive victims; she had been an active perpetrator. They had been present for one crime; she had been present for at least two, and quite possibly for three or more. Their families had contributed information about their daughters to the public record, information that gave a small and consistent shell of detail with which to construct a young life and a personality; her family had understandably been much less forthcoming. The media not only took note of the numerous gaps in their understanding of her but also used these gaps to characterize her to their readers. In a sense, what was unknown about her was used to define her. Her public essence became her mystery. "Karla Teale remains mystery woman," *The London Free Press* headlined on 7 July 1993 after her trial, adding "in court she gave no clues as to who she is and how she got there." One of the words most frequently attached to her was "secret." Cairns and Burnside of the *Sun* titled their four-page summary of her trial "Karla's Secrets" (11 July 1993). Almost a year later Nick Pron and John Duncanson of *The Star* were telling readers of "The secret wrangling behind Homolka deal" (7 April 1994).

Tammy Homolka's addition to the story added, at least for the short period preceding and during her sister's trial, a very particular set of unknowns, but again much room for hypothesis and imagination. Details of the newly presumed circumstances of her death did not begin to leak out until the months following the trial. But the more enduring complications of her addition were similar to those surrounding Karla: her presence in the story blurred the classic opposition murder narratives normally offer between killer and victim. She was the beloved sister of one alleged killer (a photo of her is said to decorate Karla

Homolka's prison cell) and the friendly sister-in-law of the other. She belonged to the group of victims, but also to the family called Homolka. To the gender treachery implicit in the charges against Karla, and the sadism implicit in the charges against Paul Bernardo, her death added dimensions of incest, sororicide, family betrayal, and betrayal of friendship.

When, the day before Homolka's brief formal trial was to begin, and after three days of preliminary argument, the trial judge, Mr. Justice Francis Kovacs, announced that he was granting the Crown's request for a wide-ranging publicity ban on the evidence offered at her trial, it was perhaps, from the point of view of public knowledge, the most unfortunate moment in Ontario history for the imposition of such a ban. Two years of limited information, imaginary transformation, and press manipulation had changed two crimes already highly charged with the drama of unjustly snuffed promise and pubescent sexuality into elaborate networks of suspicion, innuendo, whispers, and hypothetically absent information. Mistrust between a taciturn small-city police force uninterested in media relations and the commercially driven big-city media needing to have "news" even in its absence had led to a public perception of the case as an enormous collection of deceits and concealments. The victims' families were perceived as unjustly protecting their privacy and their implicit support for a permanent judicial ban on the publication of the Homolka evidence had clinched that perception. The police had come to be portrayed by the media as being interested as much in keeping the media and public from finding out about even inconsequential information as in solving the crimes. In fact they had come to be portrayed as being better at concealing information than at solving crimes. The police and Crown Attorney's offices had come to be portrayed as places where deals were made "behind the public's back," deals which might not appear to be in the public's interest should they be exposed to public scrutiny. The cases against Bernardo and Homolka had been portrayed as flimsy constructions of makeshift evidence. Homolka was likely to obtain an unjustly light sentence, it was rumoured, because the Crown had been unable to accumulate sufficient evidence against her husband to be able to dispense with her testimony. Again, it was the media that had contributed to much of this uncertainty, and it was media members who stood to profit from it when, after the trials, they were able to publish books that would then use very similar information to tell the public there was no uncertainty.

In a sense, some of the justification for a publication ban arose from the conflicting interests of the media and the police since the Kristen French abduction. The police had believed they needed to keep certain information confidential in order to advance their investigation. The media needed new information, or the appearance of new information, each day so that they could package the story as a commercially successful series. While many of the media, like the CBC or *The St. Catharines Standard*, treated the case like any other news story that their audiences might wish information about, a few journalists seemed to see it as an opportunity for personal accomplishment—a chance to make dramatic moral statements, to proclaim against police inefficiencies, or to take on a public-conscience role in forcefully defending "ordinary people" like the young victims against horrific crime. For the newspapers and journalists most attached to the story, it was a narrative that had the potential to develop and grow like a series of novels, or like episodes of a television soap, with each new instalment made more saleable by the readership built up by the previous ones. Both *The Hamilton Spectator* and *The Toronto Sun* marked the continuity of their French stories with what were in effect logos—the former using French's photograph and the latter the photographs of reporters Cairns and Burnside. Ultimately, provided it could be kept alive, the story could grow into book and movie spinoffs, much like television's *Star Trek* series had evolved into Star Trek paperbacks and movies. In their success in keeping the story alive, and in making its alleged mysteries and unknowns at least as newsworthy as actual information would have been, the media had created a situation in which—had there been no ban—all evidence presented at the Homolka trial would have been presented with fanfare, coloured pictures, front-page spreads, or dedicated broadcasts. That is, they had created desires for clarification, amplification, and melodrama which, given the competition between them, would have been extremely difficult for them to resist satisfying.

Judge Kovacs's order not only banned the publication of trial information in Canada, the only area of his jurisdiction, but also addressed the possibility that journalists in other countries might attempt its publication. In this he was prompted by the fact that much of the Niagara peninsula is served by New York and Pennsylvania television stations, whose signals are distributed in Canada by cable television companies. These U.S. border stations had already carried numerous reports on the Mahaffy and French cases. Relying on section 486(1) of the Criminal Code, which allows a judge "in the interests of public morals, the maintenance of order, or the proper administration of justice to exclude all or any members of the public from the courtroom for all or part of the proceedings," Judge Kovacs excluded the public from the courtroom except for the families of the victims, the accused, Paul Bernardo's counsel, three police officers, and the court's law clerk; he excluded foreign media; he forbade publication of the circumstances of the deaths of any persons referred to in Homolka's trial; he forbade publication of Homolka's plea; and he forbade publication of his own address to the court except for remarks on whether the accused constituted a danger to the public. However, he allowed publication of the indictment, of whether a conviction was registered, and of any sentence imposed.

In the same way the media criticised the police investigation, much of the immediate media response to Justice Kovacs's ban presented itself as the public's response to the ban. Indignant at not being able to report what they had heard in court, reporters went into the streets of St. Catharines, asking people who had been turned away from the courthouse if they were indignant. Not surprisingly, nearly all replied that they were. Much of their indignation had not to do with being unable to hear the details of the young women's suffering and death, but rather with not being enabled to understand what they perceived as Homolka's relatively light sentence. "Residents of victims' towns outraged at 12-year term," declared the headline of *The London Free Press*, a paper that had been among the most restrained in its reporting of the story. A "group of onlookers," it reported, had hurled insults at the judge, and shouted "is that what you mean by justice?" (7 July 1993). This "group," according to Christie Blatchford of the *Sun*, consisted of only seven people.

The other immediate response of the media to the ban was rhetorical. Banned from reporting what details had been introduced at the trial, it turned to describing the effect these details had had on those who heard them. The result was again to indicate the presence of an absence, to sketch the outlines of invisible and in this case unreportable narratives of horror.

> Relatives sobbed, court staff and lawyers wept, reporters cried and killer Karla Homolka choked back sobs.
>
> The day began with 25 minutes of choking details of the deaths of Kristen French, 15, and Leslie Mahaffy, 14.
>
> And followed with heart-rending victim impact statements.... (Scott Burnside and Alan Cairns, *The Toronto Sun*, 7 July 1993)

> The courtroom artists, most of whom are young women, were red-eyed and distraught. They had broken down, several of them, and wept, while Segal had read the facts into the record. Their clever hands had failed them; the sketches they had produced for their employers, newspapers and television stations, were but soft, sad pencil tracks on paper. While they cried, members of

Kristen French's family...had passed them tissues. That these people, who have endured so much, were capable of such tenderness, only made the artists weep more. (Christie Blatchford. *The Toronto Sun*, 7 July 1993)

All three of these writers seemed to be writing at or near the limits of their vocabularies: looking for a variety of ways to say "weep" in a single sentence, Burnside and Cairns exhausted themselves after "sobbed," "wept," and "cried" and had to return to "sob" to conclude it. This worked to their advantage, suggesting to the reader not only that the evidence read to the court was so bizarre and horrific that it made grown lawyers weep but also that the emotions it aroused were greater than the abilities of hardened journalists. What facts could have had such profound effects, the story moved readers to ask? What cruelties and savageries could almost silence world-weary reporters?

The court-ordered publication ban and the journalists' responses to it thus began immediately to amplify the very phenomenon that the judge had tried to prevent by imposing the ban. The small curiosity-stirring absences of information during the initial weeks of the Mahaffy and French cases had become more pronounced as the French case developed and as relationships between investigators and the media soured, and had now become an institutionally formed and judicially pronounced embargo. An absence which reporters had earlier been able to grumble and complain about had now become objectified—had become an entity which could be challenged in court, discussed on the air and in print, and ignored in foreign countries. Given a kind of legal form by the ban, the mysteries of the cases became larger, and gripped an ever-expanding number of imaginations. The ban itself became a focus of contention, mystery, and publicity, adding to the collection of mediatized elements that already existed in bewildering excess.

Moreover, while the media in general, and individual reporters in particular, protested loudly over the ban, it was also for them a wonderful piece of good fortune. Had the ban not been imposed, almost all of the absent evidence with which the public could be tantalized, teased, incensed, or with which it could be encouraged to tantalize, tease, or incense itself, would have become a single intense two- or three-day story. True-crime authors and publishers would have faced a dilemma: books about the murders would either have had to be written and published immediately after the Homolka trial, or delayed until salacious details of Bernardo's trial could be incorporated. With the ban, in a sense, it was not merely business as usual for what writer James Chatto would in a few months term "The Bernardo industry" (*Toronto Life*, May 1994), it was business better-than-ever. People who had previously taken little interest in the case began to take a new interest in its judicial issues. In the media, debate which previously had been among police officers, Ontario-region reporters, lawyers working on the case, and armchair psychologists immediately expanded to include civil-liberties experts, lawyers prominent in the profession, and national-affairs commentators. From its beginning as a southern-Ontario crime story, the case became a national legal story, and had clear potential to grow even larger.

Although there are many murders, and many sex-crimes, that are committed, quickly solved, and fade almost instantaneously from public memory, and others that are never solved and even more quickly forgotten, of all the crimes listed in the Criminal Code, murder and rape remain the ones that most powerfully encourage fantasy. The mystery novel focuses almost exclusively on murder, and the most popular of these almost never lack a young woman's body, living or dead, as a sign of sexuality on their covers. In so-called "high" literature, murder occupies an astonishingly prominent place in the most widely read works, from Shakespeare's *Hamlet*, *Macbeth*, *Othello*, and *King Lear* to Dostoevsky's *Crime and Punishment*, Dreiser's *An American Tragedy*, Eliot's *Murder in the Cathedral*, and Atwood's *Lady Oracle*. Despite polite attempts from century to century to suppress it, even rape and improper seduction have maintained a strong role in the literary imagination: Shakespeare's *The Rape of Lucrece*, Richardson's *Clarissa*, De Sade's *Justine*, Hardy's *Tess of the D'Urbervilles*, Faulkner's *Sanctuary*, Céline's *Journey to the End of the Night*, and Dickey's *Deliverance* being only a few among the more prominent. In popular literature and film, murder, violent death, violent sexual encounters, and very young women have been part of a recipe for commercial success, whether for public "blockbuster" works or for pornographic film and fiction. In both pornography and advertising, another element of the Mahaffy–French killings is prominent: the perceived sexual attractiveness of the bodies of under-age girls. Young women who are pouting supermodels and cover girls at fifteen can become anorexic has-beens by their early twenties. Celebrated teenage gymnasts, like

American Olympian Christy Henrich, can become adults who kill themselves through eating disorders while attempting to preserve a culturally desired early teenage body.

Together, these stories and images have "entertained" by focusing on some of the most taboo possibilities in human experience—by focusing on propensities which, if widely indulged, would end civilization as we understand it. The mere fact that they are taboo, as Freud noted almost a century ago, acknowledges the enormously strong and perverse desires that underlie them. More recent thinkers, such as Julia Kristeva, reflecting on the strange fascination of many of the patients in her psychoanalytic practice with their own abjection and abasement, have suggested that the very fragility of life, with the most youthful human body never more than the rupture of a blood vessel or collapse of a cell wall away from messy and painful death, has made possible the strange construction of agony as beauty, pain as seduction, and the breaking of the beautiful body as a triumph of spirit. At the heart of this fascination is the mystery of how life and consciousness occur, and of their relationship to death and annihilation. The "cesspool" of the corpse violently upsets the one who views it, Kristeva proposes, because it graphically embodies the fragility and randomness of life. It forces one to confront "the border" of one's existence as a living being. The horror of its fluids and its odours of messy decay are what one must repel each day in order to continue living.[1] Closely related to it is the equally mysterious threshold between the inside of the body and its lethal exterior, as when the woman's body opens at childbirth, and identity ruptures, bloodshed becomes life, the inside becomes the outside, the self becomes another, and horror, beauty, sexuality, and "the blunt negation of the sexual" all merge in a moment of extraordinary astonishment.[2]

Should we think such thoughts far-fetched, or at least a rare phenomenon, we need only reflect back to the medieval period when images of Christ's suffering on the cross, or of St. Sebastian pierced by a volley of arrows, or of St. John with blood gushing from his just-severed neck, or of a semi-nude St. Ursula and her virgins about to be martyred by Huns, were held among the highest artistic subjects, and numerous people, from labourers to clergy to the élites, sought through whipping, or through otherwise "mortifying" their bodies, to increase their spiritual worthiness. Kristeva suggests that with the decline of religion much of this fascination with the fragility of youth and the corruptibility of the flesh—with the thin line between being a human being and being a mere sack of rotting and pustulating meat—became secularized, but that it nevertheless continued to haunt, and continued to bring taboos upon itself.

In these taboos, one becomes aware of how similar are the human body, with its easily torn boundaries, surfaces, textures, and limits, and the social body, with its boundaries of mores, codes, and criminal penalties. The "thrill" of rupturing the law, with its attendant risk of rupturing the orderly unfolding of one's life, overlaps with those other enticing risks to the body itself, whether these be the relatively familiar thrills of dangerous driving or unprotected sexual intercourse, or the less frequently practised self-mutilation and murder. The four young Burlington teenagers, the driver newly licensed, who went out that June evening in 1991 for the thrill of driving at the highest possible speed over a hilly section of rural road—"Rollercoaster Road," in the local teen argot—were seeking pleasure both from the breaking of the law and the risk of breaking their bodies. Many of the pleasures of the disaffected young people with whom Leslie Mahaffy associated were similar—finding space outside of social boundaries, refusing to attend school, running away from home, occasionally shoplifting, organizing their own bush-party wake for the four dead teenagers, breaking curfew. These are not unusual pleasures, and we have all in some way been tempted by them. The thrill of such risk-taking gives both downhill skiing and bungee-jumping their allure. *Welcoming Disaster*, the highly respected Canadian poet Jay Macpherson entitled her 1974 selected poems. *Beautiful Losers*, Leonard Cohen entitled his widely popular 1966 novel in which the lead character courts death and welcomes as a spiritual purgation the ravages of syphilis.

What these things signal about sensational media-driven cases like the French-Mahaffy murders is their enormous power to engage the public imagination through the horrific transgressions they enact. That power is arguably as extensive as the network of taboos and codes society puts in place to curb actions like abduction, imprisonment, ███████████████████████████████ ███████████████████████████████ ████████████████ dismemberment of corpses. Abasing their own sexualities as they ███████████████ the bodies of their victims, the killers of Mahaffy and French had released and played with some of the most magical and repressed of human secrets. They had ██████████████

sexual beauty and pleasure; they had slowly and consciously broken the boundaries between the body and its
outside; they had watched life seep toward its own abyss.
They had gone farther toward darkness and death than
almost all of us care or dare to go.

Much of the fascination we, as readers, have had with
the cases and their reporting has been arguably vicarious.
Cloaked in the protection of self-righteous indignation, of
genuinely felt revulsion—we indeed would never have
contemplated committing such acts—we read and gain
unconscious access to our own remote and secret savageries and fears. And how distant are these from us: how
much should we marvel at the abrupt transformations
that have taken ordinary citizens in Bosnia, Krajiina, and
Vukovar from "good neighbour" to "ethnic cleanser,"
"strategic rapist," and "mass-murderer"? How astonished
should we be at how rapidly human corpses have been
created and amassed in Rwanda? How astonished by the
markets for at least a million child prostitutes, most of
them sold by their parents or kidnapped, many of them
even younger than Mahaffy or French, that Japanese and
Western men have helped establish in south-east Asia? Or
how astonished by crowds of white Canadians who
stoned the cavalcade bringing the sick and elderly from
the Akwesasne reserve during the Oka crisis? Perhaps we
are right to be proud of the fragile power of our taboos.

Near the beginning of *Charlotte's Web*, E.B. White took
pains to point out that under the bold, bloodthirsty, and
cruel exterior of his insect-eating spider there lay a kind
heart, and that Charlotte would prove "loyal and true" to
her friends to the very end of her story. White's focus here

51

on the deceptiveness of appearances was superficially very similar to that of journalists fascinated by Karla Homolka's physical beauty and the horrible and ██████ things she had been accused and convicted of doing. Good things or bad things, White suggested—although the journalists seem not to have been listening—bear little or no relation to human or even pig standards of beauty. A web can bring death to insects or save from death a farm animal. Acts of kindness or cruelty can reach from a barnyard to influence human households, touch audiences at a country fair, and can have unexpected consequences for future generations. Moreover, a homely spider's sense of kindness can throw the routine cruelties of human culture into a sharp new perspective.

The web of deception, cruelty, painful implication, and controversy that began emerging in early 1993 around the placid public face of Karla Homolka—an apparent antithesis of *Charlotte's Web*—was only to a small extent of her own spinning. Much of its cruelty was its culture's cruelty, and was manifested as surely in the journalistic fascination with the Mahaffy–French murders as in the crimes themselves. The initial elements of the Leslie Mahaffy case—the kidnapping of an attractive early teenage woman, her evident sexual assault and murder, and the clearly evident dismemberment of a body that could, given the latent pedophilia of our culture, stand symbolically for the sexually attractive woman—were elements of wide and secret public fascination. To become larger than a one-week story, these elements required a narrative—the narrative of an investigation or that of further crime. The Kristen French case brought both and more. It brought a crime that appeared even more transgressive: the lively young A-student was brought from even higher to even lower—a longer period of imprisonment, █████████████ ███████ and rumours of ██████████████████████. As if caught in their own unconscious fascination with the deaths, the reporters retrieved and emphasized precisely these details of rupture and transgression: the young lives of hope and promise reduced to broken corpses in a lake or ditch; a dutiful, law-abiding daughter forced to do

██

███████. The very unspeakability was enhanced by the gaps in the actual information available for reporting, so that the reader had to imaginatively participate in the crimes in order to give them any coherence or shape. Many of the media stories became, wittingly or unwittingly, invitations to do just that. Over and over in the media coverage and the viewers' imaginations the teenagers were murdered and remurdered. With the ban, and with the tantalizing stories of how the strong and grizzled were reduced to uncontrollable sobs by the evidence against Homolka, this invitation to imagine became virtually irresistible.

Some months after the Homolka trial I was browsing in an uptown Toronto men's clothing store, when a woman friend of the salesclerk dropped in to visit. "What do you think of this Homolka stuff?" was among her first questions. For the other woman the question came almost as a relief, as if she had been overfull of information. "Do you know what I heard that guy did to the French girl?" she responded at once. "He cut off her kneecaps—he just cut them off and left her there bleeding while going on with what he wanted to do to her. Can you imagine?" The woman evidently had done precisely that—she had

53

imagined. I found the conversation fascinating at the very least in its demographics. These were not people who were likely to belong to computer networks, or to be engaged in smuggling foreign newspaper articles into the country for redistribution. But they were clearly just as involved in creating and imagining a Mahaffy–French murder story as were any of the people who were by that point becoming famous for their attempts to defy the court ban. In a sense, this kind of defiance of the ban was impossible to resist. Countless other relatively law-abiding Canadians had by now sat together and mulled over the various public pieces of the Mahaffy–French puzzle, speculated about motive, personality, and other missing elements. Countless had been persuaded by the media, and by the publication ban, that there were important missing elements, that there were extraordinary things that they had not been allowed to know, and went about trying to figure out what these might be.

One of the odd things to happen when popular stories are invented—one can see this in the medieval folk tale as well as in today's popular fiction—is that the inventors tend to follow, consciously or unconsciously, a fairly narrow set of rules for telling a story. The more minimal the amount of actual detail in the story, the more the storyteller is likely to follow what he or she has learned are narrative rules or conventions. These rules tend to differ from one kind of narrative to another, so that there are certain narrative rules for a detective story, others for a science fiction story, others for a Harlequin romance, others for a story of personal success, others for a ghost story, and so on.

Apart from the few newspapers and television stations

that resisted interpreting or dramatizing the facts of the story, almost all narrators of the Mahaffy–French story told it as a Gothic story. It's fairly easy to see why. The Gothic story emerged in late eighteenth-century England as a result of at least three phenomena: a new interest in the castles, dungeons, churches, and crypts of the medieval period; an increase in the number of women novelists; and an increase in the number of educated middle-class women working as teachers, nurses, or governesses in upper-class homes. Popularized in the writing of Ann Radcliffe, Hugh Walpole, and Mary Shelley— whose *Frankenstein* is the best known of these stories today—the Gothic developed these virtually necessary elements: a stark contrast between an exaggeratedly innocent and virtuous heroine and an exaggeratedly evil and sinister villain; an attempt to abduct the heroine (who had often encountered the villain through her having accepted a position as teacher or governess) to a place of darkness and evil—the forgotten dungeons of a manor house, or the lost burial crypts of ecclesiastic buildings. The threat to the woman was explicitly sexual—to rape her and coerce her to intercourse and thus render her as ruined for marriage as the dungeons around her were ruined for habitation. The assaults took place in torchlight, among half-opened graves, or among the rusting instruments of war and torture. For a reader, the fear that drove the story was that the beautiful heroine might somehow be irretrievably damaged or broken—that the rupture between her perfect body and the horrors of the abyss might be opened—before she could be rescued. The villain here was often explicitly associated with the demonic—with satanism, sorcery, and, through the image

55

of the dungeon, with the underworld. Early twentieth-century variations on the Gothic have included numerous silent films in which the "virtue" of the tenant's daughter was lusted after by the evil landlord or mortgagee, who would tie her to railroad tracks to attempt to achieve his nasty way; in more recent times we have had books and films like *The Exorcist*, *Rosemary's Baby*, and *The Silence of the Lambs*. The genre's use in Harlequin romances was devastatingly parodied by Margaret Atwood in *Lady Oracle*.

The villain in the Mahaffy–French kidnappings was demonized in much of the media from the early reports of both killings. He was the "scruffy man" rumoured to have been seeking Mahaffy. To a priest at the St. Catharines School Board "there was no shame, there was no love, there was no goodness in the person who did it [killed French]. There was only evil" (quoted *The Hamilton Spectator*, 1 May 1992). To Christie Blatchford, writing only hours after arriving in St. Catharines, he was not human at all but a "monster" who preys on youth. All of these representations of the abductor operate, as they do in the Gothic, to make him decisively not one of us. He has nothing to do with the people we associate with everyday but exists, rather, outside human norms: he is "crazy," "loony," or outside of God's creation itself, "evil," a "monster." This perception even seems to have impaired the police investigation: the drawings they made up imagined a scowling, unshaven man who broke with social norms both by scowling and by neither shaving nor growing a beard. The witnesses and the police may also have been imagining a villain of a much different class than the two young women. The car described by witnesses as resembling an early 1980s Camaro with "no chrome on the bumper" is a vehicle most popular with working-class drivers; the car found to be driven by the eventual suspect, Paul Bernardo, a Nissan 240SX sports coupe, is more popular with young professionals. Both cars are consistent with the eyewitness descriptions.

Similarly, both young women were idealized, with not much difficulty in French's case, into being versions of the Gothic maiden in distress. Mahaffy was changed from the rebellious teen into a "flower child" and finally into a young woman "beyond reproach." The difficulties she and her parents had experienced immediately before her disappearance were written out of newspaper accounts within a few months, never to appear again. When arrests were made, this polarization between good and evil was expanded by the addition of Karla Homolka, who in some accounts would fill the role of the evil "dark woman" who in Gothic plots frequently works to deceive and betray the heroine and to punish her for having intruded upon her own relationship with the villain. In the rumours which began to circulate in various ways after Homolka's trial, the house where the girls had allegedly been kept imprisoned became a house of horrors equipped with sheltered entrances remote from neighbours, and secret, soundproof rooms. ██████████████████████████ ████████████████████████████████, and a power saw to cut up Mahaffy's body. Even early in the case, one edition of *The Toronto Sun* had reported the body had been cut up with a chain saw. A detective in the Mahaffy case had added to the horror by reporting that they were "trying to piece as much of the puzzle together as we can" (*The Hamilton Spectator*, 13 July

1991). Another insensitively had informed the *Sun* that "[t]here was no surgical precision. It certainly wasn't an expert who did it" (12 July 1991).

This recasting of the case into a mythological narrative of the assault on young virgins by inhuman monsters, with overtones of Satan's temptation of Eve and of the sadistic torture by Roman emperors of early Christian female saints, had both the individually satisfying and socially unfortunate effect of distancing the crime: of making it unusual, aberrant, freakish, with little connection to the everyday lives citizens lead. This was not a crime likely to reoccur, this narrative suggested, unless new "monsters" should somehow be spawned. Lost in the account was the fact that our society had produced all the participants in these events, including the suspected killers. It had also produced the ways of being "evil" available to the killers. While neither suspect's family could be considered a "normal" family, neither—even the conflict-ridden Bernardo family—was all that exceptional. Mr. Justice Kovacs had deemed that with treatment and a prison sentence Karla Homolka might never "commit a crime again." While it is true that one of the motifs of Gothic fiction is that the villain and villainess "look" excessively and deceptively attractive, charming, and trustworthy—in fact their attractiveness can be as excessive as their evil—what viewing them in this Gothic way deprives us of is the humanity of the accuseds' lives. It deprives us of realizations that to a great extent what they valued and desired in their lives was what we have also desired—romantic weddings, a cottage in the suburbs, wealth, repeated sexual excitement—and that some elements in their crimes are but exaggerated forms of our own desires. As in the attempts, after the Montreal massacre, to portray mass murderer Marc Lépine as a monster rather than as one more man who detested women, attempts to portray the murderers of Mahaffy and French as monsters cause us to miss the extraordinary misogyny and female self-hatred that can be observed in the killers.

It is no accident that it was young women who were ███ ██████ killed. The terrible angers that were inflicted on their bodies were inflicted on gendered bodies, ███ ██ ██████████████████. These sites included not only their sexual organs, but Kristen French's long dark chestnut hair ████████████, and the slender arms and legs of Leslie Mahaffy. These are not angers that are restricted to monsters, but show up again and again in our society, sometimes merely in male business practice, sometimes in wife-battering, sometimes in rape and murder. In women, female self-hatred much more often manifests itself in depression, anorexia and bulimia, self-mutilation, or suicide than it does in the assisting in the torture, rape, and killing of other women. But anger and self-hatred are also consequences of misogyny in our culture. Because they have resulted in murder is hardly reason to dismiss them as monstrous. One appalling implication of these crimes that almost no one wishes to confront, even when they see photos of Dorothy and Karel Homolka loyally escorting their daughter to court, is that Karla Homolka could also have been one of our daughters.

Inspector Vince Bevan of the Niagara Regional Police, head of the Mahaffy-French investigation, pictured before an image of Kristen French during the CHCH-TV "Kristen French" telecast.

MUZZLED, SHACKLED, AND GAGGED

JUDGE BOOED. COPS COVER KOVACS AS CROWD GETS UGLY (Headline, *The Toronto Sun*, 7 July 1993)

"Muzzled," "shackled," and "gagged" are words more likely to be associated with victims of crime than with news media whose actions have been restricted by a court order. Yet these were among the most prominent words the media used to describe themselves once the Karla Homolka trial judge, Mr. Justice Francis Kovacs, ordered his publication ban. In employing these words, the media were abruptly changing the structure of the story. Leslie Mahaffy and Kristen French were now to have minor roles, and even Paul Bernardo and Karla Homolka less dominant ones. In the place of the ███████ bodies of the two young women the media were now casting themselves as victims, abused, placed in bondage, rights violated by a misguided or overzealous judge. The judge, politely criticized by some of the media, implicitly termed "contemptible" by others, became cast as the new villain, displacing discussion of Homolka, Bernardo, and their alleged roles in the abductions, sexual assaults, and slayings. When the enigmatic face of Karla Homolka accompanied this new tale of assault and imprisonment, it appeared to be less that of a murderer than that of a bystander mystified by the things that could so excite the new antagonists.

61

In addition, a second victim was invited to imagine its way into the new scene of violence. The public, after months of being encouraged to identify with the victims and their families, and to shed dramatic, bittersweet tears alongside the very real ones of the victims' parents and schoolmates, was now asked to see itself as a victim of an ominous, tight-knit, judicial élite that had carelessly butchered both the public's "right" to see justice done and the media's right to free expression. Even the ubiquitously grinning Paul Bernardo was offered a small place in this new category of victim, as the media's lawyers protested that his rights to instruct counsel had been brutally and unconstitutionally infringed.

Large amounts of angry self-righteousness were thus expended over the "temporary" publication ban ordered by Mr. Justice Kovacs—a ban ostensibly intended not to threaten the media at all but rather to protect Paul Bernardo's rights to a jury trial uncontaminated by other judicial proceedings—and to guard against a mistrial. Much attention was given to how the ban could be considered to insult both media and public, and much attention also to the irony that the lawyer who represented Bernardo at Karla Homolka's "trial" did not wish such a ban, while the Crown counsel and the lawyer representing Homolka did. Much less attention was given to who was most vigorously opposing the ban, to the variety of people opposing it, to why they might be opposing it, and to the kinds of arguments marshalled against it.

Basic freedoms at core of fiery debate (Headline, *The London Free Press*, 3 December 1993)

Publication bans themselves are not uncommon in Canadian justice, and have caused little controversy when used to conceal the identities of sexual assault victims. The week of Paul Bernardo's arrest, his father, Kenneth Bernardo, was convicted of sexual offences committed some twenty years previously, with the details of the offences banned from publication to protect the privacy of the victims. There were no protests against this ban. During media appeals of the Homolka ban, closed-door inquiries were held by the Canadian military into the killing of Somali civilians by Canadian peacekeepers in Africa. Again, there were no media protests.

In general, Canadian society in the last two decades has been moving toward policies that provide both a greater openness of public information and greater individual privacy. Some early indications of this concern with such "rights" occurred with the establishment of ombudsman offices in some provinces in the 1960s and 1970s. The enacting of federal privacy legislation in 1977, giving individuals access to most government files that contained information about themselves, was followed in 1982 by the Access to Information Act, which strengthened access to an individual's own files and opened vast amounts of public policy information to applications for access. In recent years legislation such as the revised rape-shield law, which limits the kinds of information which a defence lawyer can seek in cross-examining a sexual assault victim, and the law requiring that lobbyists register and declare the interests they represent, have moved in the directions both of greater individual privacy and more open government.

The arguments around both sorts of legislation have been almost as heated and at least as complex as those that greeted the Homolka publication ban. The rape-shield law was vigorously opposed in some quarters by those who argued that it infringed on the rights of the accused to mount a full defence against the charges he faced. Its supporters held that it justly prevented the defence from setting out on fishing expeditions for irrelevant details of the complainant's sexual history—fishing expeditions that might embarrass the complainant into withdrawing her testimony, or damage her credibility as a witness. Even the possibility of having to face such questioning, the supporters suggested, infringed on a victim's access to justice by discouraging her from laying charges. The first version of the law was struck down by the Supreme Court on the grounds that in addition to preventing wide-ranging questions it also prevented questioning pertinent to the mounting of a full and legitimate defence. Access-to-information legislation was opposed for many years by governments that argued that they needed the assurance of confidentiality in order to be able to govern effectively. Even the legislation that was eventually passed contains large exemptions for both national security information and cabinet documents. Supporters of access-to-information laws have argued that citizens need as much information as possible about government policies and practices in order to be able to evaluate their political leaders and to make appropriate decisions at the ballot box. They have also argued that access to information is a matter of power—that governments should not hold a monopoly on information which gives them more power over their own lives than have the citizens who elect them, that it is unhealthy and discriminatory in a democracy for one privileged group of citizens to "know" more than others.

Concern over democratic "rights" to information was also stimulated by the passing of the 1982 Constitution Act with its Charter of Rights and Freedoms, and by the 1984 Supreme Court ruling which confirms the Charter's place as part of "the supreme law of Canada." The notion that the Charter exists to protect individuals against the excessive power of the state unexpectedly encouraged a general sense of conflict between individual and group rights and the legislative, executive, and judicial branches of governments. The Charter offered opportunities for citizens to challenge legislation (as in the Quebec Bill 101 case), cabinet policy (as in the cruise missile case), and judicial decisions (as in the Scientology case, where a libel defendant unsuccessfully argued that Canadian libel laws violated Charter guarantees of freedom of speech). In some parts of Canada in the early 1990s, particularly in Western Canada and rural Ontario, feelings of profound suspicion toward government and politicians, and of alienation from their decisions, developed out of a ground of longer-standing grievances. In the October 1993 federal election, the Reform Party, which spoke to many of these feelings of alienation and often appeared to be campaigning against politics itself, earned in ninety-nine Ontario ridings one seat and fifty-eight second-place finishes.

It was within this general climate of heightened concern for individual and public "rights," stimulated by a decade of public challenges under the Charter of Rights, of legislation that opened government records and procedures to public scrutiny, and of public calls for more such legislation—for more information about the activities of lobbyists, about the arrangements made by the Conservative government led by Brian Mulroney to privatize Toronto's

Pearson Airport, about alleged government plans to change social assistance programmes (all matters which became issues in the 1993 federal election campaign)— that Mr. Justice Kovacs made his publication ban ruling. This general concern for and sensitivity to "rights" issues provided a sort of plausible context within which many of the more dubious concerns and anxieties around the Mahaffy–French cases could be made to seem high-minded and respectable.

In the specific case of criminal justice, however, the controversy over the ban also occurred within the context of a long-standing and somewhat paradoxical belief within the Canadian and British judicial systems that publicity is both of benefit and of potential harm to an accused. Since the seventeenth century and the notorious secret trials held in Britain's Star Chamber, public knowledge of trial proceedings has been viewed as a guarantee that justice's being seen to be done can assist in justice's actually being done. Public knowledge of a democratic society's legal proceedings is believed to ensure that the judicial system can be kept free from contamination by the attempted interventions of wealthy citizens or powerful politicians; secrecy is held, on the contrary, to offer a fertile ground for bribery and political blackmail, which in turn can create individual injustice. Public knowledge is also believed to enable the public scrutiny of laws. Laws which appear not to be achieving results compatible with current social values can be identified by the citizenry, who can then pressure their politicians to make changes.

At the same time, every accused in a Canadian murder case who pleads not guilty is obliged to face trial by jury, and is entitled to a jury whose members are not predisposed to regard him or her as guilty. Such a principle is fundamental to a legal system that is premised on the theory that an accused is innocent until proven guilty. What should be particularly noted here is that the publicity that is held to benefit an accused—to ensure an uncontaminated and impartial judicial process—occurs *during* a trial; the publicity that is held to be potentially most harmful to an accused—to jeopardize by "poisoning" the jury pool his right to be presumed innocent—occurs *before*.

One aspect of the publicity-ban hearings held before Mr. Justice Kovacs that was so troubling to the media, and difficult for them to think through, was that the above principles were in conflict. In the court's view, an accused, Paul Bernardo, stood to have his opportunity for a fair trial jeopardized by continuing publicity. Moreover, the Crown's opportunities to offer him a fair trial, one in which he could actually be considered innocent at least until a jury verdict, were also potentially jeopardized. At the same time, another accused, Karla Homolka, and a public extremely interested in seeing that her case was dealt with within the full power of a just court, stood to have their rights to have justice conducted in full public view taken away. Looked at in the abstract, this conflict is fairly easy to resolve. Paul Bernardo's opportunity to have a fair and unprejudiced trial would be extremely difficult to restore if taken away, whereas Homolka's and the public's right to the public viewing of justice could be restored after a temporary suspension. But, of course, few if any legal questions occur "in the abstract." In Paul Bernardo's case, a protracted lack of information, and a press eager to dramatize and mediatize this lack, had caused mystery and mythology to grow around him. This mediatization of his case had created the very real possibility that a publication ban on Homolka's trial might result in publicity that was far more damaging to his right to a fair trial than might be the publicity that arose from full disclosure.

Partly because of this possibility, a further confusion afflicted the hearings. The lawyer for Bernardo, Timothy Breen, who could be expected to act to protect his client's rights, argued that no ban be imposed. His argument, surprisingly, was one in favour of publicly scrutinized justice: "the public is best served by open justice... in a case of this notoriety the public really does have a need to see how the system operates" (*The Toronto Sun*, 6 July 1993). He added specifically that the public was entitled to know in advance what deal, if any, had been struck between Homolka and the Crown, and of the deep, and possibly initiating, involvement of Homolka in the crimes. The Crown Attorney, Murray Segal, who might have been expected to defend the right to open justice, and to have little sympathy for the accused, requested a ban. The lawyer for Karla Homolka, George Walker, who might have wished or not wished public scrutiny, depending on how well treated by the court he perceived his client to be, similarly supported a ban.

Walker's stated grounds for his support were to avoid further distress to the victims' families and to the St. Catharines community. While one can see some value in such statements as goodwill gestures from the Homolka family, the members of which were presumably going to continue to live in the St. Catharines area, it is hard to see how the well-being of two families, or of the community, could compete judicially with the public need to have confidence in its legal system—and hard to see also on what basis Walker could argue on behalf of the Mahaffy and French families or the community. Moreover, the specifically temporary ban which the Crown had requested would end sooner or later, and expose all three families to the distress Walker had cited. In addition, his request begged the question of the families' own preferences, which foreseeably might also have been in favour of immediate public scrutiny to give them confidence that justice had been done. A more likely motive for his support of the Crown motion for a ban was his desire to protect his client from public scrutiny at a time when she was still under fairly intense psychiatric care—having reportedly been in hospital as recently as a week before the trial opened. Judge Kovacs's response to Walker was to observe, "with some regret," that a judge had "no inherent jurisdiction" on the issue of psychological distress to the victims' families (*The Globe and Mail*, 6 July 1993).

The lawyers for the media, which had profitably processed what information had been available until now, predictably opposed the ban, although on the basis of idealistic principles. The CBC's lawyers argued that full release of information would end speculation and public debate. Lawyers for *The Globe and Mail*, *The Toronto Star*, and *The Toronto Sun* argued that a ban would violate the right to freedom of expression established in the Charter of Rights and Freedoms. A *Sun* editorial argued that full release was needed so a public could know immediately how unjustly lenient was Homolka's twelve-year sentence: "the public has a right to know it. Now" (7 July 1993).

The positions of Bernardo's lawyers and of the Crown Attorney were the most puzzling. However, there is no reason to believe that Bernardo's lawyers were not being candid in opposing the ban—and the court had to assume that they were. Detailed knowledge of the case might at least have diverted some public hostility from their client and toward Homolka. But, most important, it might very well have stopped the proliferation of rumours, half-truths, and de-contextualized fragments of information that were already circulating about him. One reason for their continued circulation was their growing status as mythology—as information that was neither demonstrably true nor demonstrably false. Another was their unofficial status: to possess them was to make a social or political statement—to defy a privileged set of individuals and institutions that had not wanted you to possess them, or even to express contempt for inefficient law enforcement. Just as the introduction of legal liquor after Prohibition ended most of the bootlegging and smuggling of illegal liquor, the introduction of legal Bernardo–Homolka information might have ended the demand for rumours.

Or so his lawyers seemed to argue. In fact, it is hard to know whether open access to the Homolka trial record would have had that effect, although it is arguable that it might have led to a much better outcome than did the imposing of a ban. Repeated release of information in the John F. Kennedy assassination did not dispel suspicion that there was yet more information concealed, nor dissuade would-be investigators from seeking additional witnesses and "expert" testimony. As in the Homolka case, there were commercial reasons for keeping the case alive, and for persuading a public that mysteries existed and that "deals" may have been made.

As for the Crown prosecutors, their interest in Paul Bernardo's having a fair trial extended not only to having his right to a presumption of innocence respected but also to his being convicted of the crimes should the evidence point, beyond a reasonable doubt, to his guilt. In this the Crown appeared to represent a strong public interest that surprisingly few of the media managed to discuss: an interest in having actual criminals identified, through investigation and trial, and deterred, through imprisonment and/or rehabilitation, from committing further crimes. One of the worst scenarios for the Crown would have been for Paul Bernardo's attorneys to come to his trial and tell the judge that they had been wrong to waive his right to request a publication ban, that with hindsight they now realized that they should have requested one, and that the lack of a ban had resulted in such widespread circulation of the details of the Mahaffy–French deaths that nowhere in Canada could their client get a fair trial. Or for Bernardo to change lawyers, and for his new ones to claim the old ones had been wrong and that their client should not be forced to pay for their mistake. Or for his trial to be endlessly delayed by the difficulty of finding impartial jurors. Or for a conviction to be overturned because of questions about jury impartiality.

For the Crown, the fact that a ban would give the appearance of protecting Bernardo's right to a fair trial, and thus guard against the above scenarios, may have been more important than that the ban actually result in an absence of pre-trial publicity. In Anglo-Canadian jurisprudence, at least as much weight is given to legal principle as to public events. The fact that an accused's *legal* rights had been protected, and that strong measures had been taken to prevent prejudicial pre-trial publicity, might allow a trial to proceed and a jury to be empanelled regardless of how much prejudicial information had clandestinely circulated. In actuality, far from being confident a ban would succeed, the Ontario attorney general's office had anticipated at least two months before Homolka's trial that "U.S. interest in the Bernardo case could test the limits of Canadian restrictions on news media coverage" (*The St. Catharines Standard*, 21 May 1993).

The ban itself imposed by Mr. Justice Kovacs, however, was more than a simple prohibition of publication. It contained exclusions, nuances, and degrees, and created what *The Globe and Mail*, in an editorial that emphasized pro-democratic indignation, termed "an extraordinary hierarchy of access." The text of the ban began with a list of inclusions and exclusions.

1. The Canadian media may be admitted to the trial.
2. The public is excluded from the courtroom except (a) the families of the victims; (b) the families of the accused; (c) counsel for Paul Bernardo Teale; (d) three police officers; (e) the court's law clerk.
3. The foreign media is excluded from the courtroom.
4. There will be no publication of the circumstances of the deaths of any persons referred to during the trial.

Here the exclusion of both the general public and the foreign media was of particular interest. Exclusion of the foreign media was plausible in as much as Canadian contempt-of-court law cannot be applied extra-territorially—contempt is not an extraditable offence. This exclusion also implied a recognition of the late twentieth- century permeability of national borders to the passage of information—that in the age of fax, electronic file transmission, and satellite broadcast, information published in one nation can easily become available to potential jurors in another. It of course also implied a mistrust of foreign journalists, particularly of American journalists who had been pretty well the only foreign journalists covering the trial. Again, however, this mistrust appears reasonable. The citizens of one country frequently do not respect the laws, practices, or values of another. Canada, for example, has not respected the American trade embargo against Cuba, and has at times actively resisted extra-territorial American attempts to force the Canadian branch-plants of American companies to refuse to trade with Cuba. There was no reason to expect American journalists to obey the ban voluntarily, nor to expect the most conscientious among them to be able to, given the intense competition among various American media and among the Niagara frontier television stations. Moreover, outside the sanction of Canadian law, even the notion of "conscientiousness" was debatable. Some of the American media might foreseeably decide that conscience required them to break the ban—as some eventually did.

The barring of the public was somewhat more problematical. The concept of a public trial, and abhorrence for secret trials, as much as for "secret police," is a deeply

73

ingrained part of Canadians' understanding of justice. In addition, the trial of Karla Homolka was a kind of community event—the crime had occurred in St. Catharines, both the accused and one of the victims were daughters of St. Catharines families. Some citizens had told reporters that they felt Kristen French had become a daughter of St. Catharines. It was this aspect of the ban over which the judge had "agonized deeply," he reported to the court. For while foreign journalists could repair their loss of access to the courtroom by obtaining transcripts and eyewitness accounts once Paul Bernardo's first-degree-murder trial was over, local residents could not in any sense replace their loss of the cathartic experience of witnessing Karla Homolka enter a plea, stand trial, and be sentenced. Mr. Justice Kovacs's explanation for their exclusion, however, did seem reasonable. Once American journalists were excluded, there would be no way of knowing which members of the "public" could have agreed to become covert sources for American journalists, or of knowing which might become such sources later. Nevertheless, this part of the ruling did create a kind of hierarchy. The St. Catharines public arguably sustained a greater loss than did the American media; moreover, the American media had much greater resources, as events proved, to regain access to information than did a St. Catharines citizen.

In contrast to the reasonable distrust which the exclusion of foreign journalists implied, the admission of Canadian journalists implied a trust in their willingness to obey the ban in all its aspects. It also implied a perhaps unreasonable trust in those to whom they were legally permitted to pass on trial information. While contempt-of-court law could be used to punish overt violations of the ban, covert violations—the passing on of information to a second party who then communicated it to a foreign journalist, for instance—were more difficult to demonstrate and punish. Mr. Justice Kovacs indicated his awareness of this problem in responding the next day to media questions by stating that reporters could divulge what they had heard in court to their "editor and legal counsel."

> But when you speak with the editor, it can only be discussed in the presence of that editor without anyone else present. No secretaries, no news boys. (*The Globe and Mail*, 7 July 1993)

Considering the numbers of people involved here—that the several dozen Canadian journalists present at the trial would become three times as many information-bearing citizens once each had spoken to the "editor and legal counsel"—and the increasing amount of trust such multiplication demanded, Judge Kovacs might have reasonably added the Canadian media to his other exclusions. Such exclusion would have also put additional pressure for secrecy on the twenty or so lawyers, policemen, family members, and clerks remaining in the courtroom.

The specific banning of publication of "the circumstances of deaths of any persons referred to during the trial" was evidently deliberately ambiguous—leaving it unclear how many persons who had died were to be referred to in the trial, and thus raising the issue of whether Tammy Homolka's death might be included in the litany, without mentioning her name. The very ambiguity, however, implied that more deaths than those of Mahaffy and French were going to be referred to, and accomplished the opposite of what it had intended by making Tammy Homolka's death again a target of speculation. As a *Globe and Mail* cartoon commented generally on the ban, "Extra! Extra! Sensational Trial! Speculate all about it!" (7 July 1993).

Mr. Justice Kovacs had then followed these various exclusions with a list of clarifications.

The following may be published:

1) The contents of the indictment.
2) Whether there was a joint submission as to sentence.
3) Whether a conviction was registered but not the plea.
4) The sentence imposed.

Only the remarks of the court in passing sentence on the issue of whether the accused is a danger to the public may be published.

The order for non-publication shall apply to the *transcript* of the trial proceedings. The order as to non-publication shall be temporary until the completion of the trial of Paul Bernardo Teale on the two first-degree murder charges he is facing.

To a lay person, Kovacs's exclusion from publication of the accused's plea was extremely puzzling. With the trial proper, from charge through conviction, victim-impact statements, and sentencing eventually lasting only two hours, with no testimony being called, with a set of facts agreed upon by Crown and defence being read into the court record, and with a joint submission being made as to sentence, if she had pleaded anything but guilty it would have been the fastest murder trial in legal history ("no contest" not being an allowable plea in Canada). Given the brevity of the trial, the agreement between Crown and defence, and the lightness of the sentence, the only plausible explanation would have been a plea bargain, and a guilty plea, but the media and the public could only speculate that such was the case. The judge's official reason for forbidding publication of the plea was that the fact that she had pleaded one way or another would not constitute admissible evidence at Bernardo's trial. In law, the ruling made sense; in actuality, it seems unlikely that the jury in Bernardo's trial would not have formed their own conclusions about Homolka's plea.

The final paragraph of the ban order effectively widened the prohibition in the first section, of "circumstances of the deaths of any persons referred to," into a sweeping prohibition of all parts of the trial not otherwise specifically excluded from the ban. Its second sentence was understood by most readers as saying that the ban would end on completion of Bernardo's murder trial, but in fact it literally said no such thing. It said only that the order was "temporary until" that time; what would happen to it after that time—whether it would become extended, or even become permanent—was left troublingly open, although the intention to have it expire appeared evident from other comments Judge Kovacs had made during the hearing. Had the judge deliberately created this ambiguity, as he had in specifying how many deaths were to be covered by the prohibition? Or had he simply written carelessly?

Most readers of the order, including the media, appear to have assumed the latter, perhaps because it most accorded with the Crown's motion, or with their own hopes or expectations, or perhaps with their low estimation of the literacy of Canadian judges.

The following day, at the end of Homolka's brief trial, Mr. Justice Kovacs extended the ban still further by sealing indefinitely the victim-impact statements of Deborah Mahaffy and Donna French, the mothers of the two slain young women. Again this sealing was somewhat troublesome, although not entirely unexpected—the judge had indicated during the three-day hearing of the Crown's motion for a publication ban some "regret" that he could not show more sensitivity to the impact of court proceedings on victims' families, and at the time of ordering the ban had sealed psychological reports on two unspecified members of those families. However, if victim-impact statements are to be taken seriously—as being something other than an opportunity for a victim to "have their say" in court—then presumably they can have some influence on sentencing. Public evaluation of the appropriateness of the sentence would therefore appear to require public access to the victim-impact statements, in order that the public both understand the sentence and establish for itself how the statements had been considered by the judge. In fact, the speed and tidiness of the actual trial, and the implication that there had been a plea bargain, had already made it appear that the victim-impact statements would be glossed over in the rapidity of the process. Perhaps the legal system's receiving of the statements had been in effect mere window-dressing—or a kind social gesture.

Public dismay over the ban began in the courtroom almost at the same moment as the judge was delivering it. "No one speaks for us," *The Toronto Star* reported that a voice from the gallery called out as the judge was concluding. The judge replied, "The press acts as a surrogate of the public...but from what I have just heard it sounds like they don't have confidence in this surrogate."

> After a break, Kovacs said he received a letter from one of the spectators who had asked the judge if he could address the court about the order excluding the public.
> Kovacs denied the request.... (6 July 1993)

The questions of who speaks for the public, of what role the public has before a criminal court, and of whether the press can indeed be trusted to act as the public's surrogate were key, and it might have behoved the *Star* reporters to have reflected upon them.

The right to be given an open and fair trial, to be tried in a court of justice in which the rulings and procedures are open to public scrutiny, is a right extended by the Canadian legal system not to the public itself but to the individual charged with an offence. While there is in the Anglo-American system of justice an understanding that justice that is open to general scrutiny is in the public good, the public itself has no standing before the courts in defending that good. Such defence is left in the hands of the judiciary, attorneys general, and prosecutors, and comes into the hands of the citizenry only at election time. The public's specific "surrogate" in a criminal court is the Crown Attorney, who prosecutes the accused on behalf of the Crown, which in turn acts on behalf of the people.

Only in the sense that the press may articulate and publicize general concerns of the citizenry, and act as witness at events which most citizens cannot attend in person, does it act as a surrogate of the public. In actual fact, the press receives no public mandate to carry out such a task—no delegation of power. Its having come to appear to stand in for the public descends from the three-hundred-year history of newspapers, a history during which papers were often founded not necessarily to make direct profits but to foster the prosperity of particular social groups and their political parties by giving their opinions vigorous public representation. Even today, newspapers tend to represent not "the public" but particular classes and interests within the public. And on occasion, a money-losing newspaper, like Quebec's *Le Devoir*, may be supported by special-interest groups because they perceive the paper to bring "prosperity" to their interests. But none of the media have a formal claim to stand as a surrogate for all the public.

Thus while newspapers or other media may go to court to argue for their own freedoms, as they did in the publication-ban hearings, they have no standing to argue, for example, that the general public be admitted to Mr. Justice Kovacs's courtroom. No one, as the anonymous gallery member had observed, had been able to argue during the ban hearings on behalf of the public gallery. Moreover, while the notion that the press is a surrogate for the public may be a high-sounding one in principle, it fails before the facts of the media treatment of such a case as the Mahaffy–French murders. If anything, the media and the public were unconscious adversaries in this treatment. The media had moved the public toward specific emotional responses to the tragedies. It had created a continuing melodramatic narrative of the killings and their investigation by keeping the story alive between major developments with "human-interest" sidebars; it had transformed them from a sequence of discrete news stories—a disappearance, a murder, an arrest, a trial—into an ongoing soap opera with evolving episodes, a recurring cast of agonized relatives, distraught students, grieving townspeople, and weeping reporters.

This transformation of the case into a melodramatic mechanism for selling newspapers and attracting television viewers was so strong that it was difficult to measure actual public dismay at the ban. All of the journalist polls of people "in the street" tended to encourage the indignation which they attempted to measure. Even indignation expressed in letters to newspapers was suspect in that the writers, as readers of that paper, would have been subjected to its manipulations of the story. The question of "who speaks for us?" in such a circumstance becomes a series of other questions: "who is us?" and "what is it that 'us,' or we, want to say?"

The media's own criticism of the ban was voluminous, and took a variety of forms. In its profusion, it served the continuing purpose of prolonging and serializing the already year-old Mahaffy–French story, and conveniently filled in, or bridged, much of the time between the Homolka and Bernardo trials. One prompt response was vilification and self-pity. "Muzzled" proclaimed the *Sun* in two-inch type in its July 6th edition—creating an irony even bolder than the typeface. "Contemptible" it declared in its editorial in the next day's edition, and substituted the phrase "gag order" on each mention of the ban. Beside the editorial it ran a cartoon showing the sword of Justice having cut St. Catharines from the territory she ruled in south-western Ontario.

A similarly strong and implicitly scornful response came from reporter Norman De Bono of *The Hamilton Spectator*. Interviewed by Canadian Press, he charged that the ban was ingenuous and self-serving—that it hadn't been imposed "to protect Paul Teale's [Bernardo] right to a fair trial." Rather it had been imposed "to protect the judge and the Crown from the outrage of the public." A second reporter, Lee Ann Goodwin of Canadian Press, added that she thought the "ban was designed to protect Karla [Homolka] Teale's safety as much as Paul Teale's right to a fair trial" (*The Halifax Chronicle-Herald*, 9 July 1993).

Some of the more measured responses invoked a view of a class conflict between an élitist legal system and allegedly unenlightened citizens. Christie Blatchford in *The Toronto Sun* proclaimed that the ban had deemed the "same people who searched for French and Mahaffy ... neither trustworthy nor responsible enough to sit in the courtroom." "[I]t is the public who have been labelled unreliable, and the public who have been sent home, like bad children, and told they have no right to know."

> The ruling has gruesome implications for the justice system, which is far too secretive and clubby already. The much-despised "blue wall," the police brotherhood which is said to band together to protect its own, has nothing on the

black wall, the be-gowned lawyers and judges
who decide so much behind closed doors, away
from scrutiny. (6 July 1993)

If anyone was feeling like a "bad child" here, abused by a
"clubby" and patronizing court, of course, it was
Blatchford. With much less self-revealing passion, *The
Toronto Star* declared in an editorial that the ban was
"patronizing" to potential jurors in assuming them "unable
to separate media reports from courtroom evidence" (1
December 1993). Echoing Blatchford's feelings of class
exclusion by calling courtrooms "inherently conservative,
clubby environments," Rick Salutin in *The Globe and Mail*
then massively expanded her argument, proposing that the
ban was a continuation of the élitist campaign on behalf of
the Charlottetown Accord—"a tug of wills between the
majority of the population...and their betters." "No one
worries that judges or lawyers will have their judgment
unhinged by the straight goods," he argued sardonically.
"[I]t's just potential jurors who must be treated more or less
like children in case their little minds are affected" (10
December 1993). In fact, it was Salutin who was making
the ban into a continuation of the Charlottetown Accord
debates by making these arguments. In a similar vein, in an
article entitled "In the case of Homolka ban, the law is a
farce," Allan Fotheringham argued that the support of
Ontario Attorney General Marion Boyd for the ban demonstrated the extent to which she was a "captive of the
bureaucratic minds who are born to secrecy and revel in it"
(*The Financial Post*, 2 December 1993).

The recurrence of phrases such as "bad child," "like children," "little minds," and "captive" pointed to the huge

extent to which the media themselves felt diminished by the ruling. It also pointed to the pervasiveness in the media of the belief that they had become the new victims. The scene of the abuse the media were portraying had a striking resemblance to the Gothic scene they had earlier portrayed of the Mahaffy–French murders. The abusers were male, the place of violence was dark, obscure— behind "closed doors," a "black wall," cloaked in "secrecy." The victims were again innocents—mere "children."

In his December column Fotheringham also argued that the ban was "stupid" because it alienates the public from its court system, and "leads to further contempt for authority." This argument, which presented itself as sympathetic toward the court system and as wishing it to be held in repute even while calling the ban "stupid," was repeated both by Fotheringham in other columns, and by lawyer Patricia Jackson in arguing against the ban in the Ontario Court of Appeal on behalf of Thomson Newspapers Corporation. Calling the ban a "black box" of secrecy, Jackson told the court "If the public is to have confidence in the judicial system, it must be able to see inside the black box." Significantly, the Canadian Press article that reported her remarks lapsed into calling it a "gag order" (*The Financial Post*, 2 February 1993). Fotheringham followed with a column headlined "Judge's ruling on Homolka trial an exercise in naivete" in which he argued that the ban order "encourages the current (and potentially dangerous) high-level of disdain for authority in any guise, governmental or whatever" (*The Financial Post*, 10 July 1993). The irony here was that Fotheringham himself in his mildly acerbic columns in *Maclean's* and

The Financial Post (as in his December 18 Homolka column, in which he pronounced lawyers to be "like crabgrass—simply something you have to endure") had done as much to cast doubt on the wisdom of those in authority in Canada as had Kovacs's order.

A third approach to opposing the ban was to focus on its effects on Karla Homolka's trial. Had a proper trial taken place? The allegation that one may not have taken place was contained in De Bono's suggestion that the real reason for the ban had been to conceal an arrangement that had been made among the Crown, Homolka's defence lawyer, and the judge. It had been implicit also in Bernardo lawyer Timothy Breen's suggestion during the ban-motion hearings that there had been some sort of "deal" between Homolka's defence and the Crown, and that a plot was afoot to create the "myth" that she was "another of Bernardo's victims" (reported in *The Toronto Sun*, 11 July 1993). The clearest articulation of this argument was the *Financial Post* article, "In Canadians' eyes, Homolka has yet to be tried," which argued that because of the absence of the public and media from the courtroom, and the brevity of the process, a "real" trial of Homolka had not occurred. If she had pleaded guilty, the article proposed,

> The real "trial" or tension, one could argue...lies between the brief, predictable court process, and the critical judgement of the people who observe it both in the court, and through the media.
>
> The public are not sightseers at a circus, indulging the thrills of voyeurism (although some people do sink that low). The public has a

> duty to perform: its respectful presence ensures
> the process is fair, and the punishment fits the
> crime; in other words that the system properly
> serves society. (10 July 1993)

This approach did not hold that the trial might have been unfair from Homolka's perspective but rather from the public perspective—that the Crown might have been overly generous in laying only manslaughter charges, or in agreeing to a twelve-year sentence.

The argument that the ban was harming the defence of Paul Bernardo against charges of first-degree murder—a fourth approach to opposing it—found little expression in the media, except to the extent that media hoped that his trial would be able to occur. However, his lawyer, Timothy Breen, vigorously pursued this line of argument at both the hearings over the proposed ban and later at the Ontario Court of Appeal. Here he argued that the special circumstances of his client's case, including the excessive notoriety given the murders by overt and covert media sensationalism, made a ban do more harm than good, and cause more rather than less prejudice among potential jurors. "It is the position of the defence that the potential for prejudice has been greater with the ban than without," he said (*The Gazette* [Montreal], 7 February 1994). Lawyers for the media organizations also appealing the ban seized on this point, even though the organizations themselves had not. Bert Bruser and Paul Schabas, lawyers for *The Toronto Star*, asserted that "it is not a constitutional right of the public to assert over the rights of an accused who seeks to invoke the very publicity which assures the public of the proper functioning of the courts.

There is no precedent for banning publication of a trial where the accused submits, as he does here, that a ban will prejudice his right to a subsequent fair trial." Peter Jacobsen of *The Globe and Mail* added the related argument that "it is inappropriate for the Crown and the court to interfere in the right of an accused person who has competent counsel to conduct his own defence" (*The Globe and Mail*, 2 December 1993).

Curiously, media reporting of the action in the Court of Appeal suggested that the media lawyers had presented this point more forcefully than Breen himself. In fact, as some of the justices of the court pointed out, it was not clear that the media lawyers had the right to argue on behalf of Bernardo, even if their arguments were well founded in law. It was Bernardo who stood to be directly harmed should the ban operate to prejudice jurors, not the media or its lawyers.

The fifth and most controversial argument against the ban was that it would not work. This argument was advanced by a number of commentators, from columnist Allan Fotheringham to the respected retired Supreme Court Justice, Willard Estey. It centred on the changes to which electronic technology had subjected all human social systems. As Robert Walker wrote in *The Gazette*, it was an argument that "probably could not have been advanced 30 to 40 years ago" (7 February 1994). It was first advanced, presciently, by Fotheringham in his 10 July 1993 *Financial Post* column.

> This is the modern world, judge. Not Dickens' world. Television has made borders obsolete. The Canadian public will learn the details—through

the back door—and will further disdain court
authority.

As events unfolded, and the ban was breached not only by
television but also by other electronic media, other commentators began describing it as the impossibility it
already seemed to be. Peter Desbarats, dean of the
University of Western Ontario graduate school of journalism, writing in *The London Free Press*, commented that
"[j]udges who believe that publication bans can be effective in a world of 'death star' television satellites and innu-
merable international computer databases must still be
writing their judgments on parchment with quill pens"
(11 December 1993). The following month ex-justice
Estey, now chairman of the Ontario Press Council,
declared the ban unenforceable. "You can't order the
impossible, because it will do harm," he told *The Toronto
Star*, suggesting that the ban was tantamount to attempting to defy "the law of gravity of human curiosity" (*The
Gazette* [Montreal], 16 January 1994). This argument was
repeated by *Toronto Sun* lawyers in the Ontario Court of
Appeal, but met with scorn by Mr. Justice Patrick Galligan.
"As I understand [the argument], if the order is going to
be disobeyed, the order should not be made. I find it outrageous that the court shouldn't make an order because
someone might disobey it" (*The Toronto Star*, 3 February
1994).

Mr. Justice Galligan's anger may have been directly
related to how this argument had grown out of the
media's earlier self-depiction as childlike victims of
oppressive, secretive judges. The new scenario, in which a
gleeful media shouts "I told you so" at judges who could

now be depicted as working not only in secret dungeons but in the dark ages before technology, placed media and court in a David and Goliath narrative. Childlike and righteous David triumphantly declares the judges to be naïve, old-fashioned, to have lost their authority along with their grasp of reality. Judges previously portrayed as powerful and patronizing could now be portrayed as subverted by an ignorance their own dark, cloistered, and clubby world had brought upon them.

The Court of Appeal hearings to which most of the above arguments against the ban were eventually addressed were in many respects a comedy of cross-understandings and misdirected arguments. Many of the arguments made in both written and oral presentations to the court by the media lawyers appeared, even to a lay person, of dubious relevance to the media's possible requests of the court. One of the first anomalies about the appeal was that it was made in a civil proceeding against a criminal-court ruling. This anomaly troubled the appeal court judges enormously, with Chief Justice Charles Dubin commenting, "My difficulty at the moment is seeing how simply by tossing a blank piece of paper around you can turn a criminal case into a civil case." Judge Dubin was pointing to the fact that the media lawyers were attempting to use a civil-court proceeding to appeal a criminal-court ruling that the criminal court system itself gave them no right to appeal. Not being parties to Homolka's trial, the media had no standing in any criminal court that might review Judge Kovacs's rulings. Their bringing action in civil court was potentially viewable as an end run around the criminal system, or as a back-door attempt to achieve in civil court something which the Canadian Criminal Code precluded. In general, the appeal required the appellants to demonstrate that Mr. Justice Kovacs, in imposing the ban, had erred in law on matters that had been raised before him, or had erred in the interpretation of fact. The lawyers for Thomson Newspapers Corporation raised a question of law in arguing that Judge Kovacs had violated Paul Bernardo's Charter guarantees by imposing the ban despite his lawyers' wish to conduct his defence without a ban's assistance; however, this was a question of law which pertained to Bernardo's situation rather than that of Thomson Newspapers. It was not its legal argument to make. Lawyers for the CBC argued that there had been no evidence to show that publicity about the Homolka trial would make the finding of an impartial jury impossible: in effect that Judge Kovacs had assumed facts that were not in evidence. However, Judge Kovacs had not ruled on the basis of such evidence but had leaped to the assumption that it was self-evident that publicity would have such a consequence, noting that "widespread, massive and repetitive" publicity to date had already "made it questionable whether an impartial jury can be selected" (*The Globe and Mail*, 6 July 1993). In responding to this argument, appeal court judge Patrick Galligan, like Judge Kovacs, resorted to his own subjective judgment and experience: "I have seen the difficulty in getting jurors in some cases that have generated far less publicity than this one" (*The Toronto Star*, 3 February 1993).

One large area of difficulty in the appeal was that the case had become simultaneously one of enormous public curiosity, partly through the manner of its presentation by the media, and one of serious criminal import to both the public and Paul Bernardo. That is, it had become simultaneously a case of great civil and criminal importance. The public indeed had a large interest in seeing that justice had been done, but had no standing to protect this interest in a criminal court. As Chief Justice Dubin commented at one point, "if they [the media] were allowed to interrupt criminal proceedings to appeal judicial orders they perceived as affecting them, then almost any individual could assert the same right." Another difficulty was that the media perceived that they had been given rights under the Charter without being given any legal avenues to pursue them. Advised that their use of civil procedures to appeal a criminal-court judicial order was questionable, CBC lawyer Ian Binnie exasperatedly exclaimed, "It is not open to Parliament to create a structure that shields constitutional conduct. It is not open to Parliament to say—as in this case—that there is no appeal" (*The Globe and Mail*, 1 February 1994).

A third difficulty lay in the fact that it was virtually beyond the power of the court to take explicit notice of one of the media's main arguments—that in an age of global electronic information exchange the ban was unenforceable. Mr. Justice Galligan's scandalized response to this suggestion, however, that it was "outrageous that the court shouldn't make an order because someone might disobey it," was not quite as powerful as it might seem. Although indeed Canadian courts dutifully consider the cases that police and Crown lawyers bring before them, at other levels the Canadian legal system does from time to time stop enforcing laws that society deems unenforceable, or prefers to be left unenforced. Statutory rape charges against teenage boys are rarely laid by police, and

91

if laid rarely prosecuted. Charges of assisting suicide are also rarely laid. Before abortion was legalized, charges were often brought against those performing abortions but much less often against the female patient. Prosecution of Dr. Henry Morgenthaler on abortion charges ceased after a series of jury acquittals demonstrated that the laws under which he was being prosecuted were both disobeyed and unenforceable. Most recently, police ceased prosecuting the flagrant smuggling and sale of tobacco products when the politics of the relationship between the federal government and First Nations bands made such action impossible. More often, however, it is appropriately the legislative branch of our government that decides when laws have become unenforceable, as with Justice Minister Pierre Trudeau's famous removal of the state from the nation's bedrooms in 1968, or the Chrétien government's abrupt lowering of tobacco taxes because of the apparent unenforceability of laws against tobacco smuggling. If, indeed, global electronic communications have made judicial publication bans ineffective or counter-productive in protecting an accused's rights, then it would be as much Parliament's duty as that of the courts to find alternative ways of protecting them.

In general, it can be said that many of the attacks on Mr. Justice Kovacs's publicity ban were not done in the public interest at all but were self-serving and deceptive. Those making the most explicit attacks were usually the very media who had used the story to compete for market share. Their self-portrayal as variously gagged, shackled, muzzled, and violated was not only in poor taste but also patently not true. In most cases they continued to be able to write and speak about the case and the trial as voluminously as before, often in a different kind of language but with the similar effect of keeping public interest and speculation about the case alive. The ban, in fact, probably resulted in more stories being written about the murders and trial, and more ink being expended on them, than would have been the case had the ban not been imposed.

Perhaps most ingenuous were those parts of the media that presented themselves in the guise of the little people— of the ordinary citizens who had allegedly been turned into pathetic little children by Judge Kovacs's order—or who presented themselves as rendered powerless by the secret society of court power.

> Now courtrooms are inherently conservative, clubby environments. If you've ever been a defendant in one, you'll have noticed that all the regulars interact cheerfully with each other— judge, crown, defence, clerk, bailiff, stenographer—while ignoring you, the defendant, the reason for the whole event (and this includes your own lawyer). In this congenial atmosphere major changes in procedure and invasions from outside aren't very welcome. (Salutin, *The Globe and Mail*, 10 December 1993)

Salutin's second-person "if you've ever been" address attempts to create the illusion that the writer and reader are equals in powerlessness, both situated "outside" of an overwhelmingly powerful inside. But Salutin's power as a columnist for *The Globe and Mail*, *The Globe and Mail*'s power as both Canada's only nationally distributed newspaper and a part of Thomson Newspapers Corporation, and Thomson Newspapers' power are collectively enormously greater than the power of most of the "you-readers" who will encounter his column. There is no possibility that such institutions, with their responsibilities to their shareholders, can stand in as surrogates for the "ordinary people" which their articles and columns attempt to create. Similarly *The Toronto Star* and Torstar Corporation, the *Sun* newspaper chain, and the CBC all have much greater financial, legal, and research resources than most individuals. These resources in the Mahaffy–French cases enabled *The Toronto Sun* to buy the Bernardo–Homolka wedding photographs, allowed *The Star* and the *Sun* to conduct independent investigations, and allowed most of the large media to employ lawyers as well as journalists to attend court hearings.

The argument that the ban would cause the court system to fall into disrepute was nearly as problematical. Arguably, it was not the ban itself that might cause disrespect of the court system, but the reception of the ban in the media. The media have a large role in controlling what issues the public is encouraged to see as important, in the same way that individual members of the public have extremely minuscule opportunities to keep issues they believe important in the public eye. Organized groups in our society, from labour unions to special-interest groups to political parties, recognize this power of the media and deploy much of their resources to create media events that will attract press and television attention. In the debate over the publicity ban, the media were the only public institutions working to publicize and criticize the judge's order. No political party and no major lobby group embraced criticism of the order as its own cause. Without the media's repeated writing about their own indignation about the order, and about infringements of the ban occurring in other jurisdictions—that is, without the media making themselves their own story—much of the debate of the ban would have not occurred. The media's criticism that the ban was causing the public to be alienated from its court system was in this sense a self-criticism. As much as anything, it was the stories the media wrote about the ban that worked to alienate Canadians from their judges. A similar number of stories that praised the ban, in nationalist terms, for defending Canadian justice against foreign interference would have had a much different effect.

The argument that the ban "would not work" may in some ways have been similarly flawed. In the hearings in the Court of Appeal, Mr. Justice Marvin Catzman made the intriguing suggestion that a person or persons, quite possibly a member of the Canadian media, had leaked banned information to American and British media, and precipitated a flood of this information back into Canada. Mr. Justice Galligan added that such a person would face prosecution if apprehended (*The Toronto Star*, 3 February 1994). Judge Catzman's suggestion had the effect not only of placing the Canadian media reporters under suspicion but also of legitimizing the information being published abroad. The suggestion followed by a month a similarly intriguing article by George Bain in *Maclean's*, in which he recalled how the British press in the late 1930s, restrained by their own traditions from publishing accounts of the love affair between King Edward VIII and Mrs. Simpson, leaked stories to the Paris press, and then reported them by writing "righteous condemnations of those unprincipled Frenchmen." Bain then pointed to the unusual diligence with which the Canadian media had reported the publication of each foreign story, and declared that he couldn't "help wondering" whether something similar to the British handling of the Edward and Mrs. Simpson story had perhaps occurred (24 January 1994).

Bain's suspicion is particularly interesting in light of the detail with which Canadian media announced many of the foreign stories, often virtually inviting their readers, listeners, or viewers to seek them out. The Toronto media and the Canadian Press covered *The Washington Post*'s publication of trial details on 23 November 1993, its republication by *The Buffalo News* and the *Detroit Free Press*, its instant availability on computer database services like CompuServe, and its later availability on local Toronto computer bulletin-boards. When Britain's *Sunday Mirror* broke some details of the trial on 19 September 1993, *The Toronto Star* published not only the date of the issue but the page numbers of the article (20 September 1993). Some of the media carried advance announcements of American radio coverage of the trial, and of television coverage on CNN, ABC's *World News Tonight*, and Fox network's *A Current Affair*, thereby alerting Canadians with satellite dishes or old-fashioned antennas to tune in for embargoed information. When a small Victoria, B.C., weekly newspaper, *The Daily Victorian*, published a trial summary (15 December 1993), it was again noted in the larger media, and for most Canadians the banned details were no more than a phone call or fax away. Overall, while perhaps not directly breaking the ban, the Canadian media were effectively abetting its breaking—acting as a guide for how to get around it. By suggesting in their early December 1993 written submissions to the Ontario Court of Appeal that the ban was not working, the media were rather audaciously pointing to what was in part their own handiwork.

In hindsight it is striking how few voices were raised in support of the ban, and how limited their arguments tended to be. In part this was because the debate was by and large a media-generated one, with most of the Toronto media committed to the anti-ban position they were taking to the Court of Appeal. Few, if any, arguments were made that the Canadian judicial system is worth defending—much like during the 1990 period of intense cross-border shopping and smuggling when few arguments were made that Canadian jobs were worth defending. Few pointed out that the ban was almost certainly only temporary, and that a year or so without trial information was a small price to pay for the possibility that the killer of Mahaffy and French could be brought to justice. When journalist Iris Nowell attempted to express such an opinion, her declaration unfortunately implied that all the mediatization of the case had persuaded even her that Paul Bernardo was guilty. Speaking of a televised debate of the case in which she had participated, she wrote,

> I was heartened by the discussion...of Paul Teale's right to a fair trial. Ensuring that he receives a fair trial is essential to the public good. If he is found guilty of even one of these hideous crimes, I am confident justice will be done. (*The Globe and Mail*, 4 April 1994)

It is precisely this effect of publicity on potential jurors that Judge Kovacs had feared.

While a number of lawyers were cited as defending the ban in news articles that were otherwise skeptical of it, one of very few sustained legal arguments in its favour came from trial lawyer Edward Greenspan, in a 11 May 1994 address to the Canadian Bar Association, later excerpted in *The Globe and Mail*'s Commentary pages. Significantly, the address, as excerpted, made no direct mention of either of the Homolka or Bernardo trials. Greenspan's argument was based on a very specific notion of criminal justice: that it should be produced in "a quarantined courtroom where processes are carried out by perfect and objective rules...by rigorous and impartial procedures that a civilized society has decreed for judging persons accused of crime."

> Those procedures are designed to provide justice by due process of law, protected from the whims of people—the passions of the mob or the influence of the master. They are to guarantee that the accused shall be judged on the basis of fact and not of rumour, on a specified act and not on reputation, for a given deed and not for episodes in his past; that he not be coerced into incriminating himself; that he have the opportunity to confront the accusers and try to refute the accusations. Of equal importance among these and many more guarantees in Canadian criminal jurisprudence is the command of the Canadian Charter of Rights that a defendant enjoy a trial before impartial jurors.

Implicit in Greenspan's account is a timeless set of procedures, so refined as to be beyond the need of revision no matter what the social changes outside the courtroom. Here, there would be no need for a Law Reform Commission, or for legislative revisions to the rules of criminal procedure. The social reality of the law, and of its unfolding in a courtroom, is quite different. Concepts of how to devise "objective rules" differ from period to period, as the evolution of the recent rape-shield law, or of the Young Offenders Act, suggests. The application of such rules in the courtroom is a process of ongoing interpretation, both of the law and of the events unfolding.

But while we might find Greenspan's courtroom excessively idealized, his recitation of the principles which the judiciary and the legislative framers of the law hope to achieve is nevertheless salutary and relevant. The openness of the courtroom to public scrutiny must help prevent the interference of the powerful—"the influence of the master"—but it also should not permit the interference of mass hysterias—"the passions of the mob." The jury should make its decision not on the basis of material that would inadmissible as evidence in a court of law—including Karla Homolka's plea to the charges against her. Nor should it be influenced by hearsay evidence such as the kind that has proliferated on computer bulletin-boards, often prefaced with phrases like "My wife has a friend who works in a forensic lab and she says..." In the case of Paul Bernardo's trial for first-degree murder, the jury should not be influenced by the fact that he once faced forty-three charges in the matter of the Scarborough rapes, that he may face manslaughter charges in the death of Tammy Homolka, that charges of battering his wife with a flashlight so badly that her left eye was partially dislodged from its socket (reported in *People*, 22 November 1993) were filed against him and then withdrawn, that his St. Catharines neighbours claim that he was frequently visited overnight by young teenage girls—some of them friends of Tammy (*The Toronto Sun*, 11 July 1993), nor that a *Sun* reporter has sententiously written that he has "cool blue eyes, wherein lives no pain or surprise or amusement. No guilt. No innocence. Nothing" (Michele Mandel, 21 February 1993).

> Leaks in a gag order. Banned details of Karla Homolka's manslaughter trial flood into Canada. (Headline, *Maclean's*, 13 December 1993)

As of this writing, only one charge has been laid in connection with the defying of Mr. Justice Kovacs's publication ban, that against retired police officer Gordon Domm, leader of a small organization that seeks harsher penalties for violent crime. Dismayed by the ostensibly light sentence Homolka received, Domm has argued with great zeal that the ban is anti-democratic and set out on a campaign of civil disobedience to contest it. He began his campaign by announcing that he would make available copies of the 19 September 1993 *Sunday Mirror* account of the trial. After receiving numerous requests, he invited the media to watch him deposit 152 envelopes containing the account into a mailbox. The police intercepted him beside the mailbox, seized the copies, but did not charge him. Later Domm attempted similar distribution of videotapes of the American tabloid news programme *A Current Affair*'s two-part account of the trial, and persistently invited the police to arrest and charge him. He was eventually convicted, called by the judge a "nuisance stone in the shoe of society," and fined $4,000 (*The Globe and Mail*, 1 July 1994). Domm's case illustrates the difficulty that an individual citizen faces if he wishes to challenge a judicial order such as that of Judge Kovacs. Only if he succeeds in getting himself arrested and charged for defying it can he make legal arguments against it, and even then his arguments may be disdainfully received.

In four other instances, individuals or publications showed much more determination than Domm to actually break the ban and successfully distribute trial details (Domm appears to have been more interested in being arrested than in actually conveying banned information). Curiously, none has been charged. Ottawa's satirical *Frank* magazine published many of the details shortly after the trial. *The Daily Victorian*, mentioned above, republished many of the details from *The Washington Post* article in December 1993. That same month, a neo-Nazi telephone hotline in Vancouver allegedly made available recorded messages containing "gory details of banned trial evidence" (*The Vancouver Sun*, 18 December 1993). In January 1994, two students at Red River Community College in Winnipeg locked themselves into the offices of the closed-circuit campus radio station and read excerpts from American news reports of Homolka's conviction. All these cases appear to have represented straightforward breaches of the court order.

In Ontario, police appear to have moved only in the spring of 1994 to curtail the posting of trial information on certain computer bulletin-boards and to persuade university computer systems to close down access to the international "Internet" computer discussion groups that some Canadian users had created to collect trial details, but again—despite the ready availability of *The Washington Post* article on at least four different parts of the Internet for four months following its publication— no charges were laid. The previous November they had arrested numerous people at the Ontario–United States border who were carrying multiple copies of *The Buffalo News* or the *Detroit Free Press* that contained banned information, but had released them without charge once having confiscated all but one copy each of the newspapers. Brian Greenspan, of the Canadian Criminal Lawyers Association, had called the arrests without the laying of charges a ploy that enabled the police to confiscate the newspapers without having obtained search warrants— "an abuse of the power of arrest."

> The public does not have the right to know every single thing, because the end result is more important. (Deborah Mahaffy in *The Hamilton Spectator*, 20 July 1992)

With publicity in the cases continuing unabated, Canadian libraries and databases liberally supplied with ban-breaking material, and ban-breakers mostly unprosecuted, there seems no question now that the courts lost this struggle and that the media won. In general, it was an unequal struggle: the media succeeded both in controlling public perception of the ban, making it into their own moral issue, and in maintaining the murder story as page-one headline news. The ban may have stayed in place, but its effect on the media was positive rather than negative, and its effect on the general public knowledge of the murders distorting rather than reductive. Because of this level of distortion, public curiosity about the murders remained high enough to sustain several more rounds of intense news coverage. In the news lull between the Homolka and Bernardo trials, the media had successfully shifted attention from the trials to the ban, and public indignation from Homolka and Bernardo to a new villain, the allegedly rights-denying and soft-on-crime figure of Judge Kovacs. Portraying themselves and the public as the new victims, the media made prosecution of ban offenders extremely hazardous for the state. Such prosecution could only play into the new media script about the case, creating a longer list of martyrs to "press freedom," and amplifying the media depiction of the judicial system as contemptuous of the everyday David-figures who would defy the black-robed Goliaths of the courts by reciting facts on student radio stations or by carrying seventy-five-cent newspapers from Buffalo to Niagara Falls. The one arrest for ban-breaking seems to have been made not because the ban was broken but only because the breaker persistently dared authorities to arrest him. The overall response of the Ontario attorney general and her legal system to ban challenges was to pretend that a ban imposed was a ban with effect—that the breaches were negligible, the offenders insignificant, and their effects on the case small. This was a bluff, for which perhaps the only recommendation is that it maintained a thin illusion of judicial dignity and authority.

Culturally, whatever one's opinion of Judge Kovacs's ruling, this victory of the media over the court system was extremely dangerous. Although the media had succeeded in shaping public opinion—and public indignation—to their side in the contest, the media were not in any sense delegates or surrogates of the public. Their interests as corporations committed to increasing market share and to attracting advertising revenue may often lead them to present themselves as the "servants" of a "public," but in actuality they are merchants rather than servants, who compete in a market rather than representing a public. News is a commodity which they sell, and which they can make more attractive to some parts of the market by the codes in which they dress it—codes like reliability, excitement, glamour, or scandal. For individual citizens to lose sight of the commercial interestedness of the media—an interestedness which can lead to more or less useful reporting, depending on how the particular competitor perceives its interests—is to risk surrendering their individual power as citizens to institutions that in all likelihood place the values and goals of the financially powerful first. The ingenuousness of the media's depiction of the court system as an élite that may be an adversary of the general public rests above all in its having much more validity as a self-portrait. For while the public has little role in choosing the shareholders, directors, and managers of its newspapers and television networks, it does have an indirect role in the appointment of the judiciary, and a direct role in the electing of the cabinet ministers who oversee the judicial system and appoint its judges.

It is true that there may be difficulties inherent in the Canadian court system because of the class structure on which it is built and which it helps maintain. Despite provisions in many law schools to encourage enrolment by racial minorities and the disabled, law students are necessarily drawn from an intellectual élite within these or other "groups" of applicants, an élite defined in terms of academic achievement and the skills measured by the internationally administered Law School Admission Test. Additional admission procedures, including personal interviews, often give further advantage to self-confident, outspoken, entrepreneurial, individually motivated students over the quiet and non-abrasive. The difficulty of gaining admission to law schools, the intense nature of the programme, and the initiatory function of the articling year and bar admission examinations that concludes it, together with the fact that for three to four years the student may have close contact only with other law students, can understandably but rather ominously create a belief-system among many students that they are a special élite—an élite who have come through special trials, acquired a specialized knowledge, and are therefore "better" than other people. Moreover, some of this belief-system is reasonably founded: the knowledge a law student has acquired may very well have given him or her special advantages over others in business and political competitions.

Once in practice, lawyers face further competitive stresses and peer-group pressures. Many of the less aggressive have difficulty making their way in large firms or in individual practice. Women, who make up approximately 50 per cent of incoming law students, drop out of the profession at a much higher rate than men. Whether in single practice and facing office overhead and law society errors-and-omissions insurance that can total $40–60,000 a year for a beginning lawyer, or with a firm that rewards the accumulation of high numbers of "billable hours," young lawyers face the prospect of working long hours and spending much more time in each other's company than in that of non-lawyers. Successful lawyers, from whose ranks the judiciary are largely drawn, are often the ones who have most dedicated themselves to isolation within their own fraternity. Moreover, the legislative branch of our provincial and federal governments, which oversees our judiciary, contains an extraordinary over-representation of lawyers, typically more than 40 per cent.

But while these things may be generally or systemically "true" about the legal profession, their implications are not necessarily applicable to all lawyers. Moreover, to the extent that they are systemically true, they constitute a problem that is to be addressed, not by placing excessive trust in even less democratic institutions like the media, but by attempting social change in the profession. The fact that the lawmakers and legal profession are responsive to changes in public attitudes has been reflected over the last three decades in changes to divorce law, family law, abortion law, laws concerning homosexuality, the rape-shield laws, laws concerning native land rights, and gun-control laws, as well as in the increased sensitivity of provincial law societies to questions of ethical conduct.

For better or for worse, the court system remains a public system, a system that the public itself has created through its participation in the electoral process and in the making of public policy. Mr. Justice Kovacs's publication ban was not ordered by a sinister figure accountable to no one but a mysterious clique, but by a public official whose decisions are subject to judicial review and whose professional conduct is subject to reviews which can lead to removal from the bench. And while it is true that such reviews are conducted by what Rick Salutin might term "clubby" groups of fellow lawyers, there at least is a direct line traceable from the public that participates in the democratic process to the educational policies that produce lawyers and the judicial appointments that create judges. Citizens may not like the routes that this line takes, or how these routes may create isolation between various parts of the public community, but they are routes which they have helped create, and which they continue to have opportunities to help change. They may feel excluded and untrusted by Judge Kovacs's ban but, as individual citizens, they were not the only ones, or perhaps not even the principal ones not trusted by it. Moreover, it was also "their" ban: it was the justice system they and citizens before them had helped create that produced it. The media that would turn citizens against Judge Kovacs were also asking them to betray not only 220 years of Canadian cultural struggle but each individual Canadian's right to help govern a nation.

Karla Homolka and Paul Bernardo cut their wedding cake.

THE FANS OF
KEN AND BARBIE

> Lately...Bernardo's interests had swung to rap
> music, his landlord said. Upstairs in the house
> was a synthesizer and other equipment with
> which he hoped to record an album.
>
> "He wanted to be the white M.C. Hammer," the
> landlord said.
>
> Earlier this week, he noticed Bernardo with ear-
> rings in each ear and his normally short, blonde
> hair combed to the side in ringlets, like Michael
> Jackson.
>
> (Burnside, "Picture Perfect," *The Toronto Sun*, 19
> February 1993)

A short time after Karla Homolka's manslaughter trial
there occurred two ostensibly trivial events. One day when
Paul Bernardo was being brought to the St. Catharines
courthouse for a routine appearance, a crowd of young
women gathered and smiled, waved, and called out in
admiration. "Teale has circle of groupies," the Canadian
Press announced, noting that one of the women claimed
"she may be in love" with Bernardo, that another declared
she would forgive him if he were convicted, and that
several had begun writing to him in prison (*Winnipeg Free
Press*, 1 October 1993). And on another day, a computer
buff reportedly named Justin Wells set up the Internet
computer news group "alt.fan.karla-homolka." These two
events marked the beginning of what was to be a radical

revision to the fairly straightforward Gothic narrative which the media had so far tried to make of the Mahaffy–French murders, and of their own growing enmity toward Mr. Justice Francis Kovacs.

One could argue that the computer buff's action was a prank—an Internet colleague describes him as having acted out of "a sick sense of humour." The news category in which he had placed his karla-homolka newsgroup was one for fan clubs: among the other groups in this category were "alt.fan.frank-zappa," "alt.fan.madonna," "alt.fan.-rock.n.roll," and "alt.fan.elvis-presley." However, the category was also the home for other "sick" or darkly ironic Internet fan clubs, among these "alt.fan.g.gordon-liddy" and "alt.fan.amy-fisher." That is, Justin Wells's action in setting up his discussion group was evidently neither whimsical nor unprecedented. It followed a convention already in place: an established species of ambiguously ironic fan clubs for eccentric criminals.

One could also argue that the four or five young women who set themselves up as a kind of fan club for Bernardo outside the courthouse were merely silly girls, uninterested in thinking through the implications of their actions, or how they might be acting to trivialize the terrible deaths of which he was accused. Such an argument, however, would still not explain how they had settled on precisely this kind of silliness. For in their own minds these young women were doing significant things, both socially and individually. As psychiatrists interviewed by the media proposed, they had somewhere learned that a woman's role consists of forgiving a "bad" man, or in reforming or "saving" him, or that a potentially dangerous man could make their own small lives seem larger.

That is, acting as a "fan club," and acting as a "fan" of a criminal—as the Internet examples suggest—is a socially acquired rather than spontaneous behaviour.

Fan clubs have grown up in this century around media celebrities, particularly around musical performers. The largest and most exuberant fan clubs have been composed mostly of the female fans of male entertainers—the bobby-soxers who followed Frank Sinatra in the 1940s, the young teens whose screams drowned out the singing of Elvis Presley in his first appearances on the Ed Sullivan show, the new generation of shrieking teens that greeted the Beatles on their first tour of North America. One of the facets of these entertainers that seems to have most attracted fans and fan clubs has been the indications of transgression or rebellion which they offered. The fan-attracting entertainer must stand somewhere outside the law, whether this be the law of the family, of established musical conventions, or of general society. Parents must dislike the entertainer's work. Established media must refuse to play his records or show his films. As John Fiske notes,

> Fandom is typically associated with cultural forms that the dominant value system denigrates—pop music, romance novels, comics, Hollywood mass-appeal stars.... It is thus associated with the cultural formations of the people, particularly with those disempowered by any combination of gender, age, class and race.[1]

Vague associations with criminality also help create fans, as in the young Sinatra's public association with zoot-suiters,

James Dean's with motorcycles and black leather jackets, or the Beatles' subtle endorsements of soft drugs. In recent times this connection between celebrity, fandom and marginal criminality has become almost a commonplace in popular youth culture—as the deaths of Jimi Hendrix, Janis Joplin, Jim Morrison, and Kurt Cobain, or the heroin convictions of Keith Richards of the Rolling Stones, or the insistence of both Madonna and Michael Jackson that they are "bad," or the lyrics of rap musicians everywhere attest. At one extreme, where being a "fan" becomes the single most important factor in the fan's life, and in which the fan abandons personal relationships and educational goals in order to follow his or her obsession, membership can dissolve into female abjection, into the "groupie" phenomenon of the 1960s and subsequent decades, in which young women act out with their rock musician heroes the kinds of sexual abasement Leslie Mahaffy and Kristen French were very likely forced to endure. In the light of the alleged behaviour toward women for which Bernardo had become notable, one must wonder exactly what his new "fans" were admiring him for, and what they fantasized he might do to them.

As in John Fiske's observations, fandom is both a sign of powerlessness and a strategy for action and power creation. The fact that fans tend to be female reflects the fact that society does not encourage strong self-images in women, and at worst can create women unconsciously ashamed of their sex. Many very young fans, however, are merely very shy and inexperienced about love relationships, and find the remote, fantasy relationship they can explore with a media figure safe and imaginatively rewarding. Older female fans can have learned that nurturing is one role that can give them power over men, and can transfer this learning into relationships in which they take care of a "strong" man, or even into abusive relationships in which they see themselves protecting such a man from his own violence. Others may find association with a celebrated transgressive male helps compensate for their own sense of weakness. Or the fan may experience combinations of these feelings—a possibility which raises the question of whether Karla Homolka herself, ███████████████ ██████████████████████████████████████ ████████, was indeed such a "fan." A fifty-six-year-old Florida woman, for example, accused in 1994 of murdering her freak-show "star" husband, who had regularly beaten her, sexually abused her with a blackjack, and once been convicted and released on parole for killing their daughter's boyfriend, was described by psychiatrists as viewing "herself as passive, feminine, inferior, controlled by others and extremely nurturing" (*The Toronto Star*, 24 July 1994).

Even in such an extreme condition of abjection, however, there can be a certain amount of creativity or productivity in the fan's behaviour. Constituting oneself as a fan, or producing "fan talk" about one's celebrity, writing letters to him, or even bringing the disapproval of non-fans upon oneself, can raise one's status within the fan group. While such behaviour may appear "perverse" within the norms of general society, within the self-defined context of the fan it may seem fruitful and fulfilling.

Themes of abjection—of how awful one's life is, how vicious one's own inclinations, how much one wishes to be physically savaged, torn, and forced to suffer by love— have been a staple value of youth music at least since

Joplin, the Sex Pistols, and Sid Vicious to the present.
These themes present the same paradoxical productivity
as fandom can: the artist who claims to be spiritually and
physically wrecked and unproductive is nevertheless creating text, music, and imagery from those claims. At the
same time, particularly in the United States, we have seen
the romanticizing and media deification of numerous
gangsters and murderers, from Jesse James, Butch Cassidy,
Wyatt Earp, Billy the Kid, Bonnie and Clyde, and Al
Capone, to contemporary killers like Gary Gilmore,
Charles Manson, Theodore Bundy, Richard Speck, Jeffrey
Dahmer, or The Boston Strangler. The main feature of the
figures in both groups is the constructed perception of
them as simultaneously remarkable and transgressive, and
often as remarkable because anti-social and transgressive.
And while in the commercial economy of the mass culture the manufacturing of images of such figures can be
profitable, in the psychological economy of the fan, the
creation of an imaginary relationship with such a trans-
gressor, whom they have convinced themselves is misunderstood, saveable, or even innocent, can offer a parallel
profit of psychological satisfaction. Thus killers like
Gilmore, Bundy, or Canada's Clifford Olson can receive
love letters, or even unsolicited offers of marriage, from
women they have never met. In July 1994 convicted wife-
murderer Colin Thatcher was married in a Manitoba
prison to such a woman. Although these women frequently claim that the man they have become fixated on
is innocent or misunderstood—Bernardo's principal
"groupie," twenty-seven-year-old Lori Brown of St.
Catharines, told the press that "no one could prove to me
he is not innocent" (*Calgary Herald*, 26 April 1993)—it is

the man's having become associated with brutally transgressive crime, his possessing of an aura of transgressive strength, that has attracted them to him. They would not have noticed him otherwise.

Themes of how welcome death and suffering are, or how "delicious" it may be to suffer or inflict beatings, mutilation, or even lethal wounds, are not a special phenomenon of our century. The mystery and inevitability of death, and the unavoidable decay of the human body through injuries and aging, have made the unconscious notion that it may be somehow noble, romantic, or pleasurable to undergo pain or physical degradation a common one throughout much of human culture. Mohawk societies believed that captured warriors were given larger opportunities to display greatness of spirit the more hideous the physical tortures they were forced to undergo. Medieval Christian societies believed virtue could be shown through the willing sacrifice of bodily comforts—sleeping on hard beds, eating a minimal diet, living in unheated quarters—and by the abuse and abasement of one's body—such as undergoing flagellation or self-flagellation, or wearing the proverbial hair shirt. Medieval art celebrated those who willingly and happily sacrificed their mortal bodies on behalf of their eternal souls. In noting how this fascination with the breaking of the body has persisted in the lives of many of her psychotherapy patients, Julia Kristeva also noted how strong it has been in modern literature. Novels celebrating what might in other contexts seem sordid and disgusting lives: Genet's *The Thief's Journal*, Burroughs's *Naked Lunch*, Miller's *Tropic of Cancer*, Trocchi's *Cain's Book*, Sartre's *Saint Genet*, Plath's *The Bell Jar*, Cohen's *Beautiful Losers*, with their strange celebrations of betrayal, illness, drug addiction, and dying, have become literary classics in our culture. Here we see characters praised who have become fans of their own suffering and dying, who believe that it is purifying and cleansing to suffer, or who have become disciples of those who abuse both themselves and others. While psychologists may often attempt to explain such infatuations by suggesting that weak people are often attracted to those whom they perceive as strong and decisive, it is equally likely that what these "fans" are enacting is a fascination with being humiliated and abased similar to that noticed by Julia Kristeva in her patients (a fascination which also seems to have informed the most obsessive press coverage of the murders). Such "fans" may not be merely "weak" but be acting out imaginary dramas in which they find personal positive value—goodness and importance—in playing the long-suffering foil to another's cruelties.

Nevertheless, the fans of accused or convicted murderers tend to be a very small group. Canadians might reasonably have expected the general fascination with the Mahaffy–French cases—including the Gothic interpretation of the murders and various macabre fascinations with the suffering of the victims—to have diminished once arrests were made and faces placed on the shadowy imaginary figure of the suspected murderer, and perhaps to have virtually halted once a conviction was obtained. After all, Canada has little history of romanticizing its killers. While some recent Canadian murderers have been the subjects of books and television docudramas—Peter Demeter, Colin Thatcher, and the killers of Helen Betty

Osborne among them—they have remained life-size, and for the most part quietly despised. When Peter Worthington published an interview with serial killer Clifford Olson in *Saturday Night* (July–August 1993), and with his photo rather than Olson's on the cover, criticism that he had invited Olson to indulge in self-justification, and that he had helped him become a celebrity, rained upon him.

Yet with the February 1993 arrests of Bernardo and Homolka, the mythologization of the case increased rather than diminished. Part of the reason for this was the adversarial relationship between police and media. Another part was the continuing lack of information, and the repeated exaggeration and mystification of this lack by the media. But part of the reason also was that the accused were a *couple*—that one of them was a young woman superficially as "nice" as the murder victims. Part also was the image this couple had created of themselves to their friends and neighbours—through their appearance, their lifestyle, and the various objects and activities that had become associated with them. From the moment this kind of information about them began to accumulate in the media, and particularly in the period around Homolka's trial, they began to be perceived not so much as individuals than as a kind of representative couple— what *People* magazine in November of 1993 would describe as the "'perfect' young Canadian couple" (22 November 1993), or what Scott Burnside, during the week of Bernardo's arrest, termed "picture perfect." The image that began to circulate about them in the international press was that of Mattel's "Barbie and Ken" dolls—with its implication that Bernardo and Homolka had somehow

117

appeared to be the quintessential upwardly mobile couple next door—as in *People* magazine's "a couple so clean-cut that their neighbours in Port Dalhousie, Ont., called them Ken and Barbie" (22 November 1993). Although it was not at all in general use in Canada, this naming was usually attributed back to the Canadian media—as in this news story in Britain's most respected daily, *The Times*.

> In Canada they are called the Barbie and Ken murders, a series of horrific sex-killings allegedly carried out by a young, prosperous, attractive middle-class Canadian couple called Karla Homolka and Paul Teale. (6 December 1993)

Twenty-eight and twenty-three years old respectively, with matching blond hair, his layered and blow-dried, hers in loose ringlets, Bernardo and Homolka were now being implicitly portrayed as *typical*: as the typical underemployed, deliberately childless, late-"yuppie" young people of the 1980s. Children of European immigrant families, both were trained for white-collar work, he as an accountant, she as a receptionist. Both, from the photos that were published about them, appeared attracted to a comfortable, self-indulgent life: their rented house in a fashionable suburb (Cairns and Burnside in *The Toronto Sun* called it "a picture book house" [11 July 1993]), Bernardo's leased Nissan 240SX sports coupe, the champagne and the horse-drawn buggy of their Niagara-on-the-Lake wedding. The wedding pictures, sold by photographer Haig Semerjian to *The Toronto Sun* for a reported $10,000 and then resold to the media worldwide, show the couple riding in the horse and buggy, cutting their wedding cake, and in embraces for the camera; they were variously interpreted by the media as part of "a fairy-tale wedding." The three-tier cake, the full-skirted satin gown with seed-pearl embroidery, pinched waist, and puff sleaves, the rented buggy, and the white-tie formal-wear, were of course not "fairy-tale" at all, but the commonplace images of "fairy-tale" which numerous couples routinely purchase or rent off-the-shelf for similar occasions. In the background of the new couple's wedding-cake photo are the utterly banal full-length printed draperies of a hired hall. Similarly, the "picture-book house" was merely a one-and-one-half-storey bungalow of pedestrian Cape Cod derived styling, in a subdivision near Lake Ontario. It was more house, and more pleasantly situated, than most young couples could realistically aspire to, but highly unlikely to make anyone's "picture book." As in the Gothic treatment of their story, this isolation and romanticization of its ordinariness operated to obscure details of who Bernardo and Homolka might actually be.

In the months that followed the Homolka–Bernardo arrests, however, media coverage continued to emphasize the couple as extraordinarily ordinary, and to develop interlocking portrayals of them as typical, romantic, and obscure. As details were unearthed, Homolka was shown to have apparently been a young woman who, like countless other young women, loved animals. Her breathless remarks about her young man, whom she was said to have met in Toronto at a conference on animal care, had been published in her high-school yearbook alongside pages of similar trivia. Bernardo, like numerous other young professionals of his generation, had not found regular work. He was reported to have supported himself in

that newly arising economic phenomenon of the late
1980s and early 1990s, the underground economy. Among
the avant-garde of Reagan–Mulroney-era young entrepre-
neurs and free-traders, he was alleged in numerous stories
to have made an income by smuggling cigarettes and
liquor into Canada across the Niagara frontier. The force of
these details continued to be not to portray them as
simply run-of the-mill people—as having lives similar to
yours or mine—but rather to portray them as exceptional,
fairy-tale, better-than-average examples of ordinariness: as
being more blond, more happy, more middle-class, more
caring, more picture-bookish than you or me.

> Outside the courthouse here the watchers
> hissed at her, this pretty young woman....
> Yet Homolka was by most accounts a dutiful
> daughter—protected and loved by her parents,
> who sat at her right side throughout the hearings.
> She's an animal lover, gentle and caring; a nurse
> to sick cats and dogs....
> On its surface, Karla Homolka's very middle-
> class life has seemed to ride on still waters, with
> barely a ripple. (*The Toronto Star*, 7 July 1993)

In these various descriptions and details of the fairy-tale
ordinariness of Bernardo and Homolka were numerous
potential points of identification for the unsuspecting
reader. This was a couple that seemed so *normal*—so much
an expression of the times—that the young man and
woman could be our close friends, or could even be ourselves. They had aspired, spectacularly, to things that many
of us believe it reasonable to aspire to—the fashionable

house (even if rented), the snappy Japanese car, a childless lifestyle. The young woman had had to continue working, as in the case of most young Canadian wives, while the young man had made do, done a little wheeling and dealing, all the while waiting for the changing North American economy to open a place for him. People close to the couple were reported to have been extremely impressed with what they saw. Homolka's father was said to have told the *Sun* that he had come to love Bernardo "like a son" (11 July 1992). Their landlord told the *Sun* that Bernardo always "looked like he was coming out of church" (19 February 1993). A friend of the couple has recalled getting rides home from Bernardo and thinking he seemed like "the nicest guy you'd ever meet. I was so happy for Karla" ("Abdul," *alt.fan.karla-homolka*, 22 February 1994). When Bernardo was arrested, *The Toronto Star* described him as "[t]he boy next door" (19 February 1993); when Homolka was arrested it headlined its article about her "Homolka was 'a regular kid'" (19 May 1993). A *Chatelaine* reporter was so impressed with the couple's ordinariness that he offered this poetic evocation of it:

> Evil had not been visited upon the community, like an invasion by some alien force; it had walked and smiled and lived among them. It had said good morning at Tim Horton and good evening at the Swiss Chalet. It had dressed well and spoken well and sprinkled its face with aftershave. It had discussed the weather, the economy, the Blue Jays' pennant chances. It had shared their parks and their pints of beer and gone to sleep in a little pink house. Evil had

> become so normal that you would not or could
> not—and did not—recognize it. (February 1994)

It is perhaps worth a pause to reflect on what all these exclamations about the ordinariness and normality of Bernardo and Homolka were actually saying about "normality." Above all, normality here was being defined in terms of consumerism. To be normal was to acquire a house and a car, to eat doughnuts and fried chicken, drink beer, buy aftershave, and absorb news reports about the weather, the economy, and a prosperous baseball team. In a sense the "normal" person corresponded to the target readers and viewers of many of the media who were covering the murder story, and to the target audience of their advertisers. Moreover, the designated signs of normality were among the most bland and mass-produced possible: the subdivision house, the small sporty car, chain-store doughnuts and chicken. "Normal" consumerism was not viewed here as in any sense individualized. It did not include gourmet meals, architect-designed homes, or conversations on topics less commonplace than the weather. Instead, normality was to be understood as banality. Bernardo and Homolka were "normal" because they were deemed so utterly undistinguished and unmemorable, so empty of specific meaning. The high-school teacher who told *The Star* Homolka seemed "just a regular kid" also added that "she wasn't interested in very much." Schoolmates told the *Sun* that "Karla [had] seemed to blend in with the scenery, wallflower like, spending her time mostly with close friends" (11 July 1993). In such comments normality is understood as an absence of defining information, or as invisibility.

122

To be "normal" in this way is to do nothing that would bring a distinguishing gaze upon oneself. Homolka and Bernardo were perceived as having attached themselves only to broadly inclusive, ubiquitous, but barely visible categories—blondness, tidy clothing, regularity.

> One neighbour in Bernardo's upscale neighbourhood described him as "the most ordinary guy you'd ever want to meet.
> "He even looked like an accountant." (*The Toronto Star*, 18 February 1993)

By these criteria, of course, neither of the murder victims could have appeared normal. Mahaffy's having run away from her home several times marked her as transgressive; French's numerous community commitments and her straight-A academic record marked her as exceptional. In fact only the most empty and routinized lives would appear to qualify for this kind of normality.

However, the media's understanding of the Bernardo–Homolka normality was not only that it was banal and repetitive—characteristics which well might have quickly bored most of the media's audience—but that it was extraordinarily so: it was "storybook" or "fairytale" normality. So many times did these two adjectives get applied to the couple's lifestyle that one might have wondered what storybooks or fairy tales the reporters had been reading. The words implied that the ordinariness the couple had achieved was on the surface enviable: that the house, car, Rottweiler dog, and Swiss Chalet chicken represented not the actual lives of most other people but their best daydreams. Storybook houses exist mostly in storybooks rather than on city streets. Fairy-tale lives similarly exist in fantastic books containing magical, unbelievable events, set in lands of make-believe, and in times of legend. The word can also imply the innocence of fairy-tale characters—the naïveté of Goldilocks stumbling upon the three bears, or the blamelessness of the princess who pricks herself with a poisoned needle.

In one of the best-known stories of Stephen Leacock's portrait of his home town of Orillia, *Sunshine Sketches of a Little Town*, Leacock tells of young Zena Pepperleigh, whose obsessive reading of pulp romances of English lords and Algerian corsairs leads her to dreamily imagine her small-town life as a narrative of courtship, romantic danger, and gallant rescues. When she eventually marries her bank clerk suitor, they settle down, Leacock slyly tells us, "in one of the enchanted houses on the hillside in the newer part of town," where he "cuts enchanted grass on a little lawn in as gaudy a blazer as ever," and where "an enchanted baby" now sleeps.[2] Leacock is smilingly pointing at another implication of a fairy-tale view of life: that it can reflect a naïve romanticism that harmlessly persuades itself that unexceptional things are extraordinary or magical. In the news coverage of the Bernardo–Homolka arrests, however, it was not the people themselves who were naïvely seeing their lives as magical. It was the reporters.

The Bernardo–Homolka wedding was the most frequent focus of the reporter's fairy-tale constructions. *Maclean's*, *Chatelaine*, and *The Toronto Star* all wrote of the wedding as a "storybook wedding." *The Star* added that the wedding was "a storybook ending to a long courtship," and that their lives had thereby become a "fairy tale" (19 February 1993). *The Toronto Sun* called it an "extravagant, fantasy wedding," and "a perfect wedding" (11 July 1993). Once the *Sun* had obtained the rights to the couple's wedding photos in a bidding war with *The Star*, these photos were republished in numerous magazines and newspapers in several countries as defining images of the case. A fairly conventional formal wedding, common in middle-class families, and not uncommon in working-class ones, was thus portrayed in the media as unusual and "extravagant," and as reflecting a desire in the participants to glamorize themselves.

White weddings such as that of Homolka and Bernardo, far from having ancient "fairy-tale" antecedents, are early twentieth-century developments that reflect more a desire to emulate the upper classes than to pretend for a day to be fairy prince and princess. Much of the accoutrements of the white wedding, from the bride's elaborate gown, the groom's tuxedo or dinner jacket, and the champagne toast, to the occasional horse and buggy, reflect working- and middle-class impressions of upper-class life. The bridal party may not enjoy champagne or roast pheasant, but they insist upon them as defining symbols of the lavishness of their special occasion. For the groom, this may be the only occasion in his life that he dons a dinner jacket. This particular wedding had most of these accoutrements, but at times seems to have had not even a civil let alone fairy-tale atmosphere. The groom and his mother reportedly quarrelled so bitterly, over her strong disapproval of the roast pheasant entrée, that he determined at once to change his family name.

For journalists, the main benefit from this kind of fantasy description of the wedding was the sharp contrast it enabled them to draw with the crimes of which the couple was accused, one of which had occurred during the wedding preparations. The same day that Homolka and Bernardo were exchanging vows the various parts of the body of Leslie Mahaffy were being pulled from Lake Gibson back in their home town. While bridesmaid's dresses were being fitted, we were to believe, somewhere in a house "painted a fairy-tale shade of pink, with cute green trim" (*Chatelaine*, February 1994), Leslie Mahaffy was being███████████████████████████. While bride and groom were getting ready for their "dream" wedding, Mahaffy's body—███████████████████████████—was being rudely and bloodily ripped apart with a power saw and encased in cement. The more innocent and romantic the wedding could be made to appear, the more macabre, sordid, and ghoulish would seem the crime. The media were thus building a devastatingly sharp set of opposites— between the apparent and the real, between innocence and barbarism, between Beauty and Beast. Between these opposites Homolka and Bernardo would be allowed no other lives—they were either Barbie and Ken, superlatively, magically and representatively ordinary, or they were sadists, butchers, and monsters.

Ironically, the "fairy-tale" image contained the possibility of being a useful metaphor for describing not just one side of this contrast, but the entire paradox. The journalists employing it, however, seem to have known very little about "fairy tales" except for the popular meaning of romantic fantasy or for Disneyland versions of Polyanna and Snow White. For in most of the classic fairy tales handed down to us by the brothers Grimm or Hans Christian Andersen, evil and innocence co-exist: "monsters" are members of one's own family, like Cinderella's stepsisters or Sleeping Beauty's aunt. In Andersen's "The Red Shoes" the young orphan girl, who might be expected to embody pitiable innocence, instead becomes an unfortunate victim of vanity and social envy who must have her feet amputated by the executioner to free them of the wanton red shoes. In the tale of Hansel and Gretel, while these two young children escape, countless others have been killed in the witch's oven, and the children themselves must become killers, slaying the witch in order to prevent their own death. Actual fairy tales are not places of astonishing innocence but are rather ones where horror smiles in benign disguises, not unlike the pink house in Port Dalhousie. Bluebeard can be a plausible husband, until one peeks beyond his locked door. In fairy tales, the ordinary is likely to conceal the horrific, or even enact the horrific, rather than be, as the Homolka–Bernardo journalists expected, merely itself.

> The public may not only be immobilized by the violence found but the reasoning behind the media images being presented suggests a motivational explanation built upon individual decisions of good and evil, a nonpolitical explanation which minimizes societal factors. (Sanford Sherizen, "Social Creation of Crime News")

For the journalists following the arrests and trials, evil was to be portrayed as a shock, something unexpected in both fairy tales and society. Society, we were told, had been as unsullied as Karla Homolka's white dress until the moment Leslie Mahaffy had disappeared. Quoting a director of the Niagara Family and Children's Services,

Chatelaine told its readers that St. Catharines "had suffered a great loss of innocence, an event that will be indelibly etched on the soul of this community" (February 1994). Two years earlier the *Sun* had similarly quoted an editor of *The St. Catharines Standard*:

> Kristen's neighbourhood is white-bread, middle-class, Ozzie and Harriet. The murder was like reaching into your bathroom. The entire city feels totally violated. (26 July 1993)

In these images, the city stood in for the young women, sharing in their innocence, and suffering their violation. The violator was not part of society, but came from outside to inflict his damage on the social body.

This polarization of both the killer and society and the killer and his victim was characteristic of much of the reporting of the French abduction and killing from the beginning. Shortly after the abduction, the *Sun*'s Christie Blatchford led off with her column "The monsters prey on youth" (21 April 1992). The day after her body was found *The Hamilton Spectator* reported her school-board psychologist's praise of her innocence and condemnation of her killer as "only evil" (1 May 1992). In covering her funeral four days later *The Toronto Star* quoted the officiating priest as condemning the killer for having "chosen evil" (5 May 1992), and *The Spectator* quoted a mourner as saying "This was the act of a monster" (5 May 1992). Two months later, as the investigation slowed, *Sun* columnist Michele Mandel published an unnecessary and tasteless article—Leslie Mahaffy's mother told *The Spectator* it was "close to pornography" (28 July 1992)—in which she rather over-enthusiastically attempted to imagine the abduction, rape, and killing of French from the murderer's viewpoint. As he stalks her, she writes, he sees someone who is "so pretty, so innocent, with her Catholic school uniform...and those bright brown eyes as trusting as a doe's."

> Kristen Dawn French is everything that he is not; she is light to his darkness, innocence to his evil....
> She is as gentle as he is savage. She is a parent's dream. And a monster's fantasy. (26 July 1992)

The earliest meaning of the word "monster," the dictionaries tell us, is something extraordinary or unnatural—something that God had not intended to be a part of Creation, as in the warning on medieval maps of uncharted oceans—"here be monsters." A related and more recent meaning is a deviation from the natural order—an animal or plant afflicted with some congenital malformation. A third meaning is "a person of inhuman and horrible cruelty or wickedness" (*Oxford English Dictionary*). All three definitions place the monster outside of nature, normality, and humanity—defining it as something for which neither society nor God can be held accountable. In medieval art, as in Grünewald's depiction at Issenheim of the *Temptation of St. Anthony*, the monster is an incarnation of Satan and of the carnal sins that can afflict a Christian. In *Paradise Lost*, John Milton follows this practice in making his characters Sin and Death enormous and hideous monsters whose deformities reflect how sinful actions can deform humanity. Michele

Mandel's fictional account of French's killing makes a similar equation of the monstrous with darkness and evil, and a contrasting equation of innocence with attractiveness and light.

In the months that followed, it seemed to become difficult for many commentators to speak of French's killer without the use of words like "evil," "monster" or "devil," or without the implication that such concepts were alien to what they knew as society. Rosie DiManno of *The Toronto Star* characterized the rapes and murders of which Paul Bernardo was accused as "a trail of evil" (19 February 1993). "We know that evil exists," a Port Dalhousie bookshop owner told a *Chatelaine* reporter. "But we don't want to know it exists *here*." The reporter responded to this and other comments by St. Catharines-area residents by observing, "There was only one rational conclusion: a monster, a psychopath, was loose in the community" (February 1994). When Karla Homolka was sentenced to only twelve years' imprisonment for her role in the crimes, *Toronto Star* reporter Nick Pron moralized to the Canadian Press, "Sometimes when the crime is committed in hell, you have to have the devil as your witness" (*Winnipeg Free Press*, 9 July 1993), and one of Paul Bernardo's lawyers told *Maclean's* that "[t]he Crown may have made a deal with the devil" (18 April 1994).

The combination of the images of fairy-tale ordinariness with these images of monstrousness and satanic evil created a very specific explanation of what had happened in St. Catharines. Ordinary "Ozzie and Harriet" citizens of the city were unknowing of any possibility for such cruelty and sadism to occur. They were white ("white-bread"), dependable, church-going, and as regular as Tim

Horton doughnuts. The killers had masqueraded as similarly ordinary, renting an ordinary house, displaying ordinary hair, having an ordinary, traditional wedding, wearing ordinary clothes, and making ordinary conversations about baseball and the weather. But this ordinariness was suspect—it was too ordinary, a fantasy or parody of the ordinary everyone else knew. It was unreal—a storybook or fairy-tale ordinariness, complete with horse-drawn coach and pinker than pink bungalow. In fact it was not ordinariness at all, but a camouflage of ordinariness adopted by a couple that only pretended to be human. Under the camouflage of blond hair and pink paint lurked monsters.

Overall, this view of the crime attempts to expel it from "normal" understandings of society and thereby to absolve normal society from all responsibility for its having happened, and from having to act to diminish the possibility of its happening again. At one level it pronounces the crime a product of individual decisions of good and evil, something immune to social norms or conventions. At another and even more socially crippling level, it pronounces it supernatural and monstrous— beyond human influence or understanding.

Only a few voices spoke out against this none-too-subtle attempt not only to depict the murders as individual moral aberrations but also as aberrations outside all accepted definitions of humanity, but two of these offered extremely perceptive advice. Mae Harry, director of the Niagara Region Sexual Assault Centre, observed on the eve of Kristen French's funeral that, whoever had committed the crime, it reflected "the global and historical view of women as disposable human beings" (*The Hamilton*

Spectator, 4 May 1992). And at the funeral itself, Father Stephen Collins observed that Kristen's killer

> may well have fed himself on a diet that our society unfortunately still permits to exist. A diet of sexism, where women are toys for boys who think they're tough. He fed himself the trash and the violence we think is acceptable. He has heard the competitiveness of our society, where to dominate and suppress your opponent—whether it be in sports or academics—is acceptable. He fed himself the unemotional, irrational thing that says a man just needs to be tough and brutal. (*The Hamilton Spectator*, 5 May 1992)

Almost no one has offered similar views since Paul Bernardo's apprehension. Instead, if the alleged killer is not portrayed as a monster, he is portrayed as a psychopath or sociopath—as someone inexplicably devoid of the ability to empathize with others, unable to experience conscience, compunction, or guilt. Because of psychiatry's inability to treat psychopathy, the psychopath's crime is viewed as somehow inevitable, and the psychopath himself or herself as someone only marginally human, and as deserving full expulsion from society.

While the profile of the Scarborough rapes and the Mahaffy–French killings indeed suggests the actions of a psychopath, that is, someone with what contemporary psychiatry terms an "anti-social personality disorder," there are at least two problems with the popular view that a psychopath is a "monster" whose crimes are unconnected to society and its conventions and beliefs. One

132

problem is that not all of the roughly 3 per cent of males or 1 per cent of females with anti-social or narcissistic personality disorders become criminals. Many become legally productive citizens, albeit self-centred and manipulative ones, whose obsession with their own self-interest prevents them from committing major crimes which might later inconvenience them by obliging them to construct cover-ups or to stand trial. Others internalize prohibitions against criminality and make it a part of their own demanding self-image. Criminal psychopaths offend in a variety of different ways—not always by committing sadistic sexual crimes against women. One of the main ways in which the psychopath differs from the non-psychopath is in the psychopath's lack of impulse control; taught to dislike women, they do not stop at grumbling about them or mocking them, but carry on to extremes of violence. Another main characteristic of the psychopath is a tremendous feeling of boredom and emotional emptiness, an inability to "feel" anything except under increasingly exceptional circumstances. But again psychopaths, like the rest of us, learn from society the various ways emotional emptiness can be resolved—by watching television, ▬▬▬▬▬▬▬, shopping, making money, driving a car aimlessly, or by a man gaining power over a woman.

Father Collins's observation that it is society that undervalues women through its systemic sexism, Mae Harry's comment that human culture globally has regarded women as disposable human beings, or Tami Paikin Nolan's observation in *The Spectator* that *The Toronto Sun*'s daily "SUNshine Girl" feature encourages the very crimes, like the murder of Mahaffy and French, that their front pages exploit even as they lament, are thus no less relevant merely because the killer may have been psychopathic. Psychopaths function within the same sets of socially determined values as the rest of us, despite the obsessive narcissism and extremeness of their responses. Societies that emphasize individualism over social obligation obliquely encourage the psychopaths among them to act out their obsessions—by making self-absorption seem morally defensible. In addition, a society that, as Paikin Nolan argues the *Sun* has done, "promotes the objectification of women and reinforces the view that the streets are strewn with smiling, willing female specimens, soft and ripe as peaches newly fallen from the tree" (6 May 1992) teaches its psychopaths, together with its other citizens, how and against what targets they may justifiably direct their aggressions. Similarly, a society that eroticizes violence by dramatizing it as entertaining and emotionally thrilling—in crime shows on television or in films like the *Terminator* series—teaches its citizens both that violence can be romantic and that desires can be impulsively and violently satisfied, and thus tacitly legitimizes psychopathic behaviour. During the police investigation into the Scarborough rapes, forensic psychiatrist Dr. John Bradford, in an interview with the *Sun*, warned that the increasing violence of the rapes—in one of the later ones the rapist stretched one of the victims arms over a curb and deliberately broke it with his foot—suggested that the development of the attacks, from voyeurism to rape to rape with violence, indicated that increasingly "violence and degradation [had] become erotic for him" (Mandel, 18 February 1993), and that murder could be next. For the rapist, there was evidently both a desensitization process, in which his feelings of being emotionally empty and desperate led

134

him to need more and more violent stimulation in order to "feel" anything from his adventure, and a "learning" process, in which his experience in one attack led him to be more violent in the next one.

In Paul Bernardo's particular case, regardless of his guilt or innocence, some of his family circumstances may have been consistent with the development of psychopathy. Shortly after his arrest, a neighbour characterized the accused to *Toronto Star* reporters Theresa Boyle and Joseph Hall as having been part of a family of "losers."

> "No one wanted to go to their house to play. We rarely got invited into their house and when we did it was dirty," said the woman who spoke on the condition of anonymity....
> They were all kind of strange. The father was passive, submissive.
> And far from being proud of her son, Bernardo's mother was mean and overbearing, the neighbour said.
> "She never talked nicely to them," she said.
> "You could hear the mother screeching 20 houses away for her kids."

This was the mother whose complaints about the pheasant served at his wedding would reportedly cause Bernardo to virtually disown his family and, in his own explanation, move him to change his name to Teale. Dr. Glen Gabbard, writing for the 1994 manuals of the American Psychiatric Association, notes that "an absence of loving experience with a maternal figure," the lack of an ability to imagine a "soothing mother," "an experience of the parent as a stranger who cannot be trusted and who harbours malevolence toward the infant," and a consequent invention by the child of a pathologically self-mothering and "grandiose self," is invariably present in both anti-social and narcissistic personality disorders.[3] But again such impairment can be, and generally is, enacted by the adult subject in a variety of criminal and non-criminal ways.

In addition to banishing the alleged killers to some evil realm beyond humanity, their conversion into monsters by the media also tended to allow no differentiation between Bernardo and Homolka. Both were presented in turn as deceptively ordinary, extraordinarily ordinary, and as monsters pretending to be human and ordinary. This was a mistake even the FBI profile, with its assumption that the main killer was a rough-looking, dominating, working-class male and the second a submissive male follower who may regret his involvement, did not make. Part of the reason for the media's treating both the accused as monsters seems to have been our culture's insistence on stereotypically regarding normal women as more helpful, nurturing, and kind-hearted than men, and on regarding major deviations from such a norm as unnatural or monstrous. However, the psychiatric literature on psychopathy is consistent with the FBI's general assumptions. Persons with an anti-social personality disorder can be so powerfully persuasive that they can seduce and corrupt psychiatric staff, leading even their doctors, in Gabbard's words, to "minimize the extent of their antisocial behavior" and other staff to agree with their views of themselves and to "collude" with or even participate in their transgressions.[4]

If trained professionals can be deceived and professionally ruined by such a person, what expectations should we have of someone dramatically less knowledgeable?

The various media transformations of the case from a pair of bizarre and mysterious slayings to the work of astonishingly normal "Barbie and Ken" killers who were also monsters in disguise was accompanied by the sudden nationalization and internationalization of its coverage. Monsters, whether in Loch Ness or St. Catharines, are international news. Fans of the case and of the puzzlingly attractive couple multiplied both in the media and among their readers and viewers. What had been primarily a southern Ontario story, often followed only by two intensely competing Toronto papers, became a story prominently and repeatedly reported by every major newspaper in Canada, by newspapers in Washington, New York, Buffalo, Detroit, Seattle, and London, by American national television news programmes, and by a variety of Canadian and American news magazines. A major part of this newsworthiness, of course, was Mr. Justice Kovacs's publication ban: a news story which could not be reported became thereby a news story worthy of being reported. Moreover, news media with a prurient interest in the macabre details of the case could conceal this interest beneath a concern for the legal and moral implications of restraints on press freedom. "This story can't be told in Canada," *The Washington Post* titled its lengthy report on Karla Homolka's trial proceedings and on the public outcry over the publication ban. "Murder that dare not speak its name" was the headline of *The Times*. Both newspapers implied that the ban was ill-advised, and had damaged

Paul Bernardo's opportunities for a fair trial by preventing the factual correction of the rumours that were circulating about him. This internationalization was accompanied by an abrupt shift in focus from the victims, as the sites of fascination, to the accused killers. Few of the new large stories about the case presented photographs of Mahaffy or French, but nearly all presented photos of what *The Washington Post* described as the "attractive, well-dressed professionals" who had surprisingly become accused sadists and killers. "She was ravishingly blonde and beautiful," Britain's *Sunday Mirror* gushed about Homolka. "He was the clean-cut boy with a glittering career ahead of him" (19 September 1993).

While the new gathering of female "fans" for Paul Bernardo's trial appearances and the establishment of a "fan" discussion group for Karla Homolka on the Internet had indicated one area of perverse public fascination and identification with the accused murder-couple, this new national and international embracing of a "glittering," "ravishing" super-ordinary Bernardo and Homolka was quickly opening up the way to another. And the mediatization of the crime, the transformation of it from news to entertainment, something which had been evident from the first full-colour stories of *The Toronto Sun* and the Niagara Police/CHCH Television "special," accelerated rapidly.

Paradoxically, it was the couple's extraordinary ordinariness, the banal "fairy-tale" quality of their lives, and the numerous points of potential identification between them and the general reader which it provided that most enabled the new international media-mythologizing of the story that ensued. The anyone's-daughter image of the victims and the humble-cottage descriptions of their homes which had allowed audience identification with them had been easily displaced by this new and more interesting ordinariness provided by the high-school yearbooks and fairy-tale wedding portraits of their suspected killers. The mechanisms of "fan" identification invoked here were the commonplace ones that have operated for numerous "stars" and celebrities of popular culture. Michael Jackson may be an isolated, extraordinarily rich performer, but he enjoys the story of Peter Pan extravagantly more than other "young people"—so much so that he named his estate "Neverland." Elvis Presley so loved his mother that he bought her a mansion, Graceland. Burt Reynolds and Loni Anderson may have more access to wealth and to beautiful companions than we do but they can also weep, suffer, and mourn just like the rest of us, and have their emotions reported by the *National Enquirer*. Roseanne Arnold and Oprah Winfrey may be television celebrities, but just like ordinary people they have difficulty losing weight or in sustaining romantic relationships. For every successful star, there is some dramatic point of identification with his or her core audience, a point which allows a member of that audience to think "that person is much like me." This point of identification involves representative or general characteristics—health, family, marriage—things that most of us, stars or not, experience, and things which fan or celebrity magazines repeatedly emphasize. Michael Landon never had more fans than at the moment that he lay publicly dying of cancer.

In a sense, the media star is also a Barbie and Ken figure. The star is the super-normal, overly complete yet empty version of the "ordinary" viewer or fan who gazes upon them. Both magazines and television project an image of the star that includes, in magnified form, the elements and objects of the fan's life—romance, illness, homes, marriages, divorces, arguments, and clothing. This array resembles the accessories that Mattel makes available for Barbie and Ken, which also reflects both the actual and imaginable contexts and possessions of the ordinary person—clothing, make-up, house, car, furniture, and so on. Yet the array is also empty—the expressions on the dolls' faces are vacuous, the details of the star's life general and banal. Their extraordinariness is thus kept available to be filled by the playing child's, or the fan's, fantasies.

It was further into the company of such emblematic figures that media coverage was now repeatedly taking Bernardo and Homolka—figures who were portrayed as simultaneously remarkable and spectacularly ordinary, and accessible because of their ordinariness. They were becoming—as Amy Fisher, Charles Manson, Jean Harris, the Menendez boys, and Loreena Bobbitt had become before them—celebrity criminals. Their images were appearing in the same contexts—on the covers of newspapers and magazines, and in the pages of *People*, *Chatelaine*, *Toronto Life*, *Newsweek*, and *Maclean's*—in which the faces of famous people appeared. They were being discussed with entertainment figures in the same typefaces, in the same kinds of dramatic language, often in side-by-side columns. Their photos were appearing beside those of the stars on the same familiar glossy paper, in the same living colour, and the same formats. Overall, these representations constituted not a rendering of the ordinary features of the couple at all, but a simplifying and perversion of this ordinariness. The star is emptied of meaning as a concrete, everyday individual and given a largely symbolic reality. While Bernardo and Homolka were being exaggerated as supercharged versions of our own lives, their actual ordinariness, the ways in which their lives had overlapped with ours, and in which our own ideals had contributed to theirs, were being lost. We could identify with them, as remote glossy caricatures of things we valued, but we were not allowed to take responsibility for them as being extensions of things we had agreed to, said, and done. Above all, we were not allowed to see the violence they had done as a symptom of lesser violences and aggressions toward women to which we routinely acquiesced and in which many of us routinely participated.

Significantly, these exaggerations were occurring within a television and magazine industry that was itself being radically changed by shifting notions of the distinctions between news and entertainment. Throughout the 1980s the proliferation of cablevision choices, the expansion of all-news channels and of specialty entertainment channels, and the arrival of new kinds of television "networks"—sources of programming that lacked much of the fixed-station structure of the original big-three networks— had undermined the commercial value of network programming. Individual stations and networks were having to finance their operations on the basis of smaller audience shares. Under threat from these changes were both the traditional evening newscast, with its authoritative presentation of events of national and international significance, and many of the big-budget network series. Increasingly, networks began filling their entertainment schedules with cheap-to-produce news-story programmes presented in dramatic re-enactments: programmes like *America's Most Wanted*, *Eye Witness Video*, *Rescue 911*, *Missing Persons* and *Unsolved Mysteries*. Simultaneously, news programmes themselves began engendering longer-format broadcasts—on the model of *20/20*, or *60 Minutes*—programmes that focused on two or three stories, usually dramatizing their investigation of the stories so that the journalist became the leading actor, uncovering the facts became the major plot, and a variety of uncomfortable-looking businessmen and politicians became the villains. Some of the newer of these programmes—*Hard Copy*, *Inside Edition*, *A Current Affair*—adopted many of the strategies of tabloid journalism. They avoided most business, political, or foreign policy stories, restricting themselves to already widely publicized murders, rapes, divorces, or scandals. They included in their stories large amounts of marginally relevant "human interest" or background material—childhood videos of adult murder victims, interviews with distant relatives, photos of places they had lived. They presented hearsay evidence and innuendo that would have been legally inadmissible in court and eyewitness testimony that in court would have required corroboration and been tested by cross-examination. In June 1994 coverage of the murder deaths of football star O.J. Simpson's ex-wife, Nicole, and a male friend, these programmes variously broadcast footage of the male victim participating in a fashion show, footage of him appearing on the television "dating" programme *Studs*, an interview with the wife's psychiatrist who contributed hearsay evidence of what the wife said that Simpson had once said to her, and a poll of the audience to determine how many of them believed Simpson to be guilty. When he fled from arrest, in a white Bronco jeep, with a flotilla of police cars behind him, the fans of the crime television coverage was rapidly creating in living rooms across the continent were treated by means of helicopter video cameras to the sight of other fans of Simpson lining Los Angeles's Harbor Freeway to see him, some cheering him and calling encouragement.

A related development in the United States had been the live broadcasting on the "Court TV" channel of criminal trials, most notably the rape trial of William Kennedy Smith, the murder trial of the Menendez brothers, and the assault trial of Loreena Bobbitt for having cut off her husband's penis. While arguments can be made that the public broadcasting of important community legal matters can add to the level of democratic participation in society available to its citizens, and more widely allow justice to be seen to be done, the particular choices of lurid trials to broadcast has suggested that the coverage has at times been directed more to a prurient interest in sexual interactions and savage violence than to responsible citizenship.

The general result of these developments has been a mediatization of a great deal of the legal and social life of North America, and a transferring of these public affairs to fandom. Dramatized representations of various news stories, and stories selected for their dramatic or sensational potential, have been displacing both regular news programmes and explicitly fictional programming. Polls of viewers influenced by dubious recountings of evidence have been seriously offered in place of judicial reviews or jury trials. The Homolka portrayed through home videos,

143

the unchallenged recollections of friends, and the repeated showing or printing of an enigmatic, half-pouting, half-defiant face, is a vastly simplified version of the Homolka that the legal discourse of a courtroom would produce and sentence to twelve years' imprisonment. But it is an attractive Homolka, one that attracts by opening up readily to our fantasies of good or evil, our desires for goodness, or our fascination with abrupt juxtapositions of goodness and horror.

Front and centre in this mediatization in North America have been not only the studio television camera and the new hand-held cameras of live on-the-spot reporting but also the home video camera and its cartridges of instantly viewable videotape. Videotape, as the programme *Eye Witness Video* has repeatedly announced, has become the guarantor of authenticity, the defender of individual freedoms, the extra arm of the legal system, and—as in the Rodney King case—a check on police excesses. Contributors to *Eye Witness Video* solemnly vow to never go anywhere without the comforting presence of their video cameras. On another show, *America's Funniest Home Videos*, contestants show videos they have produced that are accidentally or deliberately amusing or embarrassing. In *Eye Witness Video* the ruling understanding is that experiences that have been processed through the video camera are somehow more reliable or authentic than those that haven't. The video camera here is a means of legitimacy—of proving the police officer did or did not abuse a motorist, of demonstrating that a room-mate has been stealing money, or of identifying the face of a killer. In *America's Funniest Home Videos* the understanding is that the videotape makes its producer or its subject "real"—that for a brief moment it places them on the national airwaves in the company of those who produce or constitute the televised reality of a continent.

In this function, the video camera follows the motion-picture camera as a means of creating legitimacy or celebrity—extending the authority of the film camera into the hands of non-professionals. The motion-picture camera was the first mechanical device to offer images that seriously challenged the status of experiential reality, offering the possibility that the filmic image might have more credibility than a directly experienced one. In the 1950s Bing Crosby arrived in Vancouver, dressed in casual clothes, preparing for a fishing trip; almost no one he met recognized him, and the up-scale Hotel Vancouver turned him away, refusing his attempts at identification. His filmic self had somehow earned priority over his experiential self. The filmic image offered authentic identity, for the sight of which fans would endure television commercials or long cinema line-ups. To become famous, you had to get in front of a camera—to "break into the movies." With home video, and its improvement in technical qualities over home movies, this possibility of acquiring personal authenticity by having one's image pass through a video camera became available to the general population. If what one saw on the television screen seemed more real that what one saw elsewhere, then one could videotape oneself, or one's family, and confer this additional reality upon them. One could have the experience of being one's own fan. One's own experiences could be made infinitely repeatable, just like the experiences on television. They could be freeze-framed, run in slow motion, run backwards. In addition, unlike still photos or motion-picture

film, videotape required no processing and thus was completely private. Couples could film their own lovemaking
and then, as viewers, become third parties to the action,
watching themselves becoming stars in their own erotic
production, and perhaps cheering or getting other vicarious pleasure as they watched. This film could become a
catalyst for further lovemaking, which in turn was filmed,
offering in theory an infinite series of technological
encounters. Or it could be viewed as if it were a professionally produced erotic or pornographic video, allowing
the couple to imagine their own activities as having the
same "reality" as those of the actors.

In the Bernardo–Homolka case, the video camera had
been prominent since the first news of the French murder
when video clips of her at school were aired on southern
Ontario television as part of the search efforts. Later in
this period videos of her with her skating club were broadcast. It was obscure precisely what function these videos
were to serve. As aids to identification, they added only a
little to what the still photos had provided. They did,
however, add complexity to the image of the missing girl,
and had the potential to engage more viewers who would
then be perhaps more attentive to whether they had
encountered her.

When Bernardo and Homolka were arrested, rumours
that ███
██
███. A few months later, as negative American responses
to the publication ban began to grow, a brief home video
of their wedding ceremony and reception was broadcast
on the American news programme *A Current Affair*. The
programme's lead journalist, Canadian-born Mary

Garofalo, boasted to James Chatto that "the beauty" of her two shows on the case had been "the tremendous wealth of video I was able to get as the first American to come in. Video of the girls, of the wedding.... We've had calls from other people who have videos they want to sell, of ball games and weddings the Bernardos attended."[5] At the same time, new rumours began to circulate that

.

What is extraordinary about the various uses of video-tape—████████████████████████████—is how clearly they reflect our society's own growing dependence on videotape and similar technologies to define and verify "reality." A society which uses videotape to make itself more real, and to allow its members to become fans of its own special moments, can readily imagine criminals who similarly use videotape to make their own lives more real. In this imagining, long before the media were to make celebrities of Bernardo and Homolka, they were already becoming stars—of their family-produced wedding video, and ████████████████████████████

██████████ In its mediatizing and celebrity-creating processes, video representation allows the creation of another self—a self that both is and is not oneself. The filmic Bing Crosby is a different self from the one that arrives in fishing clothes at the hotel desk. The act of videotaping makes external and "other" the action being videotaped—renders it done by the figures seen on the screen rather than by oneself. The people in the action become actors, rather than their usual selves. Even in family movies, the camera can have this effect, making ham actors of mild-mannered uncles and cousins. ██ ██ ██████████████████████, the two accused become much like ourselves. They too are videotaping their favourite pastimes, keeping their most exciting moments for personal posterity, building a video archive of their young marriage.

The young women who would define themselves as Paul Bernardo's fans, the ironic computer-network "fans" of Karla Homolka, ██████████████████████████████ ████████████████, or a television show creating entertainment out of rescues from near disasters are all part of a general phenomenon of our time: the theatricalization of everyday life. While technology has the potential to be, as Marshall McLuhan argued, an extension of human capability—allowing us to communicate around the world, or to "see" into outer space or deep into biological structures—it also has this powerful theatrical ability to multiply realities, and in the process to alienate us from the experiential and moral contingencies of our own actions. This translation of life into spectacle was first noted by

Walter Benjamin, contemplating the rise of the Nazi party through its translation of politics into emotionally powerful scenarios of massed bands, bravely marching armies, six-storey banners, and massed citizens shouting in unison. The citizens of Germany were in a sense conscripted into the very scenes that seduced them—as participants in mass rallies they became simultaneously actors in spectacles that would quickly overwhelm them as individuals, and fans of those overwhelming spectacles. In a sense, the individual was overwhelmed by his own action. Much the same thing happens in sports crowds, political conventions, or even in riots: individuals experience themselves as actors in events much larger than themselves; they find themselves acting in ways that they would not normally act; moreover, their own actions rebound upon them—they find themselves simultaneously moved and motivated by the very event which their participation is helping to create. The televising of sporting events or political events can extend this effect to further individuals who are enabled to "see" themselves in the responses of the crowd and respond similarly—most graphically when sports bars feature televised World Series or Stanley Cup games, where they become spectators to their own fandom.

Much has been written in recent times about the isolation many people experience in contemporary society because of such things as the demise of the extended family, the decline of small towns, or the individual mobility that is necessary to pursue job opportunities in an integrated national economy. In a society of intimate social contact, it was friends and relatives who reflected us back to ourselves—it was through social interaction that we learned both how our society worked and who we had become as individuals, or could be. To a large extent technology and technology-based media have taken on this role of reflecting ourselves back to us, or even of offering possible versions of selfhood. Children, we know, watch hours of cartoons and adventure shows each day—hours that in another time would have been spent in interactive and creative play. Someone, statistics tell us, buys the hundreds of millions of compact discs sold each year of country-and-western, rock, and rap music; someone watches the simplistic top-grossing movies, someone, the ratings say, watches the numerous afternoon soaps. There is probably nothing intrinsically "wrong" with this material; it arguably resembles the popular forms of literature—the oral tales, puppet shows, travelling theatre—that entertained large audiences in earlier times. What is different about our own time is the enormous role such material fills in telling us what we can be; in many homes a television set operates continuously through a family's waking hours. It is technology that has helped break down older communal structures of living, and helped create new structures of impersonal, "fan-club" affiliation.

Educators have had particular concern over the largely passive role in which much of this television has placed its viewers. While McLuhan may have been technically correct that a television image, composed of numerous coloured pixels or dots, involves the reader unconsciously in constructing in his or her mind an image that explains those dots, the general context in which those dots occur can leave very little to the imagination. Of particular concern in recent years have been cartoon shows built around a group of toys belonging to one manufacturer. The shows, it is feared, not only become an extended commercial for those toys, but also prescribe the specific ways in which they can be played with—the specific interactions the children can have, and the specific phrases they can speak. Much the same questions can be asked of the effect of other television and video productions on adult behaviour. Do shows like *The Young and the Restless* expand one's knowledge of how people can interact with one another, do they unwittingly make fun of a narrow range of conventional and predictable behaviour, or do they, consciously or otherwise, act to define and limit social behaviour? Do soft-porn videos stimulate one's romantic imagination or do they offer definitions of sexual interaction as routine, casual, and mechanical? Do shows like *Eye Witness Video* teach people to use video cameras to make their own lives seem more like the "realities" they see on the small screen?

The theatricalization of everyday life that occurs in such video productions not only makes the viewer both actor and fan to his or her own performance but also narrows what this viewer can see or think. A video image is extremely selective—only a portion of a scene or image or person can be screened at any one time. The image replicates the interpretive viewpoint—i.e., of what is worth looking at and what isn't—of the person holding or controlling the camera, and in turn teaches the viewer what is worth gazing upon and what is not. Some years ago, film theorist Laura Mulvey proposed a view of the popular cinema that is still widely held: that the camera represents a man's active gaze on a woman's passive body. To identify with the camera is masculine, Mulvey suggested, whereas to identify with the image is feminine. Further, a fear generated in the male viewer by the female image causes both a malevolent devaluation of the woman as a person and an idealization of her appearance. In contemporary literature the camera has frequently appeared, as in Margaret Atwood's *The Edible Woman*, as an image of male power. The lens of the camera resembles a prying, intrusive male sexuality. The person who holds the camera controls what is seen, what is considered, what is allowed to be remembered. The camera in turn objectifies and aestheticizes the female body, transforming a person into merely a desirable, two-dimensional, virtually inanimate object. This fact about the camera underlay Tami Paikin Nolan's observation about the unconscious irony that was created by the close proximity in which *The Toronto Sun* often published its crime photos of Mahaffy and French and its daily "entertainment" photo of its "SUNshine Girl."

In her novels, Atwood has frequently linked the camera held by a man with the tools and technology favoured by many of her male characters. The man who would transform his experiences into photographs is also the man who would transform deer and elk into trophies and meat, or ancient trees into lumber, or tropical islands into dictatorships. The video camera, that is, in its role as a device which reprocesses and dismantles the realities it photographs, may be closely related to the power saw.

What I'm about to write may be true, and it certainly is sick.

████████████████████████████████

████████. ("Neal the Trial Ban Breaker," contribution to *alt.fan.karla-homolka*)

████████████████████████████████
████████████████████████████████
████████████████████████████████
████████████████████████████████
████████████████████████████████
████████████████████████████████

████. Film critics have noted how the film camera in commercial movies isolates parts of the woman's body much more frequently than it does parts of men's bodies. It lingers on legs, buttocks, ankles, hair, neck, offering these as parts that are independently significant from the woman herself—performing, as it were, its own kind of dismemberment. ████████████████████████
████████████████████████████████
███████████.

These rumours, in both their accurately founded and imaginary elements, have reflected in general the viewpoints, and ████████ beliefs, and perhaps even the unacknowledged desires, of those who circulate them. That is, the very fascination with these rumours, which have appeared in newspapers and magazines, and on computer bulletin-boards, reflects a general sense that they are plausible—that it would "make sense" ██. It is here

153

that our own hungers, and our own technological ways of diminishing our own inner emptinesses, merge with those of a pathologically empty killer. In Daniel Defoe's early eighteenth-century novel *Roxana*, Defoe has his heroine, Roxana, persuade her young servant Amy to have her first sexual intercourse with Roxana's common-law husband. Roxana takes off Amy's clothes, and pushes her into her husband's bed, and watches while he has intercourse with her, and then writes about the episode in her memoirs, which of course is not her memoirs at all, but a fictional-ized memoir written as a novel by Daniel Defoe. That is, Defoe imagines his character Roxana writing an account about having assisted her husband seduce her servant. Roxana's desire to "see" her husband make love to her ser-vant has in fact not been hers, but has been instead Defoe's desire to invent and write and thus "witness" the three-way scene, which he in turn persuades us as readers to "want" to happen as we breathlessly approach this episode in our reading. In the rumours about ███████

███████████████████████████████████████
███████████████████████████████████████
███████████████████████████████████████
███████████████████████████████████████

███████████. The rumour-spreaders' pleasure in possess-ing the rumour, and in thus possessing ███████████
███████████████████████████████████████
███████████████████████████████████████
███████████████████████████████████████
███████████████████████████████████████
███████████████████████████████████████
███████████████████████████████████████

████████████████████████████████
████████████████████████████████
████████████████████████████ .

The image ███████████████████████████ also
embodies the general cultural concern with authentica-
tion, with seeing oneself and one's life reflected back in
that most legitimate and enviable of spaces, the television
screen. In the field of performance art, installation art,
and environmental art, in which artists create temporary
events or structures, sometimes in large outdoor spaces,
videography is often known as "documentation," as if the
video could make "real" and "permanent" an art form
which only has meaning through its impermanence and
temporality. The act of documentation in a strange way
parallels art's own relation to life, making the temporary
last longer, as in Shakespeare's grave assertion in Sonnet
18 that "so long as men can breathe or eyes can see, so
long" will live his sonnet and give life to his beloved. A
videotape of a sexual encounter has a similar paradoxical
relationship to what it represents, making something
which may at best have lasted tens of minutes, into something indefinitely repeatable. But the videotape goes even
further, objectifying one's own performance, placing it in
the same world of actors and stars as other performances.

This strange image of ███████████████████████
████████████████████████████████
███████ reflects back to us in the general population our
own videotape hungers—our genuine delight to see ourselves or our neighbourhood or our friends or relatives on
television. We race home or set our VCRs in advance for
these occasions which somehow authenticate some aspect
of who we are, or verify that someone that we know is

"important" and that through our knowledge of that person we also have significance. "I know him," I say, when I see an old acquaintance being interviewed on the evening news, or "I've been there" I call out when the camera in *The Graduate* pans to the front of the University of Southern California library. Or, ███████████ ██████████████████████████████, we buy our own video camera and become the stars and fans of our own productions. The time we spend being such fans, watching our old videotapes rather than making more, raises the intriguing question of whether ████████████████ ███████████████████████████████████████ ███████████████████████████████████████ ███████████████████████████████████████ ███████████████████████████████████████ ███████████████████████████████████████ ███████████████████████████████████████ ███████████████████████████████████████ ███████████████████████████████████████ ████████████████████████████?

Gatherings of groupies, a computerized fan club, a persistent mythologization of Homolka and Bernardo's blondness, blandness, and ordinariness in the popular media, and an underground fascination ███████████████ ████████████████████████████: to a large extent these were various aspects of the same phenomenon. For the media's fascination with the couple, or at least their profitable self-portrayal of themselves as fascinated, and their placing of their readers into positions of fascination as they read or viewed the media's stories, was in effect creating a nation of fans. Some of the extent of passionate

The "fairy-tale" house in Port Dalhousie where Paul Bernardo and Karla Homolka lived.

fandom that was being created was witnessed by Iris Nowell when she agreed to be a panelist for the carefully selected television-audience show focused on the publication ban. After some panelists began by stating extreme views, applause escalated to such an extent that thereafter

> any panelist who expressed a view favouring the
> ban was booed and shouted down by a raucous

157

15 or 20 audience members, some leaping to
their feet and jabbing fists in the air.

When a panelist, whom Nowell pointedly does not identify but who is most likely Gordon Domm (he "had been
arrested for distributing copies of a foreign newspaper that
carried details of the trial"), announced that he was
"going to continue breaking the ban" the audience
responded with boisterous hoorays, whistles, applause.
"'Way to go,' someone yelled."

> It got worse. There was some discussion about
> the immense publicity surrounding sensational
> murders in the United States, minus media bans,
> and at the mention of Charles Manson and Ted
> Bundy the audience applauded. Applauded!
> Palpably, the tabloidization of Canada was off
> and running. (*The Globe and Mail*, 4 April 1994)

In this scene it seemed that it was only lawbreakers who
had fans—the defiant ban-breaker, Manson, and Bundy—
and there seemed to be little discrimination being made
among them.

In effect, we were returned to the second floor of
Homolka and Bernardo's "fairy-tale" house, where in a
"sound room" on the north-east side Bernardo had
worked toward his dream of being a rap star, a "white
M.C. Hammer" whose angry, vituperative rhythmic lyrics
could bring him fame, notoriety, fans, and groupies.
Bernardo's name was being called out, and an emotional
audience yelled and applauded. With panels, editorials,
countless articles, numerous appearances of his photo on

the front pages of the *Sun*, and groupies now to his credit—not to mention at least six books in preparation to detail his accomplishments—Paul Bernardo was, at the very least, a phenomenon. And in her prison cell, Karla Homolka would be watching the frequent appearances of his face and hers on the screen of the television set that had sat so prominently in the rear of the police van that took her to serve her sentence.

Lake Gibson, where the body of Leslie Mahaffy was discovered.

THE MURDERER
IN THE MIRROR

I am genuinely pleased to see U.S. tourists
  motoring into my native land
& my only hope is that they will return home safely
before too many Canadians are killed
or too much land is bought up on lovely lakefronts.
                    David McFadden, "U.S. Tourists"

In any national culture, the interpretation of a murder
does not take place in a void, or even in the simple context of a religious disapproval of the taking of human life.
Through their histories, their popular-culture memories,
and their literatures, cultures accumulate views of how
murder is to be understood, who is most likely to commit
it, and what attitudes are appropriate toward victim and
slayer. While Cain has gone down in human history as its
first villain, Dracula has become an attractively dangerous
cult hero, and Bonnie and Clyde a tragic, overly eager
American couple.

In English Canada, however, the development of strong
national attitudes and mythologies around murder, as
around many other things, has been complicated by the
country's having grown in the giant shadow of the United
States from the moment of the American Revolution.
Canadian popular culture has been repeatedly dwarfed by
American popular culture — even as early as in the nineteenth century when cheap "penny" books and magazines
flooded into Canada, overwhelming both British book

imports and fledgling Canadian publishers. In the twentieth century, Canadian popular culture has often seemed
an underground, even regional, phenomenon, finding
limited expression in contexts like country fairs, regional
publishing houses, magazines like *Alberta Report*, B.C.'s
Raincoast Chronicles, Ontario's *Harrowsmith* and *Frank*, and
Nova Scotia's *Atlantic Advocate*, in rare moments of popular Canadian-made television like B.C.'s *The Beachcombers*,
Newfoundland's *Codco*, and Ontario's *Jalna*, *King of
Kensington*, and *Street Legal*, or in nationally fascinating
docudramas such as those on the Colin Thatcher murder
case, the Helen Betty Osborne murder case, or on
pedophilia scandals in orphanages and residential schools,
dramatized in *The Boys of St. Vincent*. Such cultural expressions, as intense as they often have been, have nevertheless flashed only briefly in a popular culture routinely
defined by American mass-market magazines, American
popular music, and American network television.

In so-called higher culture, only a very few English-
Canadian authors have been able to reach and influence
the proportions of their national audiences that American
authors have been able to reach in murder-defining books
like Dreiser's *An American Tragedy*, Fitzgerald's *The Great
Gatsby*, Capote's *In Cold Blood*, or Mailer's *The Executioner's
Song*, and only occasionally have these authors written
about homicide. The few Canadian literary works that
have grappled with murder tend to have influenced general Canadian attitudes mostly indirectly, filtering
through the society from the reading or theatre-going
experiences of those relatively few who have studied
Canadian literature at university, attended productions of
new plays, or read the new works of Canadian authors.

162

Yet a very large proportion of these works have tended to do precisely what much of the mass media has done with the Mahaffy–French murders: to define the killer or killers as alien to everyday experience, and perhaps even as alien to English-Canadian experience. The overall result has been a culture poorly equipped to read its own crimes. The literature most widely experienced by Canadians is American, and contains American interpretations and assumptions about crime. The literature which Canadians have produced about crimes tends to blame people or forces external to everyday Canadian society for crime—and often blames Americans.

One of the most frequently anthologized texts from eighteenth-century Canada is the section of Hudson's Bay Company explorer Samuel Hearne's journals in which he recounts how the Copper Indians with whom he is travelling ruthlessly slaughter a group of Inuit whom they encounter on the Coppermine River. Both Canadian high-school and university students regularly encounter this journal section in their Canadian literature courses, and encounter it second-hand through John Newlove's almost equally popular poem "Samuel Hearne in Wintertime."

Hearne begins narrating this incident in the most detached manner possible, detailing the preparations for battle and enumerating the number of Indians who set out. He reports that he "endeavoured as much as possible to persuade them from putting their inhuman design into execution"[1] but, on being accused by his Indian companions of cowardice, found himself obliged to say that he detested the Inuit even though he saw no necessity for attacking them. On nearing the Inuit camp, the Indians begin painting their shields, and taking off their clothes

163

"to make themselves as light as possible for running,"[2] and Hearne decides that, rather than stay behind and risk being attacked by fleeing Inuit, he would be safer to accompany the Indians into battle. The Indians welcome his decision, and give him a spear and bayonet for his own protection. Hearne then voluntarily takes off some of his own clothes to increase his own mobility. As Terry Goldie has noted, while Hearne began this passage insisting on his difference from the "inhuman" Indians, by deciding to accompany them, by accepting their weapons, and by stripping off his clothes, he had become increasingly one of them.

Then the Indians rush upon the sleeping Inuit and begin "the bloody massacre." However, despite Hearne's hanging back in the rear, he is soon emotionally involved in the action, and particularly in the slaying of a young woman close in age to Mahaffy and French:

> The shrieks and groans of the poor expiring wretches were truly dreadful; and my horror was much increased at seeing a young girl, seemingly about eighteen years of age, killed so near me, that when the first spear stuck into her side she fell down at my feet, and twisted round my legs, so that it was with difficulty that I could disengage myself from her dying grasps. I solicited very hard for her life; but the murderers made no reply till they had stuck both their spears through her body, and transfixed her to the ground. Then they looked me sternly in the face, and began to ridicule me, asking if I wanted an Esquimaux wife; and paid not the smallest regard

to the shrieks and agony of the poor wretch, who
was twining around their spears like an eel![3]

In his writing of this scene, Hearne seems to attempt to
detach himself from responsibility for it even as the hands
of the victim attempt to involve him. He pronounces her
"killed" even before the first spear strikes her, and takes
pains to point out that the Indians deliberately stab her
twice more before responding to his request for mercy.
The Indians seem to recognize that it is the youth and
sexuality of the victim that have engaged him—that if it
had been a man or an older woman he might have said
nothing—and tease him that he must want "an
Esquimaux wife." Their actions draw Hearne into further
complicity in the killing, in the guise of being merciful.

> Indeed, after receiving much abusive language
> from them on the occasion, I was at length
> obliged to desire that they would be more expedi-
> tious in dispatching their victim out of her
> misery, otherwise I should be obliged, out of pity,
> to assist in the friendly office of putting an end
> to the existence of a fellow-creature who was so
> cruelly wounded.[4]

Accordingly, one of the Indians plunges his spear
"through her breast near her heart," while the young
woman "made several efforts to ward off the friendly
blow."

Of course it is not a "friendly blow," despite Hearne's
attempts to view it as such. He spends the remainder of
the narrative attempting to re-establish his difference

165

from the Indians by emphasizing his own grief and by re-emphasizing the Indians' "barbarous" and "brutish" natures.

> My situation and the terror of my mind at beholding this butchery, cannot easily be con-ceived, much less described...it was with diffi-culty that I could refrain from tears; and I am confident that my features must have feelingly expressed how sincerely I was affected at the bar-barous scene I then witnessed; even at this hour I cannot reflect on the transactions of that horrid day without shedding tears.[5]

Yet even here Hearne's continuing fascination with the violence and violent sexuality of the scene betrays him. As the Indians sexually abuse their female victims, he pro-nounces their behaviour too "indecent to describe"—in a sense declaring his own publication ban on the shocking details. Yet much like the reporters at Homolka's trial who replaced the forbidden details by descriptions of their emotional impact on those that heard them, Hearne con-tinues to write, in effect implicitly describing what he already declared too indecent to be given description.

> The brutish manner in which these savages used the bodies they had so cruelly bereaved of life was so shocking, that it would be indecent to describe it; particularly their curiosity in examining, and the remarks they made, on the formation of the women; which, they pretended to say, differed materially from their own. For my own part I

166

must acknowledge, that however favourable the opportunity for determining that point might have been, yet my thoughts at the time were too much agitated to admit of any such remarks; and I firmly believe, that had there actually been as much difference between them as there is said to be between the Hottentots and those of Europe, it would not have been in my power to have marked the distinction.[6]

Hearne's description of what may well have been the rape-murder of a young woman stunningly predicts much of the reportorial construction of the Mahaffy–French deaths. The crime is committed not by oneself but by *others*—by brutes or monsters outside of normal humanity. Yet even while declaring this, the describers reveal their own fascination with and erotic involvement in the event. Their words linger too long on the victim's body and on the details of the assault, they protest too strongly their grief and tears.

Aboriginal North Americans, however, have been only occasionally the bloodthirsty savages in English-Canadian imagination that they have been in American, and very rarely at all in the last two hundred years. If English-Canadians see a culture of potential killers in North America, this culture is not aboriginal but European in origin, and lives immediately to the south. This recognition that Americans may fill the role of "enemy" in Canadian culture that aboriginals and other racial minorities often fill in American culture is articulated very early in Canada, in John Richardson's celebrated 1832 novel of abduction, murder and torture *Wacousta*. Its kidnappings, coincidentally, take place in the same Great Lakes border country with the United States as did those of French and Mahaffy. *Wacousta* has become to Canadian literature what James Fenimore Cooper's *The Last of the Mohicans* is to American literature. Canadians who have read neither it nor Richardson's other Niagara-frontier novel, *The Canadian Brothers*, can nevertheless acquire much of its anti-American mythology through another Niagara story of female endangerment: the story of Laura Secord and her cow crossing American lines to warn the British troops of the 1812 invasion.

Born in 1796 at Queenston on the Niagara frontier, John Richardson was nearly a quintessential early English-Canadian. His grandfather, John Askin, had been a merchant at Detroit, shortly after its capture by the British from the French in 1760. His grandmother had been a French-Canadian, descended, he recalled, from one of the earliest settlers of New France. At fifteen, Richardson had fought as a volunteer against the American invaders in the war of 1812, and was captured at Moraviantown in the battle at which the legendary Indian hero and British ally Tecumseh was killed.

The events in *Wacousta* take place during the 1763 Indian uprising under the chief Pontiac against Britain's newly acquired forts at Detroit and Michillimackinac. The villain of the novel, however, is not Pontiac, but a disaffected British officer, Reginald Morton, who has gone over to the Indian side to seek revenge against the British commander, Colonel De Haldimar, who two decades before had unscrupulously won and married the woman Morton loved. Assuming an Indian identity, and the name

Wacousta, he leads the uprising against the fort at Detroit which Col. De Haldimar, now a widower and accompanied by his young adult children Charles, Frederick, and Clara, commands. Wacousta is characterized by Richardson as so devastated by the loss of his beloved, and so consumed with bitterness and hatred, that he has become more savage than the Indians whom he leads. He is a man who has come to enjoy transgressive behaviour, who likes to commit it in spectacular public ways that leave his adversaries both dazzled and despairing.

Canadians who live close to American border cities have long been aware of American fascination with theatrical and spectacular crime and disaster. Southern Ontario residents joke about Buffalo newscasts that seem to consist entirely of a series of fires in Tonawanda, fatal accidents on the I-90, and murders in the city core—all excitingly described and videotaped for the evening newshour. It is this sense of crime performed for an audience that most characterizes Wacousta. In daring and vicious attacks, he twice captures the young Clara De Haldimar, attempts to rape her, and when finally thwarted, kills her in front of her father and brother, and throws her body into a ravine in front of the fort's walls before a score of untheatrical onlookers. In this novel "evil" is thus twice declared alien to most of its "Canadian" characters. The cruel, calculating, and autocratic Col. De Haldimar who commands the fort and alienates his troops represents one kind of inhumanity—a scheming and self-interested villainy that the novel loosely associates with British imperialism. The sensationally vicious Wacousta, with his blood-stained tomahawk and scalping knife, and with his lecherous "tenderness that was even more revolting than his natural ferocity,"[7] represents a headline-grabbing deformation of humanity that appals the Indian characters. Wacousta's plots to revenge himself on De Haldimar's children is the work of a satanic figure, one with a face "painted black as death," who resembles "the spirit of darkness presiding over his terrible legions."[8]

As in the media accounts of the Mahaffy–French killings, a larger-than-life "monster" abducts, sexually assaults, and kills the innocent Clara De Haldimar. A profound sexual charge infuses the narrative of this abduction, moving rescuers and onlookers to voyeurism and melodrama. At the height of Clara's sexual endangerment, her fiancé lies shackled outside Wacousta's tent, hearing both her struggles and pleas and Wacousta's macabre glee at being about to harm "a loathed enemy through the dishonor of his child."[9] Even her death, before the eyes of her family, is heightened by its theatrical context as a performance, in which the bodily plight of the young woman offers vicarious and perverse pleasure to spectators, novel-writer, and readers.

There have been few examples of such determinedly vicious and implausible killings in later Canadian literature. In part, the Gothic conventions employed both by the media in the Mahaffy–French cases and by Hearne and Richardson allow not only such murders to occur without social explanation but also the writer to depict the murder scene as one of thoroughgoing savagery and evil. There are no humanizing doubts or misgivings revealed in the murderer's mind, or hints of sympathy toward the victim. Wacousta, in fact, celebrates and boasts of his own evil. Although Wacousta's acts are partly explained, through the effect upon him some twenty years before of Colonel De Haldimar's treachery, the precisely and unremittingly vengeful and bloodthirsty nature of these acts is not. We know why Wacousta was angry, but we can never know why this anger was expressed by his becoming satanic and "monstrous." For some twentieth-century readers, however, a strong hint is provided by the facts that De Haldimar's fort is a British fort, and Wacousta's forces that besiege and harass it make their camps in dark forests that are now the equally dark streets of Detroit, Michigan, a city that has often reported the highest murder rate in the United States. Wacousta is monstrous because he has become narcissistic, theatrically violent, and "American." For cultural critic Robin Mathews, the savage and self-obsessed Wacousta is not only a prototype American but also a prototype for an individualist American society "based on anarchistic values and personally sensationalist interests."[10] The novel itself, with its conflict between the "anarchist-individualist" Wacousta and the British "authoritarian class system" represented by De Haldimar, is "at the centre of the Canadian imagination." Mathews argues that Richardson, as a Canadian who by 1832 knew the new republic all too well from having fought and been imprisoned by its armies, has placed

> in conflict, as character types, the two contending...philosophies and...reveal[ed] that neither is appropriate to Canada, and that a synthesis of them, eventuating in a new philosophy, is desirable.[11]

Although the literary use of Gothic conventions has long ago gone out of fashion, Richardson's hints that North American violence may be "American" has remained a relatively common suspicion in both Canadian popular culture and literature. One of the most violent protagonists in Canadian literature is that of Michael Ondaatje's 1970 poetic novel *The Collected Works of Billy the Kid*, later rewritten into a successful stage play. His too is a public and theatrical violence, performed before frightened crowds in gunfights on the main streets of western towns. And for a declaration almost as emphatic as Richardson's that violence is American and un-Canadian one can move 3,500 kilometres west of Pontiac's rebellion to the opening of George Bowering's 1987 ironic western novel *Caprice*. Here the Québécois cowboy, Pete Foster, has given the American cowboy, Frank Spencer, five dollars—four days' pay—to buy four bottles of whisky for him at the nearby Cariboo town. Spencer returns, drunk, with three full bottles and one with an inch and a half remaining, and claiming the nearly empty bottle as his commission. Incensed, Foster punches Spencer in the face. Bowering writes,

> He should not have done this. He was now speaking the language his opponent had learned in a lot of ranch yards and saloons in Arizona and Kansas. In that language your hand reaches for your belt, and if you have a six-gun there it speaks the next few words for you. This being a ranch outside Kamloops rather than a street in Laramie, Spencer was not wearing a six-gun...[12]

172

As in Mathews's reading of *Wacousta*, violence here is expelled from Canada, where six-guns are not worn, to America, where they are. The language of Pete Foster's punch is not a Canadian language, not even a Quebec language, but one from Arizona and Kansas. A couple of hours later Frank Spencer returns with an American-made Winchester rifle. The unarmed Pete Foster "took to running again."

> He made it halfway to the bunkhouse. Frank Spencer, now a picture of efficiency, snapped one .44-calibre bullet into the middle of Pete Foster's body, which quit moving all at once and dropped to the hard-packed earth.[13]

Immediately, other men, Canadians presumably, come running from the bunkhouse—but not to attack the fleeing, belligerent, and somewhat bewildered Spencer, but to lift Foster onto a wagon and take him "to the new hospital in Kamloops"[14] where he dies. The Canadian rescuers come not as avenging individuals with guns but as helpful citizens ready to take the victim to a public medical institution.

The implied explanation for Spencer's killing of Foster is that Spencer is drunk, and he is American. Although *Caprice* is an ironic novel that makes fun of the various stereotypes of a western novel by making its avenging hero a woman, making the mysterious Indian into a wise commentator on the action, and making the final action scene a quiet arrest by "typically Canadian" police officers rather than a shoot-out in which the villain is killed, under this parody some stereotypes remain unchallenged.

There are no successfully vicious Canadian characters. The source of arrogant gunfighter cruelty remains in the United States.

Attributing violence to satanism, aboriginals, or Americans has not been the only way in which Canadian fiction has attempted to "other" such violence, just as it has not been the only way in which other cultures have sought to explain it. Both Christianity and science have over the centuries offered to explain the existence of violence without attributing it to changeable social conditions. In orthodox Christian views, evil has its source not only in Satan's kingdom but also in our own world, which fell from grace into sinfulness through Adam and Eve's disobedience in the Garden of Eden. Our everyday world is thus a place of inevitable corruption, which can be made more bearable by social intervention but can be neither perfected nor redeemed. In Canadian fiction this bittersweet view has been forcefully represented by Morley Callaghan, whose novels like *Such Is My Beloved* (1934), *They Shall Inherit the Earth* (1935), and *More Joy in Heaven* (1937) have portrayed a Canada in which casual corruption and selfishness at all levels of society, including the church, contribute to criminals being unable to reform, and to a priest's attempts to save the lives and souls of two young prostitutes bringing him only spiritual desolation and insanity. Published internationally in their first editions, and since the 1960s a staple of both high-school and college Canadian literature courses, Callaghan's novels have been enormously influential in defining Canada to Canadians.

In *The Loved and the Lost* (1951), Callaghan portrays a

174

beautiful young woman who is ambiguously either too good or too ingenuous for the world she has been born into. Peggy Sanderson has witnessed in childhood the happiness and humanity a neighbouring black family can share, and has made it her mission to help bring happiness and racial acceptance to black people, wherever she may find them. Her efforts in Lower Montreal, however, at the Café St. Antoine, where blacks gather, bring mostly sexual jealousy and anger, and on one evening a violent brawl. A black musician who plays there comments about his own mixed response to her joyousness and kindness, and how annoyed it makes him to see Peggy "giving some no-good lavatory attendant the same glow she gave you."

> You think she offers it just for you, and then you see it's no more for you than the next guy. A bum is a bum in my race as well as yours. A girl ought to have some discrimination, not make it cheap, not for every bum; you can't just throw that stuff around. Sure you ought to be able to...well, before we all got wised up, eh?[15]

In the contrast evident here between the ideal of harmony that was lost at the Fall of Man—"before we all got wised up, eh?"—and the envy and call for "discrimination" that divides even the musician against himself, we see echoed the larger message of Callaghan's fiction about the unchangeability of the world. Even the novel's leading male character, Jim McAlpine, a young journalist infatuated with Peggy, desires nothing more than to tidy up her life and divert her from her dangerous enterprise. When she refuses him, he displays the same jealousy that the black musician expressed, and angrily withdraws from his role as her self-appointed protector. She is later found in her room, brutally raped and murdered.

Callaghan's novel doesn't quite imply that Peggy deserves such a death but, disturbingly, does imply that the world is not ready for the non-discriminatory love and warmth that Peggy had brought to it. It also implies that the violence and jealousy that Peggy's kindnesses triggered should not have been unexpected. Peggy was naïve to expect good to be returned for good, or to expect the sensual pleasures she unabashedly enjoyed in the company of those she helped would not be misread as sexual invitations. Even more than Leslie Mahaffy fearlessly walking the roads of suburban Burlington early in the morning, or Kristen French unsuspectingly approaching a car that resembled a Camaro, Callaghan's Peggy Sanderson had unwisely trusted other people, and naïvely underestimated the divisive and savage power of their passions.

Murder is not so much "othered" from Callaghan's Canadian streetscapes as excluded from the things over which human beings can exercise much control. Murder is explainable because people will "naturally" be murderers, as they will also naturally be cheaters, exploiters, and deceivers—even when they know they "ought to" do otherwise.

A similar view of murder, although based more on a biological view of human beings as subject to physiological passions than on a Christian view, appears in another staple offering of Canadian literature courses, Frederick Philip Grove's *Settlers of the Marsh* (1925). Again, as in Hearne, Richardson, and Callaghan, the imagined murder victim is an attractive woman. In this novel Niels

Lindstedt emigrates to Canada from Sweden with an over-powering ambition to acquire and develop his own farm, and with equally overpowering memories of having been neglected as a child by his hardworking single mother. Grove links both of these aspects of Niels to primitive human urges—to urges to connect oneself with the earth, and to be loved. "By some trick in his ancestry," Grove writes, "there was implanted in him the longing for the land that would be his: with a house of his own and a wife that would go through it like an inspiration."[16] After building his farm through dawn-to-dusk labour, Niels is seduced, almost as a game, by Clara Vogel, an attractive widow from the city whom he knows only vaguely but who has excited him sexually whenever he has seen her. The idealistic but unreflective young man immediately insists on marrying her, but when he takes her to his farm he finds that she needs more affection and attention than he is emotionally able to give. He withdraws to his work, and she angrily to her bedroom. After a number of painful years he discovers, to his consternation, he has married a woman his neighbours know as "the district whore." As in portraying him obsessively undertaking the development of his farm, Grove here depicts the distraught Niels as being in the grips of psychological and physiological forces that are as mysterious to him as instincts are to an animal. He describes him moving homeward "blindly, stumbling over roots and stumps." "He went on as an animal goes, wounded to death, seeking his lair ... He was in a trance."[17]

> It was as if a powerful spring inside of him had
> been tightly wound and then arrested by some

catch, either to snap under the strain or to unroll
itself in the natural way by setting some complicated wheel-work into irresistible motion, grind-
ing up what might come in its way or attempt to
stop it.

Wave after wave of hot blood went through his
body, lapping up into his brain, breaking there,
flooding his consciousness with an opaque, scar-
let flood...[18]

When Niels enters the house he finds her, as he has half-
expected, with a male companion.

Irresistibly a clockwork began to move. There was
not a spark of consciousness in Niels. He acted
entirely under the compulsion of the spring.[19]

He goes to the granary and gets his gun, and then re-
enters the house, noisily, seeing "a man's figure, half-
clad...vaulting through the open window" and a second
one fleeing into the kitchen.

The woman rose, a half frightened, half tri-
umphant smile on her face. She sought his eyes;
but she looked into the barrel of the gun.
The shot rang out.[20]

Throughout these pages Grove has, in a sense, exonerated
Niels even before he kills. It is not Niels who kills, Grove
implies, but the powerful clockwork and the "waves of
hot blood" inside him. A primitive instinct, as in a
wounded animal, drives him to avenge himself. Murder

here is "othered" to man's primitive animal ancestry, to his Darwinian impulses that overwhelm consciousness when his sexual individuality has been assaulted.

While both Callaghan's and Grove's understandings of murder come from international understandings—Callaghan's from two thousand years of Christian theology, Grove's from the wave of deterministic thought that had followed Charles Darwin's *The Origin of Species* at the end of the nineteenth century—their views of it as an act that men did, usually for sexual reasons, to women, and as something that was both an unavoidable aspect of humanity and therefore outside of an individual's control, continued to be the most prominent ones in Canadian literature. In simplified form, the Canadian message seemed to be that men can't help killing women. Three such murders depicted in novels published in the 1950s—Hugh MacLennan's *Each Man's Son* (1951), Adele Wiseman's *The Sacrifice* (1956), and Sheila Watson's *The Double Hook* (1959)—went on to become classic moments in Canadian literature. *Each Man's Son* became a book club selection in both Canada and the United States. *The Sacrifice* has gone through more than ten editions and reprintings. Each novel, in its own way, exonerated the murderer by locating the impulse for the crime somewhere outside the control of its perpetrator. At the same time, each also located this impulse within some tragic fate, or mythic fatality, that also placed control over it outside of the laws of society.

The slayings that conclude *Each Man's Son* are, like the one in *Settlers of the Marsh*, domestic. After several years away from home pursuing a failing career as a prizefighter in the United States, Archie MacNeil returns home to

Cape Breton late at night, badly battered from his most recent defeat. Unknown to him, his young son Alan has been the subject of a struggle between the local doctor, who covets the boy and hopes to gain custody of him, and the doctor's wife, who fears the boy will steal her husband's affection from her. In this struggle, she has attempted to convince Archie's wife, Mollie, that her husband will never return, and encouraged her to accept a Frenchman, Louis Camire, as a lover and as a new father for Alan. Archie's return finds Mollie and Camire together, and a terrified boy watching from the staircase—his eyes caught by the light from the parlour "like a fawn caught in the headlight of a train."[21] As this image of the boy suggests, a considerable sense of fatality and inevitability has been building up to this climactic scene in the novel. Archie's career has been following the usual and well-known path of that of an aging prizefighter. His return has been a recurrent motif of the book—longed for by Alan, feared by the doctor, denied as a possibility by the doctor's wife, and both hoped for and feared by Mollie. MacLennan has also inserted into the novel numerous allusions to one of the most famous, violent, and long-awaited warrior-homecomings in all literature—the return of Homer's Odysseus to Ithaca, where he immediately kills the numerous suitors of his wife, Penelope.

In the actual murder scene, this sense of inevitability, however, is somewhat contradicted. The scene itself in which Archie will abruptly come upon his wife and her lover in the parlour, and attack the latter violently, seems inevitable enough, but not the response of the usually evasive Camire, who smashes a nearby wine bottle on the leg of an overturned chair, and with "a sudden darting movement" thrusts the "fangs of the broken glass jabbing at Archie's face." Moreover, MacLennan's description of the developing scene is complicated by his use of the viewpoint of a young boy who is seeing almost for the first time a long-lost father he has hero-worshipped. The boy sees Camire, whom he hasn't liked, as weak and cowardly, "like a fox" that has not even its own "fangs" but has to jab with those of the broken bottle. He is amazed by his father's grace and strength. Then abruptly Alan's mother enters the scene and, almost accidentally, the father appears also lethal and savage.

> As the poker came down she was suddenly there between the two men, thin and frail as she tried to stop them. When the poker hit her head her large soft eyes rolled into her head and she seemed to sink down into the melting white wax of her own thighs and calves. The two men stared down at her. Alan stared at her. Then the house shook with the thunder of Archie MacNeil's voice. He roared as the poker swung up again and Camire darted back and forth across the room, trying to find a place to hide as he gave mouselike squeaks of terror.
>
> Seven blows landed on him, but Alan was no longer there when the Frenchman was silenced at last.[22]

It is this accidental quality in the father's violence that undercuts the larger argument of inevitability. For despite the novel's gradual building toward this scene and its violence, and the reader's knowledge of what happened to

Odysseus at Ithaca, death and murder here do not appear to have been unavoidable until Camire's response. Archie MacNeil was certain to have given him a terrible beating, but not until Camire stabbed at him with the bottle did he seize the fatal poker. His killing of Mollie was an accident of a kind that has happened in numerous Hollywood movies—the young woman shot or stabbed because she attempted to separate two men who were contesting for her. Archie's determination to kill Camire, by any means possible, appears to develop only after Mollie has fallen.

Moreover, MacLennan will soon indicate, MacNeil may not have even been in his right mind during the murder. When the doctor and other townspeople arrive at the house and batter down the locked door, MacNeil staggers toward them, one eye blind and the other "glazing." His face contorts "in a spasm of pain" and he falls to the ground in a coma from which he will not recover. The pains in his head that he has been experiencing during his long trip home have been from a blood clot caused by the beating he had suffered in his final fight.

Thus MacLennan succeeds in exonerating MacNeil in two contradictory ways. In one exoneration, MacNeil acted in the heat of passion, without intention, while suffering from brain injury, and murders only when he has accidentally killed the person most precious to him. In the other exoneration, MacNeil was only a small player in a huge mythological drama, in which the returning hero always comes home to find suitors harassing his beautiful wife, and must always—metaphorically or actually—take action to destroy them. This sense of fatality, of brooding inevitability, is compounded in the novel by the complex roles which the doctor and his wife play in creating

Mollie's infidelity, and by the necessity for the prizefighter to suffer the fate of all prizefighters—exploitation by promoters, defeat by younger boxers, brutal beatings, and brain damage. As readers, we know the likelihood of a violent ending even as we read of Archie's upcoming fight, even as we know the already written consequences of Odysseus's return to Ithaca.

The depiction of murder as being predetermined by some mythological necessity is repeated in another sexually charged killing of a woman in Adele Wiseman's *The Sacrifice*. The origin of the murder in this book lies in the pious but unreasonable conviction of its main character, Abraham, that there have been portents that God has a special role for him, and that he will be blessed by God through his children much like the biblical Abraham was blessed through his. This belief eventually causes the deaths of all three of his sons. Two are killed in a pogrom in their native Ukraine because they dared not disappoint their father by failing to return home on Passover. The third dies of heart failure after attempting to be his father's "miracle" son by rescuing the Torah from their burning Winnipeg synagogue. In the scenes that follow his death, Wiseman portrays Abraham tormented by the sudden realization that, far from being the specially blessed Jew, he may have been selfish and petty, may have driven his sons to their deaths, and have been "utterly different from that to which his soul had aspired." She shows him wandering "unaware" that others are staring at him, looking toward the sky for a divine sign but seeing "no command." Finally he begins a long climb up a staircase toward the apartment of Laiah, a happy-go-lucky and childless widow with too many male friends for her own reputation, whose life has always seemed to Abraham to have constituted a challenge or reproach to his own obsessively pious one. The staircase instantly recalls for readers the story of the biblical Abraham's climb up a mountain to offer his son Isaac as a sacrifice to God, and suggests that a certain kind of scene may be inevitable.

In many respects Wiseman makes Laiah resemble Clara Vogel, the murder victim of *Settlers of the Marsh*. Just as Clara stirs sexual feelings in Niels that he cannot understand, Laiah arouses feelings in Abraham that bewilder him, as if they were calling him to a way of life he had always firmly rejected. He dimly imagines she might have answers to great questions that have perplexed him. Once in her apartment, however, and warmly welcomed by her in the belief that he wishes to be her lover, he becomes confused. He sits there bewildered by her "vivacity," not clear in his own mind why he has gone to her apartment, and sure that her flirtatious and amorous welcome was at least not what he had expected. He hesitates, hoping to "seize the right moment to ask the right question." Trying to encourage his ardour, Laiah tells him she has been waiting for him a long time. This in turn prompts him to ask himself of Laiah, "What are you?... Who sent you to mock me?" and suddenly to consider a thought that has been waiting "electrifying, terrifying, to his mind"—to dare like the earlier Abraham to ask God directly: "One he could seek who knew, who would speak if he asked, who would give if he offered—if he had the courage to ask."[23]

Abruptly Wiseman has him convinced that Laiah's apartment at the top of a long staircase is indeed that ancient mountaintop where another Abraham long ago made an offering to God:

> ...he was lifted out of time and place. Lifetimes swept by, and he stood dreaming on a platform, apart, gazing at her with fear growing in his heart, and somewhere his Master, waiting. As in a dream, the knife was in his hand, the prayer was on his lips.... From inside a tenderness swelled toward her, and for a moment he forgot his fear and felt as though he were almost on the point of some wonderful revelation.[24]

But no intervening word from God arrives and, having entered trancelike into the ritual, Abraham cuts Laiah's throat and kills her.

Again, the murder is excessively explained and the murderer in a sense exonerated. Wiseman has offered explicit remarks about Abraham's delusions even before he began his climb up Laiah's staircase. He has not deliberately sought her out, but wandered by chance to her building. He has had no design in entering her apartment, except to have theological questions answered. He is seeking goodness, even as his hallucinations about his special relationship to the biblical Abraham lead him to shed blood. But the murder is also, as in *Each Man's Son*, heavily foreshadowed and ritualized. Like MacLennan, Wiseman has constructed her novel around another plot which the reader knows can only end in a risking of death. Ever since Abraham's convictions began that he was virtually a reincarnation of the biblical Abraham, the reader has awaited with some dread the destined moment when he will find himself on a high place, an offering beside him, and a knife in his hand.

While "othering" Abraham's violence to a mythic story, the novel paradoxically also others it to his own idiosyncrasy. His is not a cultural tragedy but a bizarre and individual one. The novel makes only an extremely mild suggestion that Abraham's obsessive and self-deluding piety may be socially caused. Religion, or at least Abraham's interpretation of his religion, does both lead him to murder and cause him to lose sight of the Jewish imperative, to "live" generously and well. In ironic contrast to Abraham, whose narcissistic religiosity has caused the loss of lives, Laiah is repeatedly characterized as a cheerful, non-religious, and pragmatic survivor, but one who above all has tried to "live" and to enjoy life. After he returns to his senses in Laiah's apartment, Abraham seems to recognize the irony, shouting "Live!" over and over again at her corpse. However, these hints that his culture may have helped shape Abraham are not developed by the novel into a social comment. No one else in the Jewish community shares his obsessiveness. It remains his own peculiarity which, while it may have its roots in Judaism, implies no criticism of it.

In *The Double Hook*, a novel that has been widely praised by critics as being one of the most influential in modern Canadian literature, Sheila Watson begins with murder—with James Potter killing the village matriarch, the "old lady" who is his mother. He pushes her down a flight of stairs to her death while announcing "This is my day. You'll not fish today." A few scenes later, he blinds his friend Kip with a whip for having tried to use his knowledge of the murder to gain possession of James's pregnant girlfriend, Lenchen, and then rides off to make a new life in a nearby town. The next day his sister Greta, realizing that she cannot inherit her mother's power over the household and over James, kills herself by locking the doors and burning down their house.

What Watson makes most interesting about these events, however, is not why the characters commit them, or how James will be punished for them—the implication is that he will not—but the mythological context in which they occur. For the murdered Mrs. Potter is no ordinary old woman, but a woman who has been monopolizing the village's supply of fish even as drought lowered the water levels in the river. After her death, the villagers see her ghost compulsively fishing all along the river bank. Through having James kill her, Watson places her novel within the frame of a "vegetation-myth" story perhaps older than the story of Abraham and Isaac, or of Odysseus's return to Ithaca. This is the story of the saving of the world from drought—an ancient bronze-age European story in which the world has become a parched wasteland because of the failing powers of a "Fisher King." A young hero must return the world to fertility and greenery by replacing the ailing king and becoming the new leader. This story is believed by scholars like Sir James Frazer, author of *The Golden Bough*, and Jessie Weston, author of *From Ritual to Romance*, to lie behind the numerous killings of fathers by sons in Greek mythology, and behind various medieval interpretations of Christ's crucifixion and resurrection.

The murder on the opening page of the novel thus becomes almost a minor element as the novel develops. The one major question of the novel becomes not whether the murderer will be punished, but whether he will return to the village and take up the leadership responsibilities which the murder has brought to him. When he does return, disillusioned by the greed and shallowness of the town, it is to a village purged by fire of the selfishness of his mother and sister. Life-giving water has already begun to seep "from under the burned threshold" of the Potter house.

> Welling up and flowing down to fill the dry creek. Until dry lips drank. Until the trees stood knee deep in water.[25]

As he nears the village, his tired horse seems rejuvenated by magical changes in the landscape. He sees the burned house, and feels as he gazes at it, Watson writes, as if "by some generous gesture he had been turned once more into the first pasture of things."[26] With his brother William, he continues to another house where most of the villagers, newly brought together by the violent events, have assisted Lenchen with the birth of James's son. The birth, and James's acknowledgement of it, act as symbolic indications of the rebirth of a hitherto fragmented community.

Murder in fact does not seem to be murder at all in *The Double Hook*. It is a necessary purging, a ritual cleansing of a community's dark, crippled, and oppressive past. It assists in the completion of a birth-death-birth cycle, ending the paralysis of a village and enabling it to return to beginnings—a new house, a child, a new leader. That is, murder is so "othered" in *The Double Hook* that there is no murder. The killing becomes less a human action than an

188

element in the rhythmic returns of natural and spiritual seasons.

What is most striking about all of these various Canadian depictions of murder is their depiction of the murderer. The murderer is male, and not at all attractive. Covered in war-paint, wearing a badly soiled suit, or aged and embittered, he visibly displays his deformed humanity. When Alan MacNeil first sees his father through the parlour doorway, he sees "[a]n ugly man with a great body in a soiled city suit, his face battered and lumpy, and his nose mashed square."[27] This deformity tends, however, to be temporary, and to be also the product of external forces that have overwhelmed the murderer. The murderer—even Wacousta—kills in a momentary fit of rage, passion, or delusion. The forces that make him kill come not from within, or from social causes, but from mysterious depths of satanic evil, or from the inevitable corruption of the fallen Christian world, or from the primitive forces of humanity's evolutionary past, or from mythologies in which the murderer is merely an actor carrying a plot immensely larger than any single actor in it. This depiction contradicts the actuality of Canadian murder, in which, as criminologist Neil Boyd notes, most murderers are indeed male but tend to be impoverished and unemployed and to kill for money and sexual power. Boyd writes that violence is not "a matter of biological destiny" but is rather "a learned response" taught by a "culture that has consistently rewarded men for aggression."[28]

The murder victims too in these depictions share a number of common features. Almost all are women. Only Clara De Haldimar is young and virginal, although even she is portrayed by Richardson as having surprisingly powerful incestuous feelings toward her brother, Charles. The young Inuit woman so cruelly killed by the Copper Indians is a stranger—Samuel Hearne can only guess at her age, and can give no indication of even whether she is married or has children—and in effect a stereotypically young, attractive, and helpless female victim. Peggy Sanderson is also an ambiguous figure. She too is young, attractive, and helpless—with her physical weakness amplified, in Callaghan's portrayal, by her naïveté about male sexuality. Her innocence is portrayed not as virginity but as spirituality—a spirituality that sees middle-class concerns about propriety and respectability as selfish and shallow rather than Christian. All three young victims, however, are highly eroticized. Their bodies, like those of Mahaffy and French depicted in *The Toronto Sun*, are hungrily surveyed by the narratives that present them. This hunger operates to heighten the reader's dismay at their deaths by inflating the lost sexual value of their corpses. The women are eroticized also by the presence in the narratives of suitors—of men like Hearne, or Jim McAlpine, who stand helplessly by while the young women are ravished and killed, and who regretfully and enviously desire them. Again, this eroticization of the murder victim contradicts the facts in Canadian crime where, psychological evidence suggests, most so-called "sex murders" are crimes of violence and dominance rather than of lust, in which it is violence that has become eroticized rather than the woman's body. Assailants often choose child-woman victims like Mahaffy or French because they are relatively powerless victims, ones whose weakness and inexperience bolster the assailant's sense of his own strength.

190

In two of the above killings, the victim is clearly killed because of her erotic attractiveness, and in the third, the killing of the young Inuit woman, her sexuality leads to the abuse of her body after her death. There is a similar link between murder and sexuality in the killings of three of the older women: Mollie MacNeil is killed because she has been found with a lover, and Laiah and Clara Vogel are killed in part because their promiscuous eroticism so offends their killers. In at least four of the slayings, it seems unlikely the woman would have been killed if she had not been perceived as a sexual being by her killer.

Like their killers, these women also tend to be portrayed in the novels as being overwhelmed by forces much larger than their individual lives. The Gothic melodrama of inflated passions, desperate escapes, and gloomy, confusing forests sweeps Clara De Haldimar from safety even as it inflates the passions of her slayer. Ancient tribal enmities kill the young Inuit woman as much as do the individual spears of her killers. Both Laiah and Mrs. Potter find themselves swept away by mythic stories in which they may never have believed themselves to have a part. Peggy Sanderson is killed, Callaghan makes clear, by the fallibility of humankind as much as by an individually responsible murderer.

Apart from George Bowering's *Caprice*, there have been in recent years relatively few widely read Canadian literary works to consider wrongful death and murder—something curious in itself, which we can consider later. But these few have tended either to further mythologize such death or to do something rather unprecedented—to insist that it be returned to social judgment and responsibility.

In many popular contemporary Canadian books—Michael Ondaatje's *Coming Through Slaughter* and David Adams Richards's *Lives of Short Duration* among the more prominent—there has also been a tendency to mythologize violence as something inevitable, poetic, or even beautiful in human life. James Reaney's portrayal of the infamous family murders in nineteenth-century Ontario in his widely staged trilogy of plays, *The Donnellys*, has suggested that the killings were more the products of enormous and tragic movements of fate than of changeable social processes.

The most popular and extravagant mythologization of death in the past three decades has been Leonard Cohen's *Beautiful Losers*. Writing against liberal views of moderation and reasonableness, and against modern emphases on individualism and individual success, Cohen creates a novel in which the characters' main goals are the annihilation of the self, and the dissolving of the boundaries—skin, blood vessels, cell walls—that keep the individual human body from anonymity and death. Behind these characters Cohen places the model of a female Catholic "saint." However, she is not a saint who has been martyred by persecutors. Kateri Tekakwitha, beatified by the Church in 1980, was an aboriginal woman who deliberately sought to sacrifice her body to her understanding of spirituality, and to the will of the Jesuits, and who may have died of illness brought on by her own rigorously penitential habits. Death in this novel, whether occasioned by sexual excesses which lead to fatal disease, or by crouching under a descending elevator, or by reaching such a state of mental annihilation that one's consciousness blends and synchronizes with the blank spots between the frames of a movie reel, as does the protagonist's mind in the final pages, is to be welcomed as an achievement and triumph. Implicit in this book, although much more emphatically rendered, is an understanding of human experience similar to that offered by Morley Callaghan. The human world is corrupt, fallen, limited, and disappointing. Cohen, however, can foresee no future "joy in heaven." The only joy in *Beautiful Losers* is in the act itself of "losing," as in brief moments of sexual pain and pleasure in which both time and the body vanish together.

Curiously, even though there is no murder *per se* in this novel, the figure of the dying woman permeates its pages and links it to those earlier novels about murdered women. Kateri Tekakwitha is arguably killed by the new Christian religion of self-sacrifice which the Jesuit missionaries bring to Canada. Cohen himself lavishly eroticizes her physical sacrifices of her own body, going beyond the written records of her life to suggest that these sacrifices might have included obscure and deliciously masochistic aboriginal sexual rituals. He also eroticizes the death of the narrator's wife, Edith, under the elevator, both by associating it with her painful seeking of sexual transcendence with a "Danish vibrator," and by having the narrator erotically recall her crushed body. Moreover, it is Cohen as a writer who creates the fictional plot in which Edith gets caught up in her husband's quest for transcendence, and who gives to her a brutal death. In this respect, he joins the other Canadian writers who have in their various ways both "killed" and eroticized the Inuit girl, Clara De Haldimar, Clara Vogel, Laiah, Peggy Sanderson, and Mollie MacNeil.

Against these eroticized deaths, and particularly against the eroticized deaths of *Beautiful Losers*, stand in bold contrast the treatment of murder in two novels by Margaret Atwood—the only major Canadian novels to regard murder and wrongful death from a woman character's viewpoint. Atwood's 1981 novel *Bodily Harm* begins with a quotation that underlines such a difference in point of view: John Berger's "A man's presence suggests what he is capable of doing to you or for you. By contrast, a woman's presence...defines what can and cannot be done to her." The quotation also gestures pointedly to the issue of responsibility: it is not myth or history or biology here that are likely to harm a woman, but a man who is actively capable of "doing" something to her.

Bodily Harm presents a roster of characters who for the most part illustrate the active man versus passive woman contrast of the Berger quotation. Among the men are a prowler, a doctor, several policemen, a surgeon, a businessman, and a drug-runner. The central character, Rennie Wilford is a "lifestyle" journalist who, rather than "doing" things, writes about what other people do. "Other people make statements, she said. I just write them down."[29] Her best woman-friend in Canada operates a second-hand clothes boutique. Lora, the woman-friend she meets on a Caribbean island, is the white lover of a feckless black politician. The opening scene begins what is in effect a long meditation on violence toward women. Rennie comes home to her Toronto apartment to find that the police have surprised an intruder, who had forced open a window and been waiting for her, with a cup of hot Ovaltine and a neatly coiled length of rope. He has fled, leaving the rope suggestively on her bed. The rope makes

Rennie think of the child's board-game of Clue, in which the players have to solve a murder, except that she understandably confuses the murderer in the game with the victim, thinking the winning solution may have become "Miss Wilford, in the bedroom, with a rope." The policemen who investigate the incident attempt to eroticize it, suggesting to Rennie that she must have unwittingly attracted the intruder's attention by not closing the bathroom curtains when she took a shower, or by having men over "a lot."[30]

Atwood adds to Rennie's life a lover whose favourite fantasy while making love to her is to hold her wrists and pretend to be raping her: "Pretend I just came through the window. Pretend you're being raped...Admit it turns you on."[31] She adds also a journalism assignment which takes Rennie to a police storeroom full of whips, rubber appliances, dildoes, an enormous home-made vibrator, and photographs of women "being strangled or bludgeoned or having their nipples cut off by men dressed up as Nazis,"[32] where the police officer in charge comments cheerfully, "Look at it this way, at least it's not for queers."[33] She finally sends the reluctant Rennie, who keeps thinking "there were some things it was better not to know any more about than you had to,"[34] on a working holiday to an obscure Caribbean island, where a revolution breaks out. Rennie, whom Atwood has had inadvertently make casual friendships with the wrong people on the eve of a disastrous election, ends up with Lora in a military prison.

Although numerous men are killed in the gunfights and assassinations that follow the election, Atwood characterizes nearly all of these as the games boys play. The games and their violence become addictive, a "hard drug," and soon the players "need more."[35] The assault on Lora—Atwood leaves ambiguous whether or not it has been fatal—is of a different kind. She and Rennie have not been players. Hoping to get to see her lover, whom she has been told is imprisoned rather than dead, Lora has been doing favours for the guards who keep promising to arrange a meeting. When she learns she has been duped, she screams and kicks helplessly at them in her anger. They quickly overwhelm her and begin silently and methodically beating her.

> They go for the breasts and the buttocks, the stomach, the crotch, the head, jumping, *My God*, Mortón's got the gun out and he's hitting her with it, he'll break her so that she'll never make another sound. Lora twists on the floor of the corridor, surely she can't feel it any more but she's still twisting, like a worm that's been cut in half, trying to avoid the feet, they have shoes on, there's nothing she can avoid.[36]

In some respects, this scene has a strong resemblance to Hearne's account of the Copper Indians' murder of the Inuit girl. It shows the two guards, like the Indian warriors, enjoying the assault, setting about it with silent enthusiasm. Like the warriors, their focus is on the sexualized parts of their victim's body—the breasts, the buttocks, the crotch. Like the girl, Lora wriggles and squirms to avoid the blows. Like Hearne comparing the unfortunate girl's efforts to the writhing of an eel, Atwood writes that her victim twists like a lacerated worm. What the scene

196

does not have is the ambivalent sexual gaze which Hearne, as a male narrator, focuses on the dying girl's body. Rather than his coy, melodramatic descriptions with their pretence that he stands apart from the violence, Atwood offers a harsh description that attributes no beauty or grace to either the action or the assaulted woman.

Repeatedly in the novel Atwood has argued the heterosexual nature of violence. It is something done by men and not by women. It is something men enjoy, and especially enjoy doing to women. Done to women, it makes male onlookers, even Toronto police officers, smile and joke. It makes male participants desire more intense and savage participation. Rennie looks through a cell window where a group of soldiers are beating a group of prisoners, merely so they can cut their hair. "She's afraid of men and it's simple, it's rational," Atwood writes, "she's afraid of men because men are frightening."[37] But there is also a strong sense in the novel that this attraction to violence may be cultural rather than biological. There are some quiet, decent men here, including the politician-veterinarian Dr. Minnow, assassinated during the election, and a cancer surgeon, Daniel Luoma, who saves one of Rennie's breasts by performing a partial mastectomy. Male attraction to violence tends, the novel suggests, to be amplified by group dynamics, as in the cultures of Canadian police forces, or of an amateurish Caribbean army. That is, although the possibility seems high that a woman in the world depicted by the novel would be assaulted by men, the violent male behaviour itself is not necessarily inevitable.

Nevertheless, while the novel does show the impulse

197

toward violence to be as strong in Toronto as anywhere, it also "others" the most extreme enactments of it to black police officers and soldiers in the Caribbean. Canadian male violence is presented as contained, potential violence—a coil of rope on a bed, a lover's half-joking pretence of rape, or a roomful of sordid appliances and photographs, walled up within a police station. Canada is where people can still pretend to be "sweet Canadians."[38] The Caribbean island is where the walls around male violence are shattered, like the back of Dr. Minnow's skull by the assassin's bullet, and where the rapist and batterer becomes the police officer who back in Canada at least posed as an upholder of order.

A similar othering takes place in the second of Atwood's "murder" books, the dystopian novel *The Handmaid's Tale*. Again, although Canada is marked as complicit in the violence, the actual site of the killings is elsewhere. This site is the republic of Gilead, the largest remaining part of the United States which, after escalating crises in nuclear and chemical pollution and in human fertility, has been taken over by a theocratic Christian fundamentalist government. The killings here are state executions, performed before separate male and female audiences after torture and secret trials have brought about speedy and dubious convictions. The Gilead theocracy and its executions are specifically marked in the novel as "American" both by their resemblance to extreme right-wing Christian fundamentalism in the United States in our own time and by their echoing of the seventeenth-century Puritan settlements at Plymouth and Salem in Massachusetts with their witch-trials and witch-burnings. As in those settlements, the men and women in Gilead are largely segregated.

Only men are allowed to hold office or own property. Clothing has been standardized to ensure sexual modesty. And to assist the failing population, fertile young women have been forced to become sexual handmaids to ruling-class couples unable to bear children. It is one of these handmaids, Offred ("of Fred"), whom Atwood has narrate the book.

Those Atwood allows us to see killed in the novel are all thus "enemies" of the new state, whose "crimes" have been invented by the state to support its policies. The first group we see are a group of white-coated doctors, left hanging on hooks at a Boston University wall, each with "a placard hung around his neck to show why he has been executed: a drawing of a human foetus."[39]

> These men, we've been told, are like war crimi-
> nals. It's no excuse that what they did was legal
> at the time: their crimes are retroactive. They
> have committed atrocities, and must be made
> into examples, for the rest.[40]

The second group are women, two handmaids and one wife, publicly executed by strangulation in front of a group of wives, daughters, and handmaids—most likely, the handmaid narrator suggests, as punishment for unchastity or adultery. The third is one man, convicted of rape—although his actual crime seems to have been to oppose the government—whom the assembled handmaids have been invited to punish in a ceremonial "Particicution." All of these executions are thus charged with sexual ambience. The state has in effect banished much of its erotic energy—otherwise repressed under drab clothing and narrowly restrictive laws—to these occasions of ceremonial murder.

The erotic nature of the executions is especially evident at the Particicution. With the handmaids assembled in a circle, the condemned man is dragged in. "We are milling around," Offred reports. "There's an energy building here, a murmur, a tremor of readiness and anger. The bodies tense, the eyes are brighter, as if aiming."[41] Shortly after "Aunt Lydia," the woman in charge, blows her whistle to announce the beginning of the ceremony, "[t]here's a surge forward, like a crowd at a rock concert in the former time, when the doors opened, that urgency coming like a wave through us." When the handmaids actually begin beating the man, Offred notes that the "air is bright with adrenalin" and that from the other young women come "growling" and "yells." At the end the guardians have difficulty getting them to stop and, when they do stop them, many of the handmaids "seem dazed" as if they had just undergone an emotionally emptying experience.[42]

Also evident is Atwood's illustration of the ways in which women have historically been complicit in their own subjugation by men. Although it is men who, in this future world, have conducted the coup which has created Gilead and its government of "Commanders," and who have stripped women of their property and employment rights, many women like "Aunt Lydia" eagerly pretend to support the coup and its policies once they see the limited power they may gain by so doing. Deprived of power, and hungry for the sense of energy and adrenalin that any hint of power gives them, they may even enthusiastically perform the state's dirty work by helping execute someone who had been working to save them.

Throughout, Atwood's emphasis on the ruthless arbitrariness of the Gilead government and its laws argues that much human violence is created by society itself, through the attempts of those who have made themselves powerful to exploit the weak. It is the male government of Gilead, encoding its own members' possessive attitudes toward women, who have defined adultery as a capital offence, who have forbidden women to hold professional jobs or to earn or hold money, and who have created the sex-slave theological category of "handmaid." The lust for blood and violence we see in the women at the Particicution, the novel suggests, is not an innate blood-lust but a deformation of positive sexual and creative energies brought about by state repression. The eagerness of the crowd at a rock concert was innocent. But blocked by the state from all expression except at public executions, this same eagerness has become murderous. The socially accepted ways in which eagerness can be expressed has been brutally altered. "It has taken so little time to change our minds," the handmaid observes in another context, "about things like this."[43]

In its depiction of men as recurrently ruthless in their efforts to concentrate political and sexual power in their own hands, *The Handmaid's Tale* offers a bleak assessment of men's ability to construct a more humane and just social order. Yet, paradoxically, in its observations that a repressive culture like that of Gilead, or of the New England Puritans, or of the covertly sexist international scholars whose conference concludes the novel, is constructed rather than inevitable, that people's minds can be changed in one direction or another, the novel is much less bleak.

In general, murder in Canadian literature is something self-righteous American men do because America makes them do such things. Or it is something helpless Canadian men do when the hand of fate or the veiled arm of mythology directs them to do it. And above all, it is what the United States makes its men want to do, or it is done to the sexual bodies of women, because that is what the fates make men do. Even George Bowering's American gunman Frank Spencer, although he manages to kill only Caprice's brother, would have done worse to her, if he could have caught her. "I just aint exactly figured out what I am going to do to her. But it's going to be awful."[44] American murderers are confident and active. Their killings are assertions of power. Canadian murderers are confused and bewildered. Their killings are signs of their powerlessness—of their inability to resist mythology, biology, or destiny. Women do not participate in murder.

In Canadian history and popular culture, murders generally tend to be given little importance, and to be so "othered" from social consciousness that they are quickly forgotten. Under the entry "murder," *The Canadian Encyclopedia* lists eleven cases, one concerning a challenge to capital punishment, three concerning landmarks in the judicial punishment of aboriginals in the Northwest Territories, and seven concerning killings elsewhere. Of these seven—the FLQ killing of Pierre Laporte and the convictions of Wilbert Coffin, Peter Demeter, Evelyn Dick, Colin Thatcher, and Stephen Truscott—all but three, curiously, involve the killing of women. Murderers themselves have rarely been treated as "notorious" except at the time of their crime. The Donnelly murderers are unacknowledged, anonymous, and largely unknown. Novelist Rudy

Wiebe and other writers have made famous the "Mad Trapper" of the Yukon, Albert Johnson, but less as murderer than as defiant and resistant hunted man. Clifford Olson, serial killer of eleven or more young people in British Columbia in the 1970s, remains well known in Canada for the moment, but, as Peter Worthington's recent experience in interviewing him points out, there is general cultural resistance to making him notorious. Southern Manitoba's Jack Krafchenko, a folk-hero in the early part of this century, is now obscure even as a regional figure.

Some Canadian murderers who might have seemed destined, if not for enduring notoriety, at least for continuing public disgust have also been quickly forgotten. In 1949, Albert Guay, with the help of two accomplices, blew up a Quebec Airways DC3, killing twenty-three people, in a plot to kill and collect insurance on his wife. Guay and the others were later convicted and hanged. In 1946, the very attractive young Hamilton woman Evelyn Dick was convicted of killing, decapitating and dismembering her husband, and of killing her infant son, so that she could be free to be with her lover. Few Canadians today could identify their names, or even that of Paul Rose, convicted in the killing of Quebec Labour Minister Pierre Laporte in the FLQ "October Crisis" of 1970. In 1966, Paul Joseph Chartier went to the Parliament Buildings intending to explode a powerful bomb on the floor of the House of Commons, but accidentally exploded it and himself in a Commons washroom, where he had stopped to smoke a last cigarette. Despite Gary Geddes's sympathetic 1976 long poem *War and Other Measures*, this would-be killer remains to Canadians at least as obscure as Britain's Guy

Fawkes is legendary. *The Canadian Encyclopedia* gives him no mention.

The only killers with enduring reputations in Canada today are two francophones whose acts continue to have strong political resonance. One, Louis Riel, personally killed no one, although his unrecognized provisional government, with his agreement, executed the defiant Thomas Scott in 1870, and Métis fighters under at least his nominal leadership killed a number of Canadian soldiers in their unsuccessful 1885 rebellion. Riel's continuing importance lies in his having, from the day of Scott's execution, become a symbol of the Catholic–Protestant and French–English conflict in Canada. His defeat resulted in Manitoba's systematic quasi-legal mistreatment of its francophone minorities—a mistreatment only partially corrected by Supreme Court of Canada decisions in recent years. With Riel's execution, under the Macdonald government in 1885, began a long-lasting francophone suspicion of both English Canada and Macdonald's Conservative Party, which did poorly in Quebec until the 1958 federal election. Numerous books vilifying Riel were written immediately on his execution and in the years following: Wilbur Bryant's *The Blood of Abel*, Sir Alexander Campbell's *In the Case of Louis Riel, Convicted of Treason and Executed Therefor*, and J.E. Collins's *The Story of Louis Riel, the Rebel Chief*, in 1885 alone. In the same year, on the francophone side, were published the anonymous works of outrage and praise *Riel pendu! l'infamie consomée* and *Louis Riel: martyr du Nord-Ouest*.

The second widely known killer is Marc Lépine, the assassin of fourteen female engineering students at Montreal's École Polytechnique in December of 1989. His has been a strange notoriety, heavily resisted by many Canadians, yet also founded in part on that resistance. The political basis of this notoriety has been the women's movement and its involvement in making crimes against women both more visible and unacceptable, together with Lépine's own suicide note in which he professed hatred toward "feminists." The women's movement has argued vigorously that his murder of the fourteen should be perceived not as the act of an isolated madman but as a political crime—as a crime that enacted a violence against women which is "systemic" to our society. He was not a monster, in this view, but a man acting out in an extreme way the social attitudes of millions of men who make coarse jokes about women, who believe the pay differentials between men and women are fair, and who perceive nothing offensive about news features like the "SUNshine Girl." At the same time, substantial numbers of women have believed it would be unjust that his name be remembered rather than those of his victims. This attitude has led to the killings being much more often referred to as the "Montreal massacre," or the "École Polytechnique killings" than being recalled in Lépine's name. Even the strong and partly successful political lobby for increased gun control that emerged from the killings, and led in part by relatives of the victims, has been done in the victims' names rather than his. Resistance to the women's movement's view that the killings were a symptom of "systemic" contempt for women has been conducted mainly in terms of the "monstrous"—i.e., through arguments that Lépine was a unique individual, from a specifically dysfunctional family, who had developed attitudes which were an aberration among generally civilized male views of women. The one forum in which Lépine's name has been remembered is the underground one which repeats his hatreds, as in words scrawled on a York University hoarding shortly after the killings: "Marc Lépine was right."

Overall, both the literary depictions of murder and popular culture understandings of it present distortions of murder and murderers similar to the distortions that plagued understandings of the Mahaffy–French killings. They offer contradictory understandings that men "naturally" kill women, that Canadian men only helplessly become killers, and that women rarely kill or help kill. The relatively few depictions of murder in the most widely read Canadian texts tend both to eroticize the killings, much like many of the media treatments of the French murder, and to depict the murder as in some way excluded from everyday human experience. The eroticization seeks to create in readers a vicarious emotional investment in the killing, to make it "pleasurable," shocking, or horrifying to them, and to make them therefore complicit in it. The exclusion of the male murderer from everyday norms makes him either a monster—a creature outside of humanity—or a person in the grips of mythologies or other predeterminations outside of human control. Canadian popular culture, far from mythologizing killers in the manner that American popular culture does, tends to forget them, and their crimes.

Murder may be in Canadian culture the crime that Canadians do not commit. It is committed on nearly every episode of U.S. television shows like *NYPD Blue*, or *America's Most Wanted*, but rarely on Canadian-produced television. It is committed routinely by people like Richard Speck, Jean Harris, Charles Manson, John Gacy, Lee Harvey Oswald, or Lizzie Borden, but when it is committed in Canada it is an aberration. It represents an Americanization of Canadian streets, a spread of violence from the south, a breakdown of Canadian values. When four gunmen invaded the popular middle-class Toronto café Just Desserts in April 1994 and casually shot a young female diner, the general Canadian response was that of a "young plumber" quoted in *The Globe and Mail*: Toronto had become "just like New York" (7 April 1994). The Toronto chief of police called the killing a type of crime "that is now appearing increasingly in the Metro area after leaving big U.S. cities like Miami and Detroit with empty, rotting, downtown cores" (*The Toronto Star*, 7 April 1994). When murder is represented on Canadian-produced television, it tends to be in the form of a docudrama, and its emphasis is not on the killing but on the need to bring the case to a just and civil ending. The killer—whether Colin Thatcher, or the teenage boys who killed Helen Betty Osborne, or Peter Demeter—is shown to be strange and abnormal despite his facade of normality. And millions, with their social consciences telling them that they are thereby being good, non-murdering Canadians, watch.

This sense that Canadians do not murder appears connected to other Canadian social myths—that Canadian streets are safe, that guns are difficult to obtain, that Canada is inherently a peaceful society—and to the dismay Canadians experience when these things are shown not to be completely true. One reason for such mythologies is the presence immediately to Canada's south of the demonstrably more violent United States, where the level of violence can make that of Canada seem virtually nil. But levels of violence are relative phenomena. Canadian streets can be only more or less safe than other streets, or more or less safe than they have been. The sense that murder is un-Canadian appears related also to the perception that has developed over the years that it and other crimes are committed not by Canadians but by strangers among us—by the Irish in the nineteenth century, by Italians in the first half of this century, and currently by Jamaican and Asian gangs. In this view it is the foreign culture that creates murder and murderers, not the Canadian one. What it overlooks, of course, is that it is poverty, low education, and limited opportunities that most often lead to crime, and it has been immigrant communities, of whatever ethnicity, that have most often been poor, jobless, and below the educational standard of the host community.

This general sense that murder and murderers are "other" to Canada was particularly inappropriate to any understanding of the arrests of Bernardo and Homolka. Both appeared to most observers as blond and Canadian "as apple pie." They were Canadian-born, and residents of the Niagara Falls area, itself virtually a Canadian myth. They lived in a pink bungalow that was effectively a parody of numerous other Canadian bungalows. They were married in a wedding that could have been nearly any middle-class "dream" wedding. How does one "other" such people? Perhaps they were too normal, was one media suggestion. Perhaps they had tried too hard to leave behind their Portuguese and Czech inheritances, tried too hard to appear stereotypically blond and successful North Americans. Perhaps they had been monstrous in

208

their feigning of normality. Perhaps they had lived too close to the fast lanes of America. But one thing was to be certain: this "fairy-tale" couple could have little to do with ordinary Canada.

Cross-border shopping for Homolka trial news.

AT WAR
WITH THE U.S.

At war with the U.S.

I surrender

I embrace you

Now
get off my back

Stand
in the light
where I can see you

George Bowering, *At War with the U.S.*

George Bowering published his small poetry book *At War with the U.S.* in 1974, during the waning months of the U.S. war with Vietnam. On the cover is a cartoon drawing by his friend, the London, Ontario, artist Greg Curnoe, of two fighter aircraft locked in aerial combat. A small stubby jet-propelled plane with red maple leaves on its wings and fuselage and a checkered pattern around its cockpit has just fired a burst of gunfire into the tail of a much larger propeller-driven P-40 marked with traditional U.S. Air Force symbols. A huge gout of black smoke streams from the rear of the American plane.

Although the cover suggests that it is Canada that is "at

war with the U.S.," the book itself suggests a broader interpretation. The poet—perhaps represented by the stubby little Canadian plane—is at war with the U.S., but so are the Vietnamese and Cambodians, and even our very planet, both in Asia and in three-hundred-year-old Canada. And Canada is "at war with the U.S." by being at war with parts of itself.

> But we trim nickel, we tame electrons
> we buzz the land. Our buttons
> break on the soil of Yankee-torn Cambodia
>
> 300 years & a few miles from stone age
> to splintered atoms, how have we
> hurt our fresh-cut home so fast[1]

A supplier of nickel to the American war effort, Canada despoils its own landscape, Bowering suggests, even as American bombs fracture Asian soil. "Americanism" in this portrayal is thus a Canadian belief system as much as it is an American one. The aerial battle on the cover of the book may as easily be one between two Canadians over how "American" Canada should be—a Canadian civil war—as one between two countries.

   The title poem, "At War with the U.S.," expands upon these suggestions. Canadians are at war with the U.S. but cannot win. They surrender, hoping this will be a winning strategy. If they embrace the U.S. sufficiently, maybe it will "get off their backs" and allow them some independence. Maybe it will even come out "in the light" where Canadians can finally see and learn to distinguish between what is American and what is Canadian.

212

The ambiguities Bowering writes about in this little
book were of course rife in Canada during the Vietnamese
conflict. Canadian industries supplied $12.5 billion of
chemicals, aircraft parts, explosives, and other materials to
the U.S. military throughout the war at the same time as
Canada refused to become officially a belligerent. Thirty-
two thousand American deserters and draft-dodgers were
admitted freely to Canada and allowed sanctuary.
Numerous Canadians journeyed south to participate in
mass demonstrations against the war; ten thousand other
Canadians went south to enlist in the U.S. armed forces
and fight in Asia. Canadian environmental groups frequently invoked the parallel between what appeared to be
a United States war against the actual Asian landscape—
the Americans' destruction of rice paddies, torching of
suspected Viet Cong villages, and systematic defoliation of
Vietnamese jungles by means of aircraft spraying
Canadian-tested Agent Orange onto the forest canopies—
and the environmental damage being done at home by
Canadian industrial practices. The widespread joke that
the United States' ultimate Vietnam policy was to "nuke
it, pave it, and build a mall on it" implied that the war
was merely an extension of American industrial and commercial ambitions—the kinds of ambitions that were con-
currently turning Canadian agricultural land into
subdivisions and shopping malls, and Canadian forests
into newsprint for American print media. Yet this kind of
"Americanism" was frequently carried out by Canadians—
not just as soldiers in the U.S. army but as industrialists
and corporate real-estate developers back home. In
Margaret Atwood's 1970 novel *Surfacing*, the "Americans"
the narrator knows to have been wantonly killing

213

Canadian wildlife in the northern Ontario forests turn out merely to be Americanized Canadians.

This combination of enmity, complicity, and fascination which writers like Atwood and Bowering showed Canadians displaying toward the United States during the Vietnam war was not unique to that war but has a long history as both an externally directed attitude and an internal conflict. At the root of this cultural phenomenon is one simple fact: Canada came into being between 1776 and 1867 because many North Americans did not wish to be citizens of the new American republic. Four of the seventeen British North American colonies did not join in the declaration of independence of the other thirteen, and some 40,000 "Loyalists" journeyed, from 1783 onward, as war refugees from the thirteen colonies to Nova Scotia, Prince Edward Island, and Quebec. Yet this choice not to be part of the American revolution and the republic to which it led was not clear-cut. There was considerable pro-revolution sentiment in Nova Scotia and Montreal during the revolutionary war, and many of the Loyalists came north because of political and family complications, or because of offers of free land, rather than because of narrowly anti-republican sentiments.

Nevertheless, the ideological differences between the two regions and their governments became fairly distinct. In the new republic grew a sense of having created a violent rupture with the past, of having established new authorities, and of having set out on an entirely "new" course. The fact that this new course was not as radical as it might have been—that it was, unlike the French revolution a decade later, a revolution led by an élite, which left

214

power and privilege in the hands of the wealthy classes that had possessed them in colonial times—did not prevent the formation of views that the new country was a place of unusual individual liberty and opportunity. In the colonies that would become Canada, the view that violent rupture with the past was dangerous and unnecessary, that change could be accomplished within existing structures in a gradual and evolutionary way, became not unexpectedly the ruling orthodoxy. Rather than a doctrine of individual, gun-bearing liberty, guaranteed by a constitution, Canadians became accustomed to having collective common-law rights protected by centuries-old principles of legal and civil organization.

Canada's first "war with the U.S." took place during some of the opening action of the American revolution—almost as if the new republic's very first thought was to seize what is now Canada. A revolutionary army under General Richard Montgomery captured Montreal in September 1775 and joined with a second army under Benedict Arnold at a siege of Quebec. American hopes seem to have been to encourage the northern colonies to join in their action and to begin their struggle by depriving Britain of its St. Lawrence stronghold. Arnold's forces were routed in May of 1776. The second "war with the U.S.," the War of 1812 between Britain and the United States, into which the remaining British North American colonies were drawn because of their British military bases, to some extent worked to solidify Canadian perceptions of being different from the United States. Declared by the U.S., and fought by British regulars and Canadian militia largely from a defensive posture, the war entrenched Canadian perceptions of the U.S. as an aggressor nation, and created the mythology that Canadian colonial militias and their Indian allies had been able to defeat American armies. Again the U.S. leaders appear to have hoped the populations of the Canadas would welcome an invasion. Sizeable numbers of Americans had emigrated to Upper Canada in the early 1800s, in search of free land and lower taxes. Instead, in the wake of the war, new military installations were constructed, and an ardent public loyalty to the Crown became the normal and demanded outlook of the Canadian colonist. Even the reform movements that culminated in the failed Mackenzie–Papineau rebellions of 1837 were handicapped by this fear of the United States and of the abrupt violence of its birth. Many colonists who opposed the rebellions *per se* later supported official institution of the kinds of government reform which rebellion leaders had demanded.

In the most influential Canadian literary writings of this period, this distaste and suspicion of things American are strongly evident, along with a hope that Canadians or Nova Scotians could find political, economic, and cultural directions distinct from those of Britain. Susanna Moodie's record of her family's emigration from Britain to the eastern Ontario area in 1832 is filled with suspicion that her new neighbours may be "Yankees," and that their desperate poverty may indicate that they are rebellion-minded republicans, disrespectful of education, manners, and middle-class privilege. Here is her portrayal of the conversation of one of her first neighbours, Mrs. Joe.

"Ah, I guess you don't look upon us as fellow-critters, you are so proud and grand. I s'pose you Britishers are not made of flesh and blood like us.

You don't choose to sit down at meat with your helps."[2]

Mrs. Moodie writes that she replied that her "helps, as you call them, are civil and obliging, and never make unprovoked and malicious speeches. If they could so far forget themselves, I should order them to leave the house."

> "Oh I see what you are up to," replied the insolent dame; "you mean to say that if I were your help, you would turn me out of your house; but I'm a free-born American, and I won't go at your bidding. Don't think I come here out of regard to you. No, I hate you all; and I rejoice to see you at the wash-tub, and I wish that you may be brought down upon your knees to scrub the floors."[3]

Throughout this exchange, Moodie portrays the American as ignorantly prideful, spiteful, and insensitive to both other people's feelings and to the decorums that constitute Moodie's own notion of civilization. On the other hand, she describes the British and their servants in terms of predictability and order: her "helps" are "civil and obliging," while she herself merely smiles indulgently at Mrs. Joe's tirade. When the 1837 rebellions break out, against administrative rule and in favour of representative government, Moodie declares unthinking patriotism as she sends off her reserve-officer husband, Dunbar, to fight this "unnatural rebellion"[4] and defend civil order. Yet when her journals are published as a book in 1852, attached to them in a conclusion written by her husband, are several comments sympathetic to the rebels and critical of the "patronage" practices which he believes had corrupted the government against which they had rebelled. Moreover, he notes that the rebellion which he had fought against had "soon produced the remedy."

> The party generally most powerful in the Legislative Assembly, and the members of which had been so long and so unconstitutionally excluded from holding office under the government, at once obtained the position to which they were entitled.[5]

But even in Dunbar Moodie's pro-rebel comments, the continuity of rule of law is affirmed. The rebellion, in his view, succeeds not by overthrowing the government but by revealing the government's lawlessness and by leading the Crown to replace it with a more "constitutional one." It has not created new rights, as did the American revolution, but has helped obtain rights to which citizens had already been "entitled."

Thomas Haliburton's internationally received comic sketches of Sam Slick, a Yankee clock salesman, published as *The Clockmaker* in 1836, contained devastating Canadian conceptions of American smugness, arrogance and bombast. At one point Haliburton has Sam Slick solemnly tell the narrator that he likes "to look up at them 'ere stars,"

> they put me in mind of our national flag, and it is generally allowed to be the first flag in the univarse now. The British can whip all the world, and we can whip the British. It's near about the

prettiest sight I know of, is one of our first-class
frigates, manned with our free and enlightened
citizens, all ready for sea; it is like the great
American Eagle...afeared of nothin' of its kind,
and president of all it surveys. It was a good
emblem we chose, warn't it?[6]

At another point, he has Slick announce to the narrator
his nation's racist and chauvinist doctrine of its "manifest
destiny" to rule all of North America:

[Nova Scotians] must recede before our free and
enlightened citizens like the Indians; our folks
will buy them out, and they must give place to a
more intelligent and ac-*tive* people. They must go
to the lands of Labrador, or be located back of
Canada; they can hold on there a few years, until
the wave of civilization reaches them, and then
they must move again as the savages do. It is
decreed. I hear the bugle of destiny a-soundin'
their retreat, as plain as anything.[7]

Haliburton's Nova Scotian narrator, often considered a
thinly disguised version of Haliburton himself, is not at all
amused by Slick's republican convictions, and replies ten-
dentiously,

The emblem is more appropriate than you are
aware of: boasting of what you cannot perform;
grasping at what you cannot attain; an emblem
of arrogance and weakness; of ill-directed ambition and vulgar pretension.[8]

Yet the narrator also covertly shares Slick's narcissistic desire to have the fastest trotting horse, and sometimes openly endorses the criticism Slick offers that the Nova Scotia legislators "don't encourage internal improvement, nor the investment of capital in the country; and the result is apathy, inaction, and poverty."[9] Like many twentieth-century Canadians, Haliburton's narrator perceives the American emphasis on individual freedom and enlightenment to be a false boast, one that ignores their nation's numerous social problems and encourages pride in being ignorant, yet he also envies American economic competitiveness. If being more American meant only being more prosperous and having a faster horse, he would like to be so. In portraying Slick as a fast-talking and successful salesman of an industrial product, Haliburton is also making a strong criticism of Canada's economic exploitation by the United States. Rather than developing their own manufacturing industries, Nova Scotians are indolently remaining an agricultural people and letting excessively-hyped American-manufactured goods easily cross their borders.

In an odd way, the position of Haliburton's narrator, horrified by the excesses of the new republican culture but also admiring of its openness, energy, and unachieved egalitarianism, resembles the position of many Canadians in the months that followed Karla Homolka's trial and Mr. Justice Kovacs's publication ban. Once again, Canadians were getting generous helpings of gratuitous advice from their southern neighbour. And much of this advice argued that the United States was a freer, more open, more democratic society, that Canadian justice was élitist, secretive, anti-democratic, and tradition-bound, that it accorded insufficient weight to individual rights. *A Current Affair*'s Mary Garofalo exclaimed, when she was admonished by some Canadian journalists for having published U.S. television material covered by Judge Kovacs's ban,

> I was dumbfounded...I'm so disappointed with those journalists who aren't standing up and fighting and violating this ban. I got a call from somebody at CFRB, and she said, Well what about the morality of it. The Morality! Fuck the morality! There's no greater immorality than talking away someone's rights! And they have the audacity to say that what I was doing was sleazy... (Chatto. *Toronto Life*, May 1994)

Here Canadian journalists were characterized as disappointing, deferential, and uncourageous. The appropriate action, Garofalo suggested, echoing the American colonies' originary disobedience against British law and proud disrespect for British tradition, is to violate the ban in as crude a manner as possible. Any morality which the judicial ban can claim is to be "fucked." Individual rights, she argued, have a higher moral claim than the orders of a legally constituted court and the civil society it represents.

Both *The New York Times* and *The Washington Post* lectured Canadians and their courts about the fundamentals of justice. The long-standing American fear of "tyranny," the American memory of their own sense of having been tyrannized by British justice in 1775, and the recurrent American fear that their own courts of law may belong to some privileged élite rather than to all the people, were all evident in the *Times'* choice of words: the ban, it announced, was "bizarre," "wrong in principle," and an "instrument of tyranny." After evoking police-state scenes of "patrols at the Peace Bridge," and "border police" stopping U.S. papers (Canada has no border police, although the U.S. does), the editorial concluded with the patronizing hope that "a regard for free expression and the folly of enforcing such a gag in today's world, will lead Canada to adopt a different course" (4 December 1993). The *Post* wrote as if Judge Kovacs's order were general and permanent rather than specific and temporary; the paper's arguments displayed a profound fear of governmental and other abuses of democratic power: "one day that business [of a court] involves a horrible murder, but the next trial could be about public corruption, corporate shenanigans, tax scandals, the sins of a rogue government agency or the depravity of a government leader." Like the *Times*, it also expressed a Sam Slick-like assumption that laws which had been adopted by the United States must necessarily be adopted in other countries: "First Amendment assumptions that are rock solid on this side of the international border are not universally accepted, even by this country's friends to the north" (4 December 1993).

Many Canadian journalists were swayed by these American arguments—or pretended to be in order to justify continued publicity about the murders—and made them part of an internal Canadian debate. Well-known for his nationalism, Rick Salutin grumpily commented that, like a stopped clock that is "right" twice every day, *The Washington Post* had been right about the need for the public business of courts to be open to public view (10 December 1993). Allan Fotheringham commented, "I do not like being lectured by Americans, but the more than puzzled U.S. press is entirely correct in its rather polite comments on this judicial ban that goes against everything the Americans fought for in their constitution after they revolted against the rule of an English king."

> The *Washington Post* is a paper that knows. This is the paper that with fantastic courage overthrew a president over Watergate.... (18 December 1993)

The Toronto Star published an editorial in which it protested that Judge Kovacs's ban "seems outdated and patronizing as it assumes potential jurors are unable to separate media reports from courtroom evidence."

> A preferable system exists in the United States, where virtually all trials are held in public—but with better safeguards for jury selection.

The editorial added the further comment that events were proving "how futile it is to suppress information in our technological age" (1 December 1993).

Two very curious things were happening in these new "Canadian" arguments and in the events that lay behind them. One was that the journalists were assuming that the ban, because of the "technological age," was unenforceable. But technology itself was doing nothing. It was the actions of American journalists, with their particular national ideological view of the Canadian courts, and the actions of any Canadians who were leaking banned facts to them, that made the ban seem unenforceable. The second was that a major element in the U.S. legal system, a product of that nation's rebellion against the more conservative and cautious British system of laws which a majority of Canadians had, since 1775, repeatedly preferred, was being offered for off-the-shelf importation into Canada. In a sense, the two things went together: the American practice of keeping preliminary hearings and trials open to media reporting was being made into an attractive-looking import because Americans were actively making the Canadian alternative appear futile and ineffective. It was as if American wheat producers had suddenly attempted to persuade Canadians that Canadian wheat was no better than animal food, and that they must henceforth eat only American wheat products.

In the years following the War of 1812, the history of American aggressive behaviour toward British North America and other territories, continued to have a determining influence on the settlements that would in a few decades be Canada. Although the United States acquired large amounts of land through the Louisiana Purchase from France in 1803 and the Alaska purchase from Russia in 1867, it also seized large amounts of land—Hawaii, California, and most of Texas, New Mexico, and Arizona— in poorly rationalized seizures and invasions. In the 1840s, under the slogan "Fifty-four-forty or fight," the United States had threatened war with Britain to obtain a north-west boundary from the Great Divide to the Pacific Ocean at 54' 40" north latitude. Through subsequent international arbitration, resulting in the Oregon Treaty, the U.S. prevented most of what would become the states of Washington and Idaho from being British Columbia territory. In 1859, in what is known in B.C. as "The Pig

War," the U.S. landed troops on San Juan Island, south-west of Vancouver Island, to enforce a favourable interpretation of that treaty. The widely announced United States theory of its "manifest destiny" to govern all of North America, declared even in the 1860 and later editions of Walt Whitman's *Leaves of Grass*, greatly unsettled Britain and the Canadas, particularly when the United States assembled enormous armies to fight its civil war. At the end of that war, a nervousness about U.S. intentions was influential in motivating the five original Canadian provinces to confederate in 1867, and in Queen Victoria's selection of Ottawa, far north of the U.S. border, to be the new nation's capital.

In 1903, there was widespread Canadian suspicion that the United States had successfully manipulated an international tribunal to grant its claim to the heads of the various inlets in the Alaska panhandle. Although Canada's attitudes toward aboriginal title to land were similar to those of the United States, Canadian expansion had, in contrast to the American, involved no aggression against European or American sovereign states. Canada had purchased the Hudson's Bay Lands in 1870, acquiring much of what is now northern Quebec and Ontario, all of Manitoba, and much of Alberta and Saskatchewan. The British colonies of British Columbia and Newfoundland entered Canada through voluntary union. And even in terms of the acquisition of aboriginal land, Canadian and American practices had differed. In the U.S., settlers had tended to travel in advance of treaty negotiators, surveyors, and lawmen, whether into aboriginal lands or the northern states of Mexico, often triggering violent confrontations with the inhabitants, which the United States army could use as a pretext for invasion. In the Canadian west, treaty negotiators, surveyors, and police officers preceded settlers, who then entered not a contested land but one already structured by civil law. The American west thus tended to produce individual "heroes"—Sam Houston, Davy Crockett, J.C. Frémont—and the Canadian west to produce institutional ones like the North-West Mounted Police and the Canadian Pacific Railway.

In the twentieth century, with most border disputes between the two countries settled, American aggression toward Canada took mostly economic and cultural form. Again, many historic Canadian decisions were taken in response to the perception of such threats. The 1928 Royal Commission on Radio Broadcasting, which led to the establishment of the Canadian Broadcasting Company in 1936, was set up both because so many small radio stations were falling under American ownership and because Canadian listeners had no Canadian alternatives to the programming that was flooding into Canada from the new networks in the U.S. The National Film Board of Canada was founded in 1939 both to facilitate the production of film in Canada and to provide documentary films from Canadian viewpoints to counter the dominance of Hollywood-produced films.

Nationalism in Canada, in fact, has been repeatedly defined in terms of anti-Americanism, and not merely as an unthinking hostility but as a recognition that Canada has represented an alternative way of being North American to that represented by the United States. From the building of the Canadian Pacific Railway as far south as possible, to prevent American encroachment and appropriation of the kind it had practised against Mexico, to the welcoming of American intellectuals discredited by the McCarthy-era persecutions of socialism, to the rage against Prime Minister John Diefenbaker in 1959 for having cancelled the building of the Canadian-designed Avro Arrow jet fighter and having replaced it with American F-104 fighters and Bomarc missiles, Canadians have tended to perceive their country in terms of its difference from the United States. Yet at the same time, we have wanted to be "as good as" the United States, and even to emulate it.

The Avro Arrow debacle very nicely illustrates many of these ambiguities. The Arrow was designed as a high-performance delta-wing interceptor to carry out a role within the American-led NORAD and NATO treaty alliances. Like an earlier interceptor, the CF-100, it was intended partly to show Canada's ability to carry out a role similar to that of the United States in opposing Communist-bloc aggression. At the same time, the Arrow was to demonstrate Canada's independence from the U.S.—its ability to build its own aircraft and to design ones that were specifically suitable for the kinds of long-range patrol and interception required by the country's vast northern spaces. It was also to help support an indigenous aerospace industry, stimulate domestic employment, and prevent the export of dollars to the U.S. for off-the-shelf aircraft. But in another sense, the Arrow was not at all Canadian but international and generic. Its main designers were British-trained engineers. In general shape and function, it resembled other planes being developed in the U.S., the Soviet Union, Britain, and France. Moreover, its economic practicability depended on Canada's ability to sell it to the country that it correctly perceived as its rival, and when the U.S. refused to purchase it, Canada was left in the humiliating position of having to purchase that rival's less appropriate aircraft, and to purchase Bomarc missiles that were effective only with nuclear warheads. The latter fact gave many Canadians persistent doubts that Canada, officially a nation without nuclear arms, actually controlled the new Bomarc installations.

> Buy American! America First! American Jobs for American People! The U.S. Congressional automotive congress went so far this week as to introduce legislation that would give $2,000 in tax credits to people who buy American-made automobiles even though 90 per cent of U.S. car dealers sell foreign-made vehicles.
>
> So what is the Canadian response to our recession?
>
> Cross-border shopping.
>
> (*The Vancouver Sun*, 1 February 1992)

The ambivalent position of Canada toward the United States, both fearing it and envying it, both disdaining it and seeking to compete with it on its own terms, has usually been portrayed as a cultural phenomenon—even the Arrow has been converted in Canadian consciousness from a military aircraft into a cultural symbol. Attempts to defend Canada against the United States have far more often involved cultural actions than military ones. But underlying the ambivalence are some starkly significant material realities. The economy of the U.S. is almost ten times larger than that of Canada. The economies of scale within which it can produce everything from fighter aircraft to compact discs are vastly more efficient than those possible in Canada. Its large and relatively concentrated population has enabled its industries to establish distribution networks for its products—whether chains of retail stores or chains of movie-houses—which have much greater financial power than comparable distributors in Canada, and therefore much greater power to purchase their competitors. Canadian producers of goods, services, or cultural products interested in attaining similar scale must try to succeed in the United States market by setting up a branch-plant operation like the Reichmann brothers, licensing their products to American producers as the Labatt and Molson breweries have often done, or moving to the U.S. as Mary Pickford, Lorne Green, William Shatner, Michael J. Fox, and John Candy did.

For Canadian governments, the overwhelmingly larger scale of the U.S. economy has made Canada extremely difficult to govern. A rise in United States interest rates can quickly kill any attempt at a low-interest-rate Canadian policy. A United States failure to institute a national health-care system can undermine Canadian attempts to retain its own universal health-care system, particularly after the 1988 free trade agreement, which enabled Canadian businesses to move their operations to the U.S. and avoid the cost of paying for mandatory medical coverage to Canadian employees while still enjoying access to the Canadian market. Canadian governments can attempt to reduce the consumption of cigarettes by raising tobacco taxes, and then discover that low taxation of tobacco products in the U.S. is causing widespread smuggling of them into Canada. They can similarly raise gasoline taxes in an attempt to reduce the consumption of gasoline and to encourage the search for alternate energy sources, and find that unchanged American taxes are causing Canadians who live in or near border towns to buy their gasoline in the U.S., and Canadians travelling cross-country to drive most of the distance through the northern states.

These indirect or inadvertent American constraints on Canadian governments to set their own monetary and taxation policies are often exacerbated by direct American attacks on Canadian government practices. The Canadian practice of charging stumpage fees to companies for the right to harvest the timber on crown lands has been challenged by U.S. lumber producers who argue that the U.S. practice of auctioning timber rights results in a more competitive market, and that therefore duties should be levied against Canadian lumber exported to the U.S. The Canadian Wheat Board, established by the Conservative government of R.B. Bennett in the early 1930s, has been similarly challenged by U.S. grain producers as constituting a subsidy to Canadian farmers. In each case the challenge implies, as in the *Times* and *Post* Homolka editorials, that the U.S. practice is superior to, and more "fair" than, the Canadian one, and that the U.S. one should be imported into Canada. In each also, the American ideology of individual freedom and of free-market competitiveness is placed against a Canadian ideology of state-supported collective action.

The Mahaffy–French murders took place not only against a background of increasing trade disputes but along a stretch of the international border with a long history of military and economic conflict between the two nations. No fewer than seven battles took place on the

Niagara Peninsula in the War of 1812, and both Niagara-on-the-Lake, the site of the Bernardo–Homolka wedding, and Buffalo, the site of some of the major ban defiances, were burned by American and British forces respectively. In recent times the American side of the Niagara River has been the focus of extreme Canadian anger over the continual polluting of Lake Ontario: the Love Canal chemical dump continues to leech dioxins and other chemicals into the American Niagara Falls. In the 1990–1992 period of the murders, the peninsula was also the site of major attacks on Canadian taxation and social policies. Gas stations in Canadian border towns were driven out of business by the low gasoline prices immediately opposite. Cigarette and liquor smuggling from the U.S. into Canada, spurred by the sharp differential in taxes that made U.S. prices as low as half of the Canadian, burgeoned.

Moreover, even trade in general goods, of which the U.S. prices were often marginally lower because of different conditions and practices, was affected. U.S. retailers began constructing on their side of the border shopping malls for which the only possible market could be visiting Canadians. They also began advertising in Canadian newspapers and on Canadian radio and television. Some Canadian newspaper readers protested that the papers were being unpatriotic in accepting such advertising, and threatened to stop purchasing them. The price differentials, where they existed, were caused by a variety of factors, all in some way related to the particular situation of the Canadian economy. One major factor continued to be the economies of scale enjoyed by the American wholesale and retail distribution systems. Another was the higher cost of operating a business in Canada due to

231

chronically higher interest rates and to the medical, pension, and unemployment benefits that Canadian employers were required to add to their payrolls. Yet another was the Canadian requirement for bilingual English/French labelling, which often meant that imports of American products like bedsheets had to be repackaged. Sometimes the differential in price was an illusion created or fostered by American advertising, and vanished once the exchange rate between the Canadian and American dollars was taken into account. Whatever the reason, Canadians on one-day shopping trips began returning to Canada with more dutiable U.S.-bought goods—an estimated $3 to $5 billion worth annually by February 1992—than Canada Customs staff could process. Long line-ups occurred on the American side of border-crossing points. Every month, Canadian newspapers would carry stories about yet another increase in "cross-border shopping" and about the damage "un-Canadian consumers" were doing to local industries and retail businesses.

Although the media did not often interpret the "cross-border" phenomenon as such, it was undoubtedly a national crisis. Collectively, Canadians had decided many decades before through their governments that they would accept higher levels of taxation in order to have a greater level of service from their governments. They had supported the institution of Unemployment Insurance in 1940, of the Canada Pension Plan in 1966, and of medicare in 1966. They had also supported high taxation of liquor and tobacco products in the belief that such measures acted as social controls against alcohol abuse and against the early addiction to cigarettes by young people. They may have been "correct" or "incorrect" in making these decisions, but as citizens they had a right to make them and to expect them to be acted upon. Ideologically, of course, these measures entrusted to the state certain actions which American citizens had traditionally believed better left to the individual. In the United States it was generally believed to be the individual's responsibility to prepare for his or her retirement, pay for medical bills, and to avoid the abuse of alcohol and resist tobacco addiction.

Although, in light of the numbers of people involved, this Canadian resistance to higher-priced goods appeared to be a collective disobedience, it lacked the organization and cohesion of actual collectivity. Partly encouraged by the publicity the Canadian media gave to the phenomenon and by American advertising, the cross-border shopper made personal or family decisions to participate, and made these on the basis of individual rather than collective economic advantage. Most seemed oblivious to the fact that their actions, by undermining the Canadian taxation system, could be jeopardizing some of the Canadian social programmes many of them relied upon. In this individual or entrepreneurial motivation and disregard for collective consequences, the cross-border shopper had become "Americanized," and when interviewed by the Canadian media would usually claim that he or she, as an individual, could no longer afford to pay Canadian prices or taxes.

At another level of Americanization were the professional smugglers, who at Niagara ranged from individuals who made regular automobile or boat trips across the border with cartons of cigarettes or cases of liquor, to gangs who used false documents to bring in tractor-trailer loads of contraband. Here the frontier attitude of many Americans in California in the 1830s, that Mexican law was irrelevant to their personal commercial goals, was repeated in the individual's cavalier attitude toward Canadian law. In several newspaper accounts of Paul Bernardo's life in St. Catharines, it has been alleged that he made much of his living not as an accountant but by smuggling cigarettes into Canada across the Niagara River. A darker side to this international exchange was suggested by an allegation on the second Mahaffy–French programme of *A Current Affair* that the FBI was investigating possible connections between Bernardo and several deaths in the U.S. At the time of Bernardo's arrest, *The Toronto Sun*, in an article that attempted to associate him with other murders, had reported that his car had "apparently made numerous trips across the border and the U.S. Customs computer, TECS, will be searched for information" (19 February 1993).

In late 1993, after *The Washington Post*, *Newsweek*, *USA Today*, *The Detroit Free Press*, and *The Buffalo News* had all published information banned by Mr. Justice Kovacs's order, another kind of cross-border shopping busied the Niagara area. Following the same route Paul Bernardo had allegedly taken many times before, numerous Canadians hurried to Buffalo to purchase and bring back banned details of Karla Homolka's trial. After running out of copies of *The Buffalo News*, some news vendors sold photocopies of the Homolka article. The conflict that was evident here was similar to that evident in the earlier crisis in cross-border trade: individuals were refusing a social decision which their society had collectively made through its institutions and were asserting instead their personal abilities to take separate action. The entrepreneurship of the U.S. media in obtaining the banned details was reflected in both the initiative of the news vendors who made and sold photocopies and that of the Canadians who drove to Buffalo.

At virtually the same time as Customs agents, the police, and the Ontario attorney general were attempting to stem this flow of newspapers, Canada's federal government was wrestling with the growing problem of cigarette smuggling. Increasing numbers of tax-free cigarettes were being exported by Canadian tobacco companies to unscrupulous distributors in the U.S., being re-sold to Canadian smugglers, many of whom were residents of an Indian reserve that straddles the border, and distributed on Canadian streets. The result became a street price for smuggled cigarettes that was less than half the $7.00 per pack price charged for legal cigarettes by most retailers. *The Globe and Mail* estimated that 70 to 75 per cent of the cigarettes being sold in Quebec in late 1992 and early 1993 had been smuggled from the United States, and 20 per cent of those sold across Canada. Government attempts to stop the smuggling by imposing a prohibitive tax on Canadian cigarettes exported to the U.S. had been thwarted by tobacco company threats to close their Canadian factories, put their employees out of work, and begin manufacturing the same brands in the U.S. The possibility of ending much of the smuggling by arresting aboriginal smugglers on their reserves was dismissed by governments out of fear of provoking tribal violence.

In both the case of the Homolka trial information and the case of the cigarettes, the fundamental question concerned the ability of Canadian governments to govern. If, because of the proximity of a powerful and ideologically different United States and the presence of dissident, entrepreneurial citizens within Canada, those governments were no longer able to enforce significant parts of their legal system and taxation policies, the sovereignty of those governments was significantly compromised. In early February, the federal and Quebec governments capitulated on the tobacco taxes, with the federal government offering additional matching tax reductions in any province that wished to offer their own tax reductions. With low-tax, interprovincially smuggled Quebec cigarettes threatening to overwhelm their markets, Ontario, New Brunswick, and Nova Scotia soon made similar reductions. A high-tax policy supported by most Canadians—one that was undoubtedly regressive in taxation terms but which had succeeded in lowering smoking rates across the country—was effectively thwarted by a few thousand smugglers and their short-sighted customers. Interestingly, some observers hailed the attempts at tax reduction as a triumph for democracy and American-style individual freedom—including the parish priest of St. Eustache, Father André Daoust: "People are just looking out for themselves by buying the contraband cigarettes. The taxes are too high," he told *The Globe and Mail* (Mackie, *The Globe and Mail*, 26 January 1994). But in terms of Canadian history, it could more easily be viewed as a defeat for democracy—for the ability of the nation to govern itself through the policies of its elected representatives. For the purchase of contraband wasn't occurring because taxes were "too high." They were occurring because the taxes and overall prices were much higher than they were south of the border. In a column headlined

"Tobacco teaches a lesson," *Toronto Star* writer Donna Laframboise also argued that the tax reduction indicated the power of a "democratic society," and that

> all three levels of government have behaved largely as though there were no real constraints on the levels of taxation they could impose. The tobacco smuggling issue has demonstrated clearly that there is a limit, that after a certain point ordinary people can and will find ways to rebel. (2 May 1994)

In fact, the smuggling issue had demonstrated no such thing. It had only demonstrated that Canadian governments were powerless to adopt tobacco taxation levels that were significantly higher than those in the United States.

In the Homolka case a similar capitulation seems to have occurred—one even more serious, not only because it concerned the ability of the Canadian state to guarantee an individual the right to a fair trial, but also because it called into question Canada's ability to maintain its own judicial system. Mr. Justice Kovacs had imposed the ban because he had agreed with the Crown's contention that the public revealing of the details of Homolka's conviction could damage Bernardo's prospects for a fair trial. However, with private importation and circulation of the American newspapers, with the presence of these and several other American publications containing banned material in Canadian libraries, often on microfilm, and with the ban being broken regularly elsewhere by electronic means, the details would appear to have been publicly revealed. At least in a technical sense, the situation that the Crown predicted would jeopardize Bernardo's right to a fair trial had come about. Yet only the symbolic defiance of Gordon Domm was prosecuted. The ban breaches of *Frank* magazine and *The Daily Victorian*, and of individual citizens at the Niagara and Windsor borders, were unprosecuted. As in the cigarette-smuggling case, the Canadian state had apparently lacked the power or will to enforce its own rule.

This apparent powerlessness of the state to protect the rights of an accused which it had set out to protect, despite his not having wanted them protected, may in the long term be more important than the actual technical infringement on Bernardo's rights. For the most serious effect of the small flood of newspapers and photocopies into the Niagara area seems to have occurred in St. Catharines itself. Here, Michael Posner reported in *Chatelaine* (February 1994), could be found "well-thumbed copies of British and U.S. newspapers that defied the publication blackout; and pirated videocassettes of the Fox network's show *A Current Affair*." But a change of venue could appropriately remedy this difficulty for the accused. Elsewhere the number of people actually interested in joining the Internet Homolka fan club, or in searching out copies of *Newsweek* or *The Washington Post* at their libraries, seems to have been small. Overall, Mr. Justice Kovacs's ban would appear to have succeeded. Although it was unable to stop the continuing mythologization of the case and of its major figures, it was successful in preventing the trial details from becoming a part of these self-continuing Canadian news stories. What is more troubling, however, are the indications for the future, when the electronic transmission of news from extra-national sources may be even more extensive than today—when the kind of news printed by *The Toronto Sun* may come to most homes by direct satellite transmission rather than from a local print source.

That is, one significant implication of the Homolka case and Judge Kovacs's publication ban is that various government efforts over the past thirty years to "protect" Canadian culture haven't been only about the protection of Canadian produced music, television, and books. Culture in its larger sense concerns the production of social meanings and values. To protect a nation's "culture" is to protect its opportunities to determine for itself what it deems valuable: what priorities its government should have, what legal practices its courts should follow, what social policies it should have for its children, its aged, and its sick, what kinds of educational, professional, and artistic options it should make available, what options for distinct development it should permit for its minorities and its regions. In Canada, part of the protection of culture has involved the state making it possible for certain kinds of cultural expressions—books, magazines, radio and television programming—to circulate in a society whose distribution system for such things would be bought up in a flash by American investors if there were no state protection. In some areas, such as film distribution, the Canadian state has failed dismally, and the result is that national debates among Canadians about who and what they would be cannot be conducted in that medium. The Homolka case brings into particularly sharp focus the efforts of the Canadian Radio-television and Telecommunications Commission to regulate television signal broadcasts. Without regulation, the very existence of

Canadian radio and television media, whether Canadian- or foreign-owned, and with them the existence of Canadian broadcast views of domestic events such as the Homolka trial, would be doubtful. Without it, the only network television news circulating in North America about the trial—as about the Simpson trial—could have been from CNN, *Hard Copy*, or *A Current Affair*.

The trial also brings into some focus the CRTC's concerns about direct satellite transmission. In a future world in which the orbiting satellites of multinational corporations transmit television signals directly to private homes via miniaturized, low-cost satellite dishes already in existence, not only would Judge Kovacs's ban be even more unenforceable than it was, but the very existence of Canadian interpretations of a ban would be doubtful. In much the same way that Judge Kovacs lacked jurisdiction over United States media, the CRTC will have no direct jurisdiction over multinational "deathstar" technology. Perhaps only by threatening to ban the Canadian possession of miniature satellite receivers would a Canadian government be able to ensure the presence of Canadian channels among deathstar offerings. Proponents of individual rights, of course, would decry such measures as draconian infringements of private initiative, just as they have decried the effect of Judge Kovacs's order. The alternative, however, might be to surrender forever the collective rights of Canadians to use television broadcast in the production of their own cultural values.

Throughout the long war Canadians have had with the United States over Canada's protection of its publishing and broadcast institutions, there has been one constant. In the same way their newspapers have tried to export to

Canada the First Amendment rights of the U.S. constitution, American politicians have tried to export to Canada the view that culture is a commodity. American negotiators took this position at the free trade negotiations in 1987–88, at the NAFTA negotiations in 1992–93, and at the recently concluded Uruguay round of the GATT talks. The argument implies that culture has nothing to do with values, or with ideological choices, which are in this view, unlike culture, permanent and beyond debate. Culture here does not involve debates about individual rights, freedom of speech, or freedom of information, because these things are held to be, as in the language of the U.S. constitution, "self-evident." Instead it involves ideologically neutral entertainment, spectacle, and other "cultural industries." Such a view allows deep American indignation when U.S. cultural exports are spurned, as Eurodisney has been spurned in France, or as American films are spurned in many Islamic countries. It allows the U.S. to portray such spurnings as ideological, while continuing to regard its own productions as neutral and natural. This view, moreover, is not purely "American." It also exists among Canadians, again making Canada's continuing "war with the U.S." a kind of civil war. *Globe and Mail* columnist Andrew Coyne's expression of this view is representative:

> If there is an economic incentive to publish Canadian books, or distribute Canadian films for that matter, it is surely the same, whether the publisher or distributor is Canadian, American, or Tanzanian. If there is no such incentive, that, too, applies without regard for nationality. (4 July 1994)

241

In actuality, as numerous long-suffering publishers and filmmakers—from Canadians like Karl Siegler and Douglas Gibson, to American Steven Spielberg—will attest, publishers, filmmakers, and distributors in any country make unconscious and conscious cultural decisions every day, often preferring to seek economic gain with books and films with whose ideologies they agree rather than with ones they detest. Even Coyne's preference for profitable books is an ideology.

In the Homolka case, a view such as Coyne's allowed American commentators to portray as a freedom of speech issue what was for many Canadians a cultural issue— would Canadian courts have the power to make their own determination of how best to protect both Bernardo's rights and Canadians' right to have him stand trial? For the American media, "freedom of speech" was not merely one good among many, to be negotiated in each new context, but a sacred principle, beyond negotiation, cultural difference, and ideology. In their view, Canadians did not have the cultural right to overrule such a transcendent principle. The Canadian court had accepted a very different view of freedom of speech—one articulated by Crown Attorney Murray Segal: "There must be a balance between freedom of expression and the proper administration of justice regarding a fair trial. The right of freedom of speech does not exist in a vacuum to other rights. Freedom of speech sometimes clashes with other rights that are also protected by law" (*The Toronto Star*, 5 July 1993). Unlike the American First Amendment, which prohibits Congress from passing legislation that infringes on freedom of speech, and proclaims freedom of speech paramount in all circumstances, the Canadian Charter insists

on balancing one "good" against another, and thus pro-
viding for socially contextualized rather than absolute
decisions. Both Murray Segal's arguments and Judge
Kovacs's ruling were consistent with a Canadian cultural
tradition of balance, consultation, and negotiation. Many
of the media arguments against the ban were, in contrast,
American arguments, based on absolute principle and
"inalienable right."

The reasons for the Canadian media's resistance to the
publication ban, and the enthusiasm with which they
adopted the American "freedom of speech" arguments,
are elusive. Were the media seriously proposing modifica-
tions of Canadian law to bring it into line with American
practice, as *The Toronto Star* editorial of 1 December 1993
seemed to indicate, with its declaration that the United
States had a "preferable system"? Or were they merely
pragmatically invoking the doctrine of freedom of speech
to advance their own commercial interests in being able
to write about the case? Peter Lynde, writing in *The
London Free Press*, suggested the latter, arguing that while
"claims about the rights of the public and the freedom of
the press all sound noble," what the newspapers were
actually publishing suggested that their goals were
"increased circulation" and "increased revenues." He also
pointed out that the media had not become exercised
over similar publication bans, not even over the concurrent closed-door official inquiry into the killing of
unarmed civilians by the Canadian military in Somalia.

> Why have the media virtually ignored this case
> and all of its subsidiary but serious issues,

243

including that of press censorship? Because the practitioners of journalism understand what is key to the battle for market share in the world of modern media: Sex—especially when combined with torture, murder, and victims who are under-age. (12 January 1994)

On the other hand, the American media's puzzlement by the ban and their faith in the appropriateness of their constitutional First Amendment seem to have been genuine. Moreover, the letters-to-the-editor in various Canadian papers indicate that at least some Canadians have taken the criticisms of the Canadian judicial process seriously.

The actual differences between the Canadian and American criminal justice systems involve both the legal proceedings themselves and the practices current in the two nations governing the behaviour of lawyers and the media. Unlike in Canada, which is governed by a single federal Criminal Code, American criminal law and procedure generally fall under state jurisdiction, and differ in detail from state to state. In most states, criminal cases of the seriousness of the Homolka case begin with closed-door consideration by a grand jury, which evaluates evidence gathered by the prosecutor's office, submitted under oath by complaining individuals, or gathered by its own investigators, and determines whether this is sufficient for the issuance of an indictment. Suspects can be compelled to testify at such hearings, subject to the self-incrimination protections offered by the Fifth Amendment to the Constitution. They or their counsel, however, cannot cross-examine witnesses. Alternatively, in some states the prosecutor's office may issue a complaint and cause the individual to appear at a preliminary hearing, open to the public, to determine whether there is sufficient evidence to proceed to trial. Here the defendant cannot be compelled to testify, and has the right to participate through counsel in the proceedings and to cross-examine witnesses.

In the Canadian legal system, the normal steps for the prosecution of a serious or "indictable" offence begin with the issuing of an "information" or charge by the police. The accused generally has a right to request a preliminary hearing, held, as in the U.S., to determine whether the prosecutor has sufficient evidence to justify proceeding to trial. Here the defendant has similar protections to those in the U.S. preliminary hearing, with the exception that the hearing is normally subject to a publication ban so as to prevent the evidence from becoming public knowledge before a jury trial. The public, however, except in extraordinary circumstances, may attend. As an alternative to holding a preliminary hearing, a provincial attorney general can take the extremely rare step of issuing a preferred indictment that sends the case directly to trial, which is what later happened to the case of Paul Bernardo.

The differences in the general behaviour of police departments, prosecutors, lawyers, and the accused in the two countries have tended to be as much cultural as legal. One major difference between the Canadian and the United States systems is the fact that many sheriffs, district attorneys and lower-court judges in the United States are elected rather than appointed. Elected sheriffs and district attorneys need to maintain a high profile as effective law-enforcement officials in order to assure themselves of re-election, or to use their office as a stepping stone to other elected political positions. Lawyers with electoral ambitions can also find the creation of publicity around the cases they undertake politically useful. Senior judicial appointments in the United States can often be as politicized as are appointments to the Canadian Senate, with appointees usually belonging to the party that holds executive office and, in the case of Supreme Court appointments, having been obviously selected to help the executive branch achieve ideological goals. This politicization is aided by the American practice of obliging its registered voters to declare a party affiliation if they wish to vote in primary elections. The general result of these factors has been to help create a legal culture in which publicity routinely plays a significant role.

In Canada, there are no elected law enforcement officers. Prosecutors' and Crown attorneys' offices are staffed with civil service appointments, which in the large provinces are free of political patronage. The judiciary are appointed to the lower courts by the provincial attorneys general and to upper courts (which include the superior courts of each province, as well as the Supreme Court of Canada) by the federal minister of justice. With only a small fraction of Canadians formally affiliated with political parties, most of these appointments seem non-political, although in the case of many lower-court appointments past work behind the scenes for the political party in power is often rumoured to have contributed to the appointee's selection. Here publicity, if anything, may be a hindrance to a lawyer who wishes judicial appointment. One's publicly known political affiliations can offer a potential embarrassment to governments which seek publicly to maintain a myth that such appointments are made strictly on merit.

The general value accorded publicity in the American legal profession is amplified as well by the career enhancement which a well-publicized trial can offer to a criminal lawyer. Lawyers like William Kunstler, F. Lee Bailey, Alan Dershowitz, and Melvin Belli have become national figures through their work in high-profile cases, allowing them not only to enjoy more prosperous practices but also to earn significant additional income as talk-show guests, convention speakers, and authors. Because of the scant development of Canadian pop culture media, overpowered as it is by American pop culture, such opportunities can rarely tempt a Canadian lawyer. The large and lucrative American media market, with its increasing tendency to convert news into inexpensive-to-produce entertainment, also offers lawyers opportunities to earn commissions from the client's media earnings. The result, as Edward Greenspan commented in his 11 May 1994 address to the Canadian Bar Association, has been that a "race to the microphones has become almost common practice among defence lawyers in high-profile cases in the United States."

> ...the era of the lawyer as press agent is in full swing in the U.S. with some defence lawyers seeking book and movie deals for clients as vigorously as they do material witnesses. In a recent tour de force that has left members of the legal community gasping in either horror or admiration, the New York lawyer Michael Kennedy arranged for a client to give his version of why he

killed four women to the ABC-TV news program *Prime Time Live*—before the client surrendered to police.

Greenspan finds very little of such activity among Canadian lawyers, who both face less temptation and are subject to tighter ethical rules. Where he finds a similarity between American and Canadian criminal trial practices is in the press conferences held by police departments, often with arrays of captured weapons or packages of heroin or cocaine laid out for the media's cameras. While the public is encouraged to associate this undoubtedly impressive evidence with the alleged criminal, it is given no indication about whether the items will be admissible in court, or whether the context in which they were found will lead a jury to link them with the accused. Greenspan's conclusions about these press conferences is blunt: "They are designed to do one thing and one thing alone: to interfere with a fair trial."

An instructive American comparison to the media and court handling of the Homolka case is offered by the O.J. Simpson case, arguably as grisly and celebrated as the Bernardo–Homolka ones. Whereas Homolka and Bernardo had to be made into celebrities, Simpson's case began with a high level of media coverage because he was already a media figure, as a football player in the 1960s and '70s and as a sportscaster and actor in recent times. The day after the murder of Simpson's ex-wife, Nicole Brown Simpson, and her companion, Ronald Goldman, the mediatization of the case began—but at this point not by the media but by the police and Simpson's defenders. Simpson's lawyer, Howard Weitzman, informed the media that Simpson was "shocked by the crime" and "had nothing to do with this tragedy." Meanwhile the first of numerous "leaks" from the police investigation occurred with the release of information about Simpson's pleas of no contest on a 1989 spousal battery charge. On Tuesday, the following day, there were more police leaks—information about bloodstains found in the Simpson driveway, scratches said to have been found on Simpson's body, a bloodstained ski mask, and a bloodsoaked glove found somewhere on the Simpson premises and said to match one found at the murder scene. "Unofficial police sources" were also said to have released information that police had been called several times to Nicole Simpson's townhouse to settle domestic disputes. Although the Los Angeles police chief stated that Simpson was not at that time a suspect, other "police sources" were quoted as saying that the evidence pointed to Simpson as the killer. Weitzman again met with the media, assuring them that Simpson had been travelling to Chicago at the time of the murders. The media themselves began unleashing their own formidable investigative resources, the first result of which was an interview by KCBS television with Nicole Simpson's therapist, who reported having been told by her patient that Simpson had threatened to kill her.

The apparent leaking of police details here was not all that different in kind from the details that had leaked from the St. Catharines police department during the early stages of its investigation of the French abduction, although the speed of the release was much faster. Again some of the details leaked, or said to be leaked—in this case concerning the ski mask and the scratches on Simpson's body—turned out later to be false. The Los

Angeles police seemed to be signalling to the media not only that it was hard at work—the message that the St. Catharines department seems also to have wanted to convey—but also that it believed Simpson to have been responsible. Simpson's lawyer responded as if already in court, denying the allegation and pleading his client innocent. Although the police appeared to have the investigation well in hand, the media responded as they had in St. Catharines, setting up their own rival investigations. The overall result was a trial that was being conducted in public, subject to no rules of evidence, no swearing of witnesses, and no cross-examination.

The remainder of the week saw the continuation of this public "trial." On Wednesday, the head of the Hollywood division of the Los Angeles city attorney's office, while being interviewed, read aloud four police reports of an investigation into a 1989 New Year's Day incident at the Simpson home in which they had found Nicole Simpson with her lip cut, left eye swollen and blackened, and with hand imprints on her neck. *The Los Angeles Times* reported that police had removed a bloodstained swatch of carpet from one of Simpson's cars. Simpson responded by hiring a new lawyer, Robert Shapiro, who told the media that Simpson had been waiting for his airport limousine while the murders were happening. On Thursday, Simpson presented himself at the nationally televised funeral of his ex-wife as a grieving ex-husband and solicitous father. The media revealed that two Los Angeles police investigators, equipped with metal detectors, were searching a field near Chicago's O'Hare Plaza Hotel, where Simpson had stayed the night following the killings. Friday was a day of competing news conferences, climaxed by a dramatic nationally televised car-chase that many reporters compared to a movie scene. Shortly after Simpson first evaded police, who believed they had arranged to arrest him, Los Angeles police commissioner David Gascon held a news conference to condemn his flight. Simpson lawyer Shapiro then held his own press conference at which Simpson friend Robert Kardashian read a rambling, melodramatic "farewell" note from Simpson in which he again protested his innocence. Los Angeles district attorney Gil Garcetti then held another news conference during which he affirmed the strength of the evidence against Simpson. The low-speed car-chase around the Los Angeles freeway grid, filmed by twelve media helicopters, eventually ended after dark with a tense hour-long standoff and surrender. Throughout, as an estimated 95 million Americans watched, commentators made egregious comments about the fall of an American hero and the tragedy of a violent marriage— most of which communicated a sad acceptance of Simpson's guilt.

By the next week it was perhaps not surprising that many television news shows were polling their viewers about whether they believed Simpson guilty or innocent, and that CNN had added to the public trial an "electronic jury." Although the public arguments and counter-arguments continued, many of the media had clearly decided on their own verdicts. On Sunday, Shapiro told the media how a depressed Simpson had spent Father's Day weeping for children he is not allowed to see, and District Attorney Garcetti, interviewed by ABC television, predicted that Simpson would soon confess and plead diminished responsibility. On Monday, the L.A. police were reported to be searching the Chicago field for a knife, jacket, shirt, and shoes. Tuesday, Shapiro told a news conference that four doctors had examined Simpson and found no evidence of the "body scratches" rumoured to have been found by police on his body. Media reports said that "sources" had given them a detailed account of the injuries to the victims—that Nicole Simpson was virtually decapitated and repeatedly stabbed in the chest by a killer who showed "no mercy," and Goldman stabbed more than twenty times. The media also reported that their own investigations had discovered a golf caddy who said that Simpson had uncharacteristically lost his temper while playing golf the morning of the murders, and a cutlery dealer who said Simpson visited his shop several times but that employees could not remember making a sale. Even more compromising to Simpson was police release of a 911 emergency service tape recording from the previous year in which an alarmed Nicole Simpson reported that he had broken through her back door and was verbally threatening her. An angry and incoherent male voice raged in the background. The tape played hourly on virtually every television and radio news broadcast in the U.S. and Canada.

Media headlines now implicitly declared Simpson guilty. The June 27th *Newsweek* featured on its cover his official mugshot with the caption "Trail of Blood." *Time*'s cover presented the same photo with the caption "An American Tragedy"—an open reference to Theodore Dreiser's classic American novel about a young man who killed his pregnant girlfriend. *People* ran on its cover a photo of O.J. and Nicole Simpson with one of their children, and the caption "Love and Death." Even in Canada, belief in his guilt was being openly expressed. In *The Montreal Gazette*, in an article titled "Domestic violence: anyone can be a victim or a perpetrator," Ludwig Kay wrote,

> this was a tragedy you could see coming for years. The records show that Nicole Brown Simpson called police to protect her from her husband during their marriage not once but eight times. (21 June 1994)

By Friday, the grand jury considering the charges against Simpson was in some trouble. Its members were exposed to the same information, leaks, misinformation, speculation, and polls as the rest of the population, and at least two of its witnesses had concluded contracts for tens of thousands of dollars to give their stories to the media before coming to testify. Even the prosecution, which had initiated much of the trial by media, was concerned that the integrity of the jury might be in question. After questioning the jurors, the presiding judge announced that "some jurors have become aware of potentially prejudicial matters not officially presented to them by the district attorney" and that "to preclude any unintended consideration of prejudicial matter and protect the due process rights of Mr. Simpson and the integrity of the grand jury process" he was dismissing the jury and sending the charges to a preliminary hearing. Legal observers told *The New York Times* that such dismissal was without precedent.

The similarities to the Canadian experience with the Mahaffy–French killings were striking, despite the much quicker pace of the Simpson events. In both cases the media were eager to act as investigators into the murders, and eager to present the events to their publics not as news but as entertainment. In both it was the tabloid media—in Canada *The Toronto Sun* and in the U.S. the tabloid television news programmes *A Current Affair*, *Hard Copy*, and *Inside Edition*, which regularly packaged news as entertainment—that most aggressively followed the stories. In both cases the police set out to mediatize their investigations, and attract public involvement in their work. In turn, the media set out to mythologize the crimes and their alleged perpetrators. In Canada they made saints and monsters out of the victims and their accused killers; *The Toronto Sun* eventually titled some of its coverage of the case "The Crime of the Century." In the U.S., as early as the Friday-afternoon car-chase, the media began comparing Simpson's situation to that of Shakespeare's *Othello* or Homer's *Agamemnon*, as if somehow, rather than resulting in ghastly death for the victims, the crime had resulted in a greater nobility for the accused. Because of the long delay in the Canadian case in identifying and arresting suspects, the defence was slower to play its media cards. Nevertheless, Bernardo defence lawyer Ken Murray was the most willing of all the lawyers engaged with the case to meet the press, and was particularly adroit at joining his own arguments about his client's rights to direct his own defence and his indignation over the closing of Homolka's trial with the media's concern about press freedom.

But the differences between the American and Canadian cases, particularly in the degree of the police and prosecution's mediatization of their investigations, are also notable. In Canada, although there were police press conferences and leaks of police drawings and other information, there were few press conferences after the arrests and certainly no trial by press conference. Although the media made rival bids for the rights to such things as the Bernardo–Homolka wedding photos, they are not known to have offered to pay witnesses large sums for sensational evidence, or to have risked the attendant tainting of evidence that occurred in the Simpson case. The Crown lawyers were particularly discreet about the evidence they were going to present, and at the Homolka trial as scrupulous about preventing prejudicial publicity as the Los Angeles district attorney's office had seemed determined to create it. One legal commentator, Monroe Freedman of Hofstra University, even suggested that the creation of prejudicial publicity had become a prosecution tactic permitted by the U.S. Supreme Court:

> Unfortunately, pretrial publicity by the prosecution is all too common and, I believe, scandalous. The United States Supreme Court has established that inflammable, inadmissible material does not prejudice a trial. It is virtually impossible for a prosecutor, in constitutional terms, to prejudice a trial. (*The Gazette* [Montreal], 25 June 1994)

Moreover, as the above observation suggests, the defences against the mediatization of justice and prejudicial publicity it creates are visibly much less strong in the U.S. than in Canada. Bar association rules of professional conduct, which in Canada through conservative interpretation can restrain lawyers from acting so as to damage "public respect...for the administration of justice," permit considerable grandstanding in many American states. Whether

255

because of First Amendment protections to freedom of expression, different understandings of harmful publicity, or the much larger range of questioning allowed to the defence in jury selection, the accused's right to a fair trial is differently defined. The fair trial itself rests on the optimistic expectation that an untainted trial jury can be assembled and, through sequestering if necessary, be kept free from public influence. This expectation in turn encourages both district attorneys and defence counsel to fight the case in public, in the hopes of influencing jurors in the court of media opinion before having to persuade them in the court of law.

These differences were again apparent when the Simpson case, a week after the grand jury dismissal, began its preliminary hearing. In Canada, a publication ban in a case such as Homolka in which the evidence is closely related to that in another case yet to be tried is highly unusual, but a publication ban in a preliminary hearing is routine: the accused has the right to request and receive one. The reasoning behind the latter ban is that much of the evidence presented at the preliminary hearing may eventually be presented to a jury, and that this jury should, in fairness to the accused, receive the evidence in the context of a trial, and according to the rules of evidence, rather than through the interpretations, commentaries, or complaints of the media. Moreover, during jury selection, both the Crown and the defence are limited in the questions prospective jurors can be asked to a list of— on average—five or six questions pre-approved by the court. Certain kinds of specific questions that might contradict the prospective jurors' undertakings that they believe themselves capable of delivering a fair verdict, such as a question pertaining to possible racial prejudice, have been excluded from the process. Also routine is the exclusion of television cameras, still cameras, and tape recorders from Canadian court proceedings of all kinds. Even in the Canadian parliament, television cameras are permitted to focus only on the speaker and forbidden to show the reactions of other parliamentarians. In Los Angeles, however, even though excessive publicity had already caused an unprecedented dismissal of a grand jury that had met behind closed doors, the Simpson preliminary hearing was obliged to be held in public, with television cameras in court focusing on witnesses, lawyers, the accused, and on spectators, and with even the afternoon soap operas cancelled so that their networks and stations could air the court broadcast.

There is little doubt that the televised preliminary hearing into O.J. Simpson's murder charges allowed justice to be "perceived" to be done, or that the legal commentary offered by the networks enabled some viewers to have a larger understanding of the legal issues and procedures at play; such things are, in a general sense, public goods. But with up to 95 million viewers watching media coverage of these hearings, and of his trial by media and of his arrest, either live or through news shows like *A Current Affair*, *Crossfire*, or *Larry King Live*, it is very doubtful that Americans can ever be sure that a jury was able to consider the evidence against him within the rules established by their nation's laws. Once the possibility of such jury consideration has been taken away, it would appear impossible to restore.

Because of his wealth, Simpson was able to continue to

play the media game after the preliminary hearing had ended, hiring additional and newsworthy lawyers, as well as public-relations experts, posting a half-million-dollar reward for information, and having his defence team publicly accuse the principal police investigator of racism. Meanwhile, many tabloid media, finding that their stories about Simpson's guilt had gone stale, began to publish stories that he had been framed, or that others were guilty. Far from restoring the possibility of an impartial jury, however, these actions merely made more complex the "poisoning" of the jury pool, and displayed starkly the different relationships to media "justice" which differences in wealth can create. The Simpson verdict consequently offered absolutely no assurances about the health of the American and Californian judicial systems. Nevertheless, making civic choices, and making compromises among legal possibilities, are the prerogatives of any nation, and if American citizens consciously prefer the results of their choices and compromises, such preferences are their civic right.

There is also little doubt that the Homolka trial, held in the presence of only courtroom artists, Canadian journalists enjoined to temporary silence on key matters, and the families of the victims and the accused, offered no immediate assurance to the public that justice had been served. But there is also little doubt that, despite the coverage of *The Toronto Sun*, much less prejudicial publicity about Paul Bernardo was circulated in Canada, and to fewer people, than was circulated in a much shorter time about O.J. Simpson in the United States. Even the numerous electronic and word-of-mouth rumours that circulated about Bernardo tended to create, through both their outrageousness and their ambiguous status, as much uncertainty about the details of the case as doubt about his innocence. Indeed, where the damage to Simpson's right to an unbiased jury was difficult to restore—at best it could only be redressed by his lawyers' extra-judicial

Grace Lutheran Church and parking lot in St. Catharines, from which Kristen French was abducted.

259

spreading of counter-prejudicial evidence, replacing a fair judicial trial with a haphazardly balanced media one—the damage to the Canadian public's "right to know" what occurred at the Homolka trial was eventually repairable, even if the possibility of "immediately" knowing was gone forever.

Unlike Americans—who tend as a group to be fans only of their own country—many Canadians have now attended with nearly equal emphasis to both criminal cases, and are perhaps in a better position than ever to make reasoned judgments about not only which legal system produces the best entertainment but also which produces the better justice. However, Canada's undeclared war with the U.S. raged throughout it all, and with ominous effect. For, with the ban-breaking efforts of the American media, and the continued sensationalizing of the Mahaffy–French killings by Americanized parts of the Canadian media, Canadians nearly got the less attractive elements of both legal systems—the prejudicial publicity of the American, subverting the possibility of fair trial, and the extreme discretion of the Canadian, preventing immediate and accurate public knowledge. Such an outcome would not have been a democratic social choice. Meanwhile technological change will continue to increase the strength and subtlety of American incursions into Canadian civil space. American databases can already store entire movies, pornography included, for downloading into home computers. The U.S. flag no longer arrives on P-40 aircraft or carried by musket-bearing soldiers. It comes on direct-broadcast satellites that render Canadian law powerless; it comes on a direct-purchase "information highway" that runs from American producer to Canadian buyer without passing through Canada Customs. In a short time Canadians will not even remember that they once possessed alternatives to the American First Amendment or to CNN justice.

Message 237
From daemon@anon.penet.fi Mon Feb 21 06:27:39 1994
To: jsmith@musica.mcgill.ca
From: an74361@anon.penet.fi
X-Anonymously-To: an67345
Organization: Anonymous contact service
Reply-To: an74361@anon.penet.fi
Subject: The Faq (at last!)

****

The Paul Teale/Karla Homolka Frequently Asked Questions List (FAQ)
Version 2.1 - February 1, 1994

****

Q. What is the story behind the newsgroup "alt.fan.karla-homolka and this
FAQ?

1. The "alt.fan.karla-homolka" Newsgroup

In July 1993, Judge Francis Kovacs ordered a publication ban on one of the
most sensational manslaughter trials in Canadian history. The accused,
Karla Homolka, had been sentenced 12 years for manslaughter for her
involvement in the grisly deaths of Kristen French and Leslie Mahaffey. The
ban itself had been imposed "to insure a fair trial" for her accused husband
/accomplice Paul Teale, but was hotly contested by both Canadian and
American media, and also by Teale's attorney.

As a response to the media ban, Justin Wells (stem@io.org) created the
newsgroup "alt.fan.karla-homolka". Justin's self-admitted sick sense of
humor put the group in the "alt.fan" hierarchy, and he did not expect the
group to last more than two months. How wrong he was.

At first there was a trickle, then there a torrent. "Alt.fan.karla-homolka"
became a home for resident ban-breakers, as new rumors were posted
regularly in the group. The most famous of these early ban-busters was
"Neal the Trial ban breaker". His rumors provided shocking insights into the
trial that nobody was supposed to know anthing about, and made him a
celebrity in Canadian newspapers such as the Toronto Star and the Calgary
Herald.

The alt.fan.karla-homolka *"FAQ."*

ALT.FAN.KARLA-
HOMOLKA

2–233 *alt.fan.karla-homolka* Why are there so few
hot, exhibitionist, S&M women?
                    Eric Braun, *The Internet Directory*

The "word" that may most resonate in future years in
Canada around the Mahaffy–French slayings may not be
Mahaffy, nor French, nor even Bernardo, but *alt.fan.karla-
homolka*. Most Canadians, however, may still not be familiar with such a "word," or have at best vague notions that
it has "computer" associations. Some may indeed recognize it as the name of an on-line computer-world discussion group, similar to those in which they participate as
academics, business people, or hobbyists in the "news"
offerings of the multi-user computers which they otherwise connect to for electronic mail. Some of them may
know that those news offerings come via a global network
of multi-user computers called "Internet." A very few will
understand the computer-language "tree" structure of the
word itself: how it consists of a series of binary delimiters
linked by "dots" or periods, each one subdividing what
has gone before, so that "fan" indicates a category within
the larger category "alt," and "karla-homolka" indicates a
small and specific category within the category "fan."

This wide variation even in knowledge of the "word,"
and how it is structured, contributed significantly to the
impact which *alt.fan.karla-homolka* had on the case, and
on the large aura of cultural confusion and nervousness

263

which surrounded it after Mr. Justice Kovacs's publication ban. For *alt.fan.karla-homolka* suggested that something had changed in the nature of knowledge itself. Something had changed in the way people could know, in the way knowledge could be transmitted and created, and in the way knowledge interacted with national culture. Something had also changed in how one became "in the know." In reporting on the journalists' panel discussion on the subject of the ban, participant Iris Nowell recounted the experience of D'Arcy Jenish, who had attended the trial. Jenish, Nowell wrote,

> tried to make the point that some of the U.S. newspaper accounts he had read differed greatly from what he had heard in the courtroom. That got a woman on her feet asking why he had been able to read all those out-of-country newspapers. Wild applause. "Who are you?" she shouted, to even wilder applause and cheers. (*The Globe and Mail*, 3 April 1994)

Like many people, Jenish had been able to read many of the U.S. newspaper accounts on computer database services. As he wrote in the 13 December 1993 *Maclean's*, *The Washington Post* story on the Homolka trial had been available in computer form on the database service CompuServe, which has approximately 45,000 Canadian corporate and individual subscribers, many hours before the paper itself was distributed, and at least a day before Ontario authorities appeared aware of the printed version.

Within a couple of days of publication, that story

was also available to users of university computer systems across the country.... They could obtain the *Post* account through Internet, a rapidly expanding computer network that links universities, research institutes and businesses and is used by up to 30 million people in 135 countries— including an estimated 100,000 in Canada.

The woman's question, "Who are you?" reflected a new awareness and indignation that technology, wealth, and education had created a new kind of citizen, one who had access to knowledge that other citizens did not have, who could make assessments and judgments that others could not make, and who had power—power which even a court order could not curtail—that other citizens might not even be able to imagine. This last aspect—the inability of some Canadians even to imagine the power other Canadians might have, or the implications of that power, created considerable bewilderment and unease. "Who are you?" the woman asked, not only as if Jenish had somehow exceeded his democratic privileges, but also as if he were perhaps some new and ominous species. And the audience supported her with "wilder applause and cheers."

For many Canadians the sudden jolt they received from the Karla Homolka trial, and from the ease with which its publication ban was broken, was the first concrete indication that the news stories over the past few years about an "information revolution" concerned something real. The fact that journalists were submitting stories to newspapers by transmitting computer files over their home telephones had not created any visible difference in the newspapers people read. The electronic exchanges of information by university and corporate researchers on Internet had been no more visible to most Canadians than the protons, electrons, and quarks studied in a physicist's laboratory. Even being thrown out of work by a computer or computerized robot had not meant a great change in people's lives. Technology had been eliminating jobs in the western world since the industrial revolution. Moreover, the displaced workers usually didn't get to see the machines that had replaced them. If they had, many of these machines would have looked relatively innocent. A desk-top computer looks deceivingly like the typewriter it has replaced. An assembly line with robots has much the same structure as a traditional assembly line.

> The Teale Tales Mailing List is dedicated to preserving freedom of information in Canada's court system. Write for more information.

For other Canadians, however, *alt.fan.karla-homolka* meant something quite different. It meant new avenues of liberty—perhaps even new ways of resisting state power. The impulse toward classical anarchism—where anarchy is understood not as chaos but as spontaneous self-government through responsible citizenship—had been a dominant element of the international culture of multi-user computer systems for almost two decades. The first "networks" connecting university, military, and commercial computers had been established in the United States on a co-operative model, and with a minimum of administration. The model had been provided by Bell Laboratories, creators of the UNIX operating system for large, multi-user computer systems. Bell had realized in the 1970s that relatively instantaneous communication between multi-user computers in different parts of North America could be of enormous assistance to their own researchers—as well as a sales feature in Bell's attempts to market the UNIX operating system to universities, the military, and research-oriented corporations. In this model, each member of the network would agree to underwrite the cost of forwarding electronic mail and newsgroup messages from their multi-user computer to neighbouring multi-user computers in exchange for being able to receive messages and news from other "sites" on the network. Administrative costs would be extremely low because the system would be, in effect, managed by its participants. No one would own the network and no individual or institution be given the power to regulate it. This model was supported by the U.S. military, which would benefit from close computer contact with its commercial suppliers, and which recognized the proposed non-hierarchical structure as one which would be relatively impervious to attack or sabotage. In the early stages of the network, to send a message from one side of the continent to the other required the sender to name, in succession, the "sites" through which the message was to be routed. Because the network was indeed structured like a net, the sender could choose sites known for their efficiency, and avoid sites known to be bottlenecks. Such routing on the contemporary Internet, for both e-mail and newsgroups, is now fully automated—with the consequence that the system can automatically "repair" itself when attempts are made to censor contributions. The original newsgroup provisions of UNIX, known as "usenet," now form the basis of such groups on the contemporary Internet. At the beginning, the main function of these was to allow researchers to brainstorm about a topic from different parts of the continent as if they were carrying on a conversation at a seminar or conference. Multiple participants could "post" responses to a topic, read each other's responses, and comment on them; each participant would automatically receive the complete ongoing discussion on his or her local multi-user computer as the discussion unfolded. This research role of usenet diversified quickly, however, as participants realized the suitability of the newsgroup for equally wide-ranging discussions of their hobbies, favourite entertainments, or political concerns. The newsgroups have grown to become a maze of strangely coded discussion titles from *rec.arts.erotica* to *alt.fan.spinal-tap*.

Because of the co-operative nature of this network, there was minimal control over what was sent or what was posted to newsgroups—the participants served as contributors, editors, and readers. While each participating multi-user computer had its own administrator, there was—and still is—no central network administrator. Local administrators might refuse to forward material to specific sites, or refuse to include certain newsgroups, but peers exercised the majority of the control over what was written on the network. The network, in effect, developed its own somewhat conservative unlegislated culture—its own "common law" about what could be ethically done or said. Enforcement involved an electronic blitz of condemnation in the public space of the newsgroups: in usenet parlance, the miscreant was "flamed." At an extreme, it could take the form of one's local system administrator cancelling one's access to the computer. To some extent this new common law developed because the users of the new electronic network were all from similar backgrounds. Almost all had academic training. The corporate and university researchers had advanced degrees. Most led, or aspired to lead, comfortable, middle-class lives. Most also were accustomed to working for employers who gave them a great deal of latitude in how they conducted their work, and considerable responsibility for getting it done. These were efficient, "can-do" people—people accustomed to writing their own software programmes to get a balky computer to perform, accustomed to rewiring their personal computers, accustomed to "kludging" together mismatched pieces of computer hardware to do tasks unforeseen by their manufacturers. The very term "to kludge"—to rearrange software or hardware in an unorthodox, awkward, but effective way—reflected the dogged sense of independence that was their main characteristic.

The overall result was a culture that had enormous pride in its own ability to devise solutions and to police itself. The structured concepts of academic freedom and collegial discipline that one finds in universities were re-created in the Internet computer culture in idealized and unsystematic forms. At the same time that this culture relied on collective values and collective pressures, it was fiercely anti-authoritarian. As the cost of computer technology declined, projects and activities that were not allowed on one computer system could easily be started on a new system, which itself could be connected to the Internet. All you need is your own "box," people in the culture would say of the advantages of managing one's own multi-user computer.

Much of the ideology of this 1980s computer culture, with its excitement about technology, its conviction about the ability of computer aficionados to police their own activities, and its insistence that information should be free, has been transferred into the contemporary period of increased commercialization of computer services and increased participation in Internet and other computer-communications services by non-academic users. Eric Braun, for example, begins the 1994 edition of *The Internet Directory* with instructions on "the conventions of proper behavior on the Internet." His repeated use of words like "proper" and "correct" in this preface displays his belief that there is a consensus in computer-culture about what does constitute acceptable behaviour.

> There are no Internet police as yet, and none are needed because the proper observation of neti-quette by most Internet visitors makes the Internet a nice "small town" place to be, despite the fact that millions of people "live" in it.[1]

His instructions tell about how to observe "correct manners" by not using unnecessarily large amounts of computer resources, by making sure that one's comments "add quality, not quantity, to any discussion," and by avoiding "excessively long signatures." "If you must respond to something you strongly disagree with, be civil. And remember that keeping an open mind is a crucial part of being a good citizen."[2] This emphasis on good citizenship reflects the long-standing utopian computer-culture view that a computer user can offer a new higher version of the ordinary citizen, one who is self-directing, self-disciplined,

270

responsible, and able to function without the intrusive presence of authority. Again, this concept is more American than Canadian—connected more to a frontier mythology in which citizens created their own justice than to one in which officials marked the territory and established rules before settlers could enter. Braun, in fact, dedicates his book to the independent citizen:

> This book is dedicated to citizenship, because every freedom has responsibilities attached, without which it would be meaningless.[3]

Because this view of the citizen is still the basis for the *laissez-faire* usenet and Internet structures, it is effectively required by them. In his article (*Maclean's*, 13 December 1993) about electronic breaches of the Homolka ban, D'Arcy Jenish quoted University of Ottawa computing director David Sutherland as saying that "neither governments nor university computer systems specialists can control the information available on Internet because users put the equivalent of 25 medium-sized novels into the system every day. 'We don't pretend to maintain control,' he said. 'The technology has outgrown us completely.'" Much the same can be said about the commercial information services such as CompuServe. Yet David Sutherland's remarks were also somewhat disingenuous. It is not merely the huge mass of material that is e-mailed or posted on the Internet network that makes it so uncontrollable. It is also the fact that Internet was from its earliest stages designed to be inexpensive and uncontrollable, by people who believed that the collective will and wisdom of the users was superior to the arbitrary power of supervisors. Internet, CompuServe, and other services today are much like publishing houses in which the readers serve also as writers and editors.

Users of these services come from a much greater variety of backgrounds than they did in the early 1980s. They may still constitute a small, upwardly mobile, and relatively privileged segment of the population, but with the simplification of software achieved by Macintosh and Windows technology and the continued decline in computer prices, the numbers of users without ongoing connections to universities has increased sharply. Private individuals, political parties, small businesses, and special-interest groups are all capable of purchasing, for a few thousand dollars, their own multi-user "box" and having it operate as a 24-hour on-line "node" in the Internet. For a few hundred dollars, individuals can purchase desk-top computers obsolete for other purposes and use them to "dial in" to these new Internet nodes. School boards have set up their own networks for the participation of children, and connected these to the Internet. Businesses have started sending junk mail on the Internet — a practice that horrifies traditional users but which the anarchic user-determined ethics of the network has only haphazard power to prevent.

The spread of "free-nets"—multi-user computer services connected to the Internet, sponsored by local institutions, and made available free to large numbers of computer users—has further democratized Internet use. But the organizers of free-nets, and of commercial "nets" like CompuServe and America Online, share by and large the traditional view of the computer community as self-policing. The result has been that a co-operative and trusting approach to computer ethics is currently offered to many users unfamiliar with the utopian, academic understandings of individual freedom, self-reliance, and self-governance with which it was first associated. The adoption of pseudonymous computer identities, particularly among newer users who experience the Internet primarily as entertainment, has spread. Originally, such pseudonyms allowed the user to enjoy artificial or fictional identities— to invent himself or herself in ways difficult in everyday interpersonal contact. Joe Ficklesport could have a long, elaborate, and essentially harmless e-mail affair with Wanda Wonderweaver without either believing they were creating more than a role-playing game, and without even needing to know whether each was indeed of the sex or age they represented. In recent times, less transparent pseudonyms have been used to involve the unwary in investment frauds and child-pornography seductions. The new capability of computers to transmit colour photographs by e-mail, or even short colour film clips, has been of special advantage to pedophiles.

In the Karla Homolka newsgroups, for obvious reasons, pseudonyms like "Neal the Trial Ban Breaker," "Abdul the Electronic Gordon Domm," and "Lt. Starbuck" were widely used. For further protection, many of the participants, including those with the above pseudonyms, worked through a computer site in Finland which allowed them to establish anonymous electronic identities from which they could contribute material to the Internet. The electronic identity of Abdul the Electronic Gordon Domm, who called himself also the moderator of the Teale Tales Mailing List, was an72135@anon.penet.fi— where "fi" is the Internet address for Finland.

Until 1899, when Guglielmo Marconi established wireless telegraphy communications between Britain and France, and 1901, when he established it between Cornwall in England and St. John's in Newfoundland, nations had enjoyed almost absolute control over whether or not public messages crossed their borders. By the 1930s, when Marconi's invention had become both long-wave and short-wave wireless radio, not only was the sending of public messages across national boundaries possible but such messages were relatively inexpensive and convenient both to send and to receive. This technology had two main effects: it diminished the importance of place in human interactions, and it reduced the power of the state to regulate the information which its citizens could receive or circulate.

The diminishing of the importance of place, however, was two-edged. On the one hand, one no longer had to travel to a specific place to listen to an opera or hear a national leader speak; on the other hand, one's own opportunities to speak or perform on this new technology depended very much on one's being in a place where its messages originated. Moreover, the new technology's ability to allow millions in different places to hear a single performance implied that, over all, fewer performances and performers would be needed to entertain the same number of people, and thus that fewer people might be able participate in the creation of their own cultures. It was to deal with this issue that Canada first acted in the 1930s by setting up the Canadian Broadcasting Corporation and later the Canadian Radio-television Commission. If Canadians did not own their own radio stations and their own broadcast facilities, they would presumably become a nation that listened only to other nations' broadcasts or, later, that watched other nations' telecasts. Individual Canadians would not get the opportunity to become broadcasters or performers, or to have their scripts aired on nearby stations. Culturally, they could become a nation of passive electronic consumers. At first glance, the reduction in the power to regulate the information that crossed its borders was not, for a democracy at least, a significant problem. Very few books, magazines, recordings, and films had been banned from entry before foreign radio waves began routinely to penetrate Canadian air space. Most of these, for commercial or cultural reasons, were unlikely candidates for foreign broadcast, and, even if they had been broadcast, the lack of home tape recorders among the general public in the 1930s and '40s would have limited their audiences. The materials banned included those considered obscene or pornographic under the Canadian Criminal Code and those considered treasonable, seditious, immoral, or indecent under the Customs Tariff Act. The obscenity provisions kept out of Canada not only crude pornography depicting violence or pedophilia but also modern literary classics like James Joyce's *Ulysses*, D.H. Lawrence's *Lady Chatterley's Lover*, and Henry Miller's *Tropic of Cancer*.

As long as cultural standards in the United States remained similar to those of Canada, the broadcasting of both pornography and books like *Ulysses* into Canada on the popular AM band was extremely unlikely. Seditious material was broadcast into Canada on the less popular and less accessible short-wave radio bands from Japan, Germany, the Soviet Union, and other countries during World War Two and the Cold War, but was generally considered more amusing than dangerous. Regarded much

275

more seriously was the entry into Canada of various kinds of gambling equipment, particularly slot machines. While the banning of such equipment may not seem like a censorship issue, such machines can in fact be seen as primitive information-generating and culture-shaping devices, and their banning can be connected to state sensitivity about private possession of more elaborate information-generating devices, such as satellite dishes, decades later.

While not banned, devices involved in radio broadcast in Canada in the early years were closely supervised and monitored. The Radio-Telegraph Act of 1913 began not only the required licensing of broadcasting stations but also a one-dollar licence for each receiving radio set. The licensing of radio receivers continued until after World War Two.

In the area of taxation, trade and copyright protection, the new permeability of international borders by broadcast signals was very problematic. For a whole other area of import controls on information had focused on excluding books and magazines not on the basis of their content but on the basis of copyright ownership, place of manufacture, and place of taxation payment. While the new technology's devaluation of place as a significant element in human life brought all Canadian listeners closer to Carnegie Hall, it also allowed broadcasts and recordings "made" in another place to be available in Canadian places without passing through Canada Customs checkpoints. The significance of Canada as a "place" within which Canadians could expect to benefit financially— through sales or through government taxation revenues— from the activities conducted within its borders had been considerably diminished. One of the central challenges in

Canadian culture and politics since the first penetration of Canadian airspace by foreign broadcast signals has been the attempt to regulate such things as American owner-ship of Canadian broadcasters, Canadian content on Canadian airwaves, Canadian advertising broadcast by U.S. border-city stations, and more recently American advertising on American television signals redistributed by cable within Canada.

For most democratic governments and their citizens, the new diminishing of national sovereignty through radio-wave penetration of national boundaries has seemed like a good thing. Confident in the economic and political power of their cultures, they have argued for freedom of information and have eagerly exploited the new technolo-gies to broadcast politically destabilizing material to their non-democratic rivals. At the same time, many of the European democracies have been protected by linguistic difference from the kinds of commercial and cultural flooding that can arise when two nations speaking a common language share a border and broadcast space. Even these nations, however, have often attempted to keep tight control on internal broadcasting. Britain has limited to four and France to five the number of television networks licensed to broadcast within their borders, and have thus been able to give certain advantages to state-owned broadcasters. They have also regulated cable and satellite broadcasting, limiting them to the kind of generic services—news, sports, movies, children's programming—the CRTC permits on Canadian cable. Indirectly, such reg-ulations act to create culture—creating what appear to be "natural" proportions of class representation and offering prominence to topics that might appear insignificant within an environment of thirty channels or more. July 1994 figures show that in British homes equipped to receive satellite or cable signals, the original four channels still claimed more than 71 per cent of the viewing hours, with the two BBC channels taking 31.8 per cent. British regulators were particularly incensed in the 1980s to find a pirate station broadcasting to Britain from outside their jurisdiction. Israel's broadcast regulations effectively kept certain political views about relationships with the Palestine Liberation Organization off the air, as well as PLO spokespersons, and again were challenged by a pirate broadcaster, operating from a ship anchored outside its territorial waters.

An example of what can happen when two rival cultures share both a common language and a common broadcast space is provided by East and West Germany after the erection of the Berlin Wall in 1961. Despite East German efforts to block some West German signals, the relative prosperity of East Germany within the communist bloc led to the spread of television receivers within the country, and their reception of images of West German culture—particularly those broadcast deep within East Germany from Berlin. The images of material abundance in West Germany eventually led to the extraordinary images in 1989 of long cavalcades of East Germans hungry for even an afternoon in the West German "paradise."

In Canada, much of the CRTC's regulatory activities have served, directly and indirectly, a cultural as well as economic function. Recent decisions have rejected the concept of a sectarian religious television channel similar to those offered by Protestant fundamentalist broadcasters in the United States, as well as specific proposals for a

channel specializing in ballet and theatre and one specializing in cartoons. Older decisions allowing Canadian
cable systems to substitute Canadian advertising for the
American advertising contained in the originating signal,
or allowing them, in cases in which American and
Canadian channels are broadcasting the same show, to
substitute the Canadian signal for the American, have not
only increased the revenue of Canadian broadcasters but
have diminished the cultural saturation of Canada with
American commercial messages. Specific Canadian content regulations requiring, as a licensing provision,
Canadian radio and television stations to broadcast certain amounts of Canadian-originated material have benefited the Canadian music and film industries and
increased the amount of Canadian-made conceptions of
experience available to Canadians.

By and large, the regulation of Canadian broadcasting
has been designed not to exclude foreign signals but to
increase the opportunity for Canadian-made material to
be broadcast. Some desultory attempts have also been
made to discourage the emulation of American broadcasting models in Canada. These have been successful, as in
the case of the religious-channel applications, when
directed toward specific kinds of channels, but largely
ineffective when directed toward the programming policies of general-interest channels. The American model of
airing children's shows in the morning, soaps and game
shows in the afternoon, news at supper hour, situation
comedy and crime shows in prime time, and talk shows
and movies in the late evening, has long been emulated
in Canada—with many of the most popular American
shows bought off-the-shelf and broadcast in the same

time-slots as in the U.S. At its extreme, this policy allows censorship and confiscation. Unlicensed broadcasters are theoretically subject to closure and confiscation of equipment—a rule without which the general licensing policies of the commission would be meaningless. And except in areas of the country not served by Canadian broadcasters and cable companies, the private possession of satellite receiver dishes for television reception is also illegal—a policy again which is necessary if the commission is going to pretend to have any authority over what signals are sent or received within the country.

Yet in actual fact, both regulations are weakly enforced. Much as Canadians who broke Mr. Justice Kovacs's court ban went largely undeterred and unprosecuted, fundamentalist religious groups in western Canada have continued to operate small transmitters, rebroadcasting American religious programming, in open defiance of the CRTC. Small numbers of satellite dishes can be seen on Canadian rooftops in both city and country, and seem likely to proliferate as improvements in technology reduce both the costs and the necessary diameter of such dishes from a few metres to tens of centimetres. The lack of enforcement appears to stem from divided opinions among Canadians themselves: many would complain loudly about religious persecution or abuse of individual freedoms were the CRTC to act, while others would applaud this action as a defence of Canada. Thus, when the long awaited "500-channel universe" delivered by "deathstar" satellite technology arrives, with the satellite transmitting to Canadians from far outside Canadian airspace, it is difficult to see what the CRTC will be able to do to help any Canadian broadcasting to survive—other than hope, as it does now, that Canadians will develop a rival satellite system. If the commission lacks the political will now to close down small religious broadcasters, or to enforce its ban on satellite receivers, it is unlikely to have any stomach for the draconian measures that would be necessary to attempt to regulate the incursions of a foreign direct-broadcast satellite.

Ironically, in the Homolka case, CRTC regulations designed to protect broadcast integrity and limit commercial messages contradicted the legal requirements of the publication ban. The CRTC regulations forbade cable-system operators to delete any portion of the broadcast signals they received except for the substitution of Canadian commercials for American ones. The Ontario attorney general's office, however, instructed the cable operators to delete any portions of U.S. news shows that contained banned Homolka trial details. The result was that both sets of instructions were broken by cable operators, who accidentally overlooked some broadcasts of banned details, and defied the CRTC by deleting others. In neither case were they prosecuted.

One of the primary inhibitors of CRTC action against illegal broadcasting and satellite signal reception, and of Ontario's enforcement of the Homolka ban, was a set of restive, semi-rebellious, anti-authoritarian political feelings in Canada that can be loosely termed populism. While these feelings have shared the individualist bias of the more recent multi-user computer culture, until recently their class and occupational markers have been decidedly different. Populist feelings have always had some strength in Canada because of the openly conservative character of

Canadian society, with its emphases on the continuity of legitimate government, on the prestige of government institutions, and, in recent times, on the creation of large publicly funded frameworks for social services. They have also been stimulated from time to time in western Canada by the perception that Ontario and Ontarians enjoy undue privilege. While populism was not a known term in the early nineteenth century, the anti-élitist feelings currently associated with populism were very much evident in the animosity Susanna Moodie recorded among "Yankee" immigrants toward middle-class British immigrants like herself, and in the rage many supporters of the 1837 rebellion in Upper Canada felt toward the governor and the "Family Compact" of Tory merchants and landowners whose wishes and interests the governor favoured. In this century populism had been until recently an agrarian phenomenon, visible primarily on the prairies and in rural Quebec. Its first large political impact came in 1921, when in the federal elections the newly formed Progressive Party won sixty-five seats in the West, Ontario, and New Brunswick on a platform that opposed high tariffs and proposed replacing parliamentary authority with various instruments of direct government by the electors. The Progressive Party offered two of the main ingredients of Canadian populism: a suspicion of wealthy, upper-class Ontario manufacturers, protected by high tariff barriers that prevented other Canadians from being able to buy cheaper imported goods, and a suspicion of parliamentary "élites," believed to be dominated by politicians from the big cities and the central provinces.

While the Progressive Party collapsed by 1926 because of its own unwillingness to have an "élite" leadership or to otherwise organize its fractious and independent members into a coherent party, populism quickly re-emerged in the West in the form of Rev. William Aberhart's Social Credit party. Again this was a party that asserted grass-roots and folk wisdom against big-city know-how and, when in power, attempted to challenge federal law on monetary and other issues. To the Progressive Party's general outlook on politics it added a fierce support for individualism and condemnation of both big business and trade unionism. The Social Credit citizen, whether a small businessman, a farmer, or a worker who sold his labour, was above all an entrepreneur who could only weaken himself or herself by joining unions or commercial associations. In Alberta from 1935 to 1971, and in British Columbia from 1952 to 1972, Social Credit ruled with majorities based mainly on rural constituencies. In the 1990s populism reformulated itself in Alberta under Ralph Klein and the Progressive Conservative party, and won election, again mainly in rural constituencies, on an anti-big-government, anti-social-programmes platform that emphasized the traditional family, the citizen as an individual, and balanced government accounts. Constituted in the 1980s as the federal Reform Party, under Preston Manning, the son of former Alberta Social Credit premier Ernest Manning, yet another western populist movement campaigned for direct democracy through referenda and town meetings, and greater individual responsibility for health-care, pension, and unemployment provision. Expressing general contempt for the "élites" that had been governing the country, this movement won not only fifty-two parliamentary seats in the 1993 federal elections, all but one in the West, but also nearly 35 per cent of the popular vote in rural Ontario.

One major change, however, in Canadian populism in the late 1980s and early '90s was its development of its own "élites," with their own institutions or institutional connections, and their own media voices. These élites included academics like David Bercuson and Douglas Morton of the University of Calgary, businessmen like Conrad Black, and senior journalists like Peter Worthington, Barbara Amiel, and Kenneth Whyte. Their institutions included *Alberta Report*, the *Toronto Sun* chain with its papers in Ottawa, Edmonton, Winnipeg, and Toronto, and most recently *Saturday Night*, owned by Black and edited by Whyte. In the electronic media they included numerous open-line radio hosts, such as Vancouver's Rafe Mair and Calgary's Dave Rutherford. The principal functions of these populist élites were to tell the reader or listener in simplified terms what was wrong with government policy or regulation, and then also to tell them that they *already knew* and had already known what they had just been told. The criticisms were thus presented as common sense—as something ordinary people instinctively knew. And the readers and listeners themselves were congratulated and flattered for having already possessed such wisdom.

For many of the new populist experts, particularly the columnists and open-line hosts, the payoff for this process was the increased size and loyalty of their audience, higher ratings, and more secure careers. For the owners of the media, the rewards were different and potentially larger. Reducing government regulation over individuals could increase business opportunities for corporations. Increased access for individuals to the American marketplace could increase access for businesses. Lower rates of individual taxes, achieved by cutting back social and cultural programmes, could increase the disposable incomes of consumers. Less regulation over television broadcasting, including lower Canadian content requirements, could make the operation of a television network less costly. Elimination of bilingual labelling requirements could make the packaging of goods in Canada less expensive. A general climate favouring the reduction of regulations over individuals tended also to favour the lowering of regulations over business.

In the 1980s the main focuses of populist sentiment were bilingualism, cultural subsidies, gun control, the 1988 free trade agreement with the United States, and the Meech Lake and Charlottetown accords. Because of the high value populism places on the individual, and because of the mythological primacy of the individual and his or her "inalienable rights" in the United States, many of the populist arguments invoked United States examples, or even proposed directly that Canada should more closely resemble the United States. Canadian populism to a large extent widened the ongoing internal "war with the U.S." that has been a continuing part of Canadian politics.

The Christian fundamentalists who operate illegal television stations in Alberta, for example, import from the United States not only their programming but also their arguments about religious freedom. Anglophone-rights activists who complain about French being "shoved down their throats" are not only mistaking the nature of their exposure to French in Canada but are imagining as the alternative a homogenously anglophone society such as that implied by United States currency or cornflakes boxes. The gun clubs that argue against increased controls over Canadian guns and ammunition, and against proposals that gun possession be prohibited except in rural areas, import many of their guns and their arguments about gun owners' "rights" from the United States and its ambiguous constitutional provision about the "right to bear arms." In fact, Canadians have no "right" to own firearms, any more than they have a "right" to a driver's licence, a right to consume alcohol, a right not to encounter French on their soup cans, or a right to shop in the United States. Under Canadian law such things are at best privileges granted by society, which citizens have the "right" to seek and the state the right to grant and regulate.

In the 1988 free trade debates much of the populist sentiment was directed to perceptions that the tariff-protected state disadvantaged individuals by forcing them to pay artificially high prices for goods in order to shelter both industrial and cultural élites. Historically, this concept went back to the arguments made in the Maritimes since Confederation, and in the West at least since the 1920s, that a tariff-protected economy benefited Ontario and Quebec manufacturing by shielding them from American competition while forcing the rural areas to pay inflated Canadian prices for manufactured goods cheaply available south of the border. Overlooked in this argument was the fact that a prosperous Central Canada stimulated Atlantic and Western economies by employing their surplus labour, investing in their industries, and buying their products. Nevertheless, individual consumers, forbidden to purchase automobiles thousands of dollars cheaper in the U.S. or clothing 30 per cent cheaper, saw these things as infringements of individual

286

rights rather than as strategies to protect and foster their economic opportunities. Similarly, the free trade agreement implications for increased competition between Canadian and American companies, and for increased pressure to equalize the tax burden on such companies in order to create a "level playing field" for them, were also confused by sentiments about individual rights. While such tax changes could in the long term endanger the Canadian social programmes they financed, Canadians who desired above all their "right" to lower prices in the short term chose to ignore such a possibility. In cultural areas also, the free trade agreement was misunderstood and misrepresented as an individual-rights issue. Sixty-two self-styled "Artists and Writers for Free Trade" announced in *The Globe and Mail* that they were "not fragile," that they could take the rough and tumble of international competition, and that they didn't want their ability to create to depend "upon the denial of economic opportunities" to their fellow citizens (19 November 1988).

Ideologically, these arguments resembled those implicit in the actions of the million or more Canadians who during the 1989–93 cross-border shopping crisis—possibly in the company of Paul Bernardo—exercised their individual "rights" to buy and smuggle back from the United States cheaper clothing, cigarettes, food, liquor, and gasoline. They also resembled those motivating the information-age individualists who cleverly and resourcefully obtained banned details from Karla Homolka's trial by fax, electronic mail, and satellite transmission.

In the case of the Meech Lake Agreement (1987) and the Charlottetown Accord (1992), much of the anger that was

287

directed against them, and incited against them by the
populist media, was based on the argument that these
were agreements constructed by the "élites" against the
wishes of the ordinary people. Paradoxically, the more
political parties and political leaders supported the agreements, the more this perception grew—that they were
products of conspiracies of privileged people against the
general citizenry. The fact that these leaders had been
elected by the citizenry in legitimate electoral processes—
that these so-called élites were the people's own creation—was lost amid a general sense of paranoia toward
political leaders. The more the general media pointed out
that fact and expressed their support of the agreements,
the greater became the populist conviction that it was all
part of a conspiracy of the privileged. Pressure for a referendum on the Charlottetown Accord—a referendum
being a direct-government instrument argued for in the
1920s by the Progressive Party and in the 1980s by the
Reform Party—grew directly from this suspicion of one's
own elected legislators. When after the October 1992
defeat of that referendum Justice Minister Kim Campbell
pointed out to a Harvard audience how the accord had
been favoured by all party leaders and by the educated
and the affluent, Kenneth Whyte in *The Globe and Mail*
continued in this paranoia, accusing her of élitism, "a politics of condescension," and of being "thick with the old
Mulroney gang" (20 March 1993).

Similar suspicion-laden images of an élite ganging up on
the ordinary people followed Mr. Justice Kovacs's ban,
which seems to have raised much the same feeling as
Campbell speaking at Harvard. Rick Salutin complained of
being ignored by a courtroom club that condescended to

288

the public as if they were children. Christie Blatchford called judges and lawyers as "secretive and clubby" as the "much despised" police brotherhood. Both, she suggested, were perceived to "band together" to protect their own. Allan Fotheringham raised images of a judicial bureaucracy that revelled in its own isolation from the public. Many of the contributors to the on-line computer discussion groups expressed similar anger toward a judge whom they believed had been condescending and contemptuous toward ordinary Canadians—not trusting them to be able to act as conscientious jurors, nor to deal with the horrific details of the murder in an adult way. Like the politicians who had negotiated the Charlottetown Accord, the judge had acted, in this scenario, like a pre-emptory and self-important parent, pretending to "know better" than a free and democratic citizenry.

Much of this kind of controversy has been created by the far-reaching penetration of Canada by American culture that government bodies like the CRTC have been attempting to deflect and regulate. Every day Canadians read more magazines about American political and cultural events than they read about their own. On television they encounter more images of America's anglophone culture than they encounter of their own bilingual one, more depictions of American police forces operating under American constitutional provisions than they encounter of Canadian police forces, more depictions of American courtroom practices than of Canadian ones. Consequently they are more familiar with the wording of American police "Miranda" cautions to an arrested person than they are with Canadian ones, with American understandings of individual rights, with American fears about crime, with

American traditional attitudes toward "big" government, with the mythology of the American state, than they are with the corresponding elements of Canada. If the crime rate grows in the United States, Canadians falsely assume it has grown in their own country and call for stiffer legal measures. When Kim Campbell told her Harvard audience that the defeat of the Charlottetown Accord was partly due to the ignorance of Canadians about their own history and system of government, which was known more to the élites than to the general population, she may have been condescending, but she was also largely correct. American domination of Canadian popular culture, through film, television, books, and magazines, has alienated many Canadians from their own histories, communities, and political traditions. It has made the Canadian judiciary appear remote and mysterious because in fact, by comparison to the availability of images of the American judiciary at work, they are remote and mysterious. It has made anglophone Canadians who venture into federal politics and meet actual living and breathing French-speaking compatriots, and come to understandings of their cultural goals, seem like bizarre "élites" to Canadians whose only media images of the world contain no Québécois, and represent "French" with Francois Mitterrand, croissants, and Jacques Cousteau.

A U.S. computer magazine is using technology to openly defy the publication ban on details of Karla Homolka's trial.

"Information wants to be free," said Louis Rossetto, *Wired*'s publisher and editor about his decision to put the article on the Internet. "We

wanted people to see what the article was that
resulted in our not being available to Canadians."
(*The Gazette* [Montreal], 27 March 1994)

While technology has enabled much of the American
domination of Canadian popular culture, it has also in
the recent events of the Karla Homolka trial proven to
have vastly empowered the resultant Americanized grass-
roots opinion in Canada, amplified the ability of the
Americanized citizen to act individually, and even subverted the power of a national state. *Alt.fan.karla-homolka*
has implied the coming into being of a global information
universe which may be dominated by American culture,
because of its size, but which may also be containable by
no national boundaries, not even American ones.

In such a global information universe the nation-state
promises to be threatened both from without by a new
borderless commercial culture and from within by individual citizens who hope for unfettered access to global
opportunities. It is here that the separate interests of
multinational corporations, which have lobbied for the
level playing fields of the GATT and for multilateral free
trade agreements, coincided with those of the Internet
computer culture and the populist individual. Although
some populist opinion may have been enraged by D'Arcy
Jenish's privileged access to the Internet—as an employee
of *Maclean's*—by and large the *alt.fan.karla-homolka*
Internet users have displayed the same populist attitudes
toward restricted freedom of data as prairie populists have
displayed toward gun control or parliamentary gover-
nance. *Alt.fan.karla-homolka*, in fact, appeared to make
visible the end of Internet as an élitist, self-governed

291

phenomenon and its beginning as a populist one—its movement out of the academy and into the world of restless, indignant, "ordinary people." Populism, it revealed, was now beginning to go seriously electronic, and to exhibit the same resentment toward authority and representative government that it had as a print phenomenon.

Moreover, the regulations that prevented the individual from importing goods indiscriminately into his or her home country, from receiving any television signal or computer data he or she wishes, or from owning various firearms, were also the regulations that inhibit multinational corporations from unrestricted sale into various national markets. Laws that forbid individuals from importing overproof liquor, automatic rifles, or automobiles without adequate emission controls also prevent corporations from profiting from the import and sale of such products. Laws that keep television viewers from unrestricted access to foreign television signals or from establishing their own television stations also keep corporations from dominating the Canadian television market with cheaply purchased foreign programming and from monopolizing Canadian advertising revenue. This is why newspapers, like *The Globe and Mail* and the *Sun*, whose owners or investors have strong ties to the corporate sector, editorialize from time to time against CRTC regulation of television broadcasting, support free trade agreements, and oppose Mr. Justice Kovacs's ban as an infringement of individual liberty and of freedom of speech.

At the same time, however, because this new globalization of trade and information limits the power of national governments to legislate in some areas, it also limits the power of individual citizens to work and lobby for social change—an effect most populist thinkers seem blind to. Under the Canada–United States Free Trade Agreement, for example, the Canadian government cannot establish new social programmes without paying compensation to the American-owned companies that already provide those services for lost current and future profits. The expropriation of any American-owned business also requires compensation beyond fair market value. The prohibitive nature of such compensation appears to have effectively blocked the establishment of a government-operated automobile insurance programme in Ontario, and to prevent the renationalizing of any government services once they have been privatized and funded by American investment. Any future government of Alberta, for example, may be prevented under this provision from returning the retail selling of liquor to state control. In turn, the provision limits individual rights by making the efforts of individual citizens to lobby for such things as state-administered automobile insurance or possibly a national day-care system futile. (It also has the ironic consequence of offering greater protection for American investors than for Canadian ones.) Certain social choices previously open to citizens at provincial or national levels, such as having a government-administered automobile insurance system or establishing a national day-care system, have simply been foreclosed.

The lobbying avenues that remain open to citizens become increasingly difficult to navigate as goals that were previously attainable through municipal, provincial or national legislation now are achievable only by international agreement. National environmental standards are subject not only to the global spread of pollutants but also to trade agreements that limit national power to exclude particular products for environmental reasons. Ontario's efforts to exclude or discourage the sale of beer in cans in preference for beer in returnable bottles has faced serious challenges from the United States, which interprets it as a trade rather than environmental restriction. Various nations that have hoped to build or retain national car industries have been deluding themselves, according to Britain's *The Economist*.

> ...the car industry—along with such other areas of national championry as airlines, steel, chemicals and even stock exchanges—now stands in the way of two winds of change that pay no heed to borders: free trade and technology. The first, through organizations such as the European Union and the General Agreement on Tariffs and Trade, is opening up protected domestic markets to competitors from other countries; the second is calling into question whether a car company is needed to make cars at all. (1 February 1994)

In the United States, local lobbying to protect indigenous agriculture and industry from lower-priced Canadian products like steel, wheat, and softwood lumber may soon be rendered futile by new GATT rules that limit a nation-state's application of anti-dumping laws. Individual or group lobbies at an international level are not only expensive but require the mastering of volumes of new rules, procedures, and practices, which in turn are often so complex that they require teams of full-time lobbyists to understand and explore them. Canadian farmers, fearful that the new GATT provisions would prevent the Canadian government from maintaining egg, milk, wheat, and poultry marketing boards, sent demonstrators and lobbyists to Europe in 1993 in an attempt to influence GATT negotiations, and to establish links with European farmers.

Interestingly, the concept of knowledge-creation held by the early designers of usenet and the Internet closely resembles the contemporary economist's sense of how automobiles or chicken markets are produced. On the usenet, knowledge was created from the bottom up—by unplanned interactions between groups of researchers in different locations all contributing to the same discussion group. In the global economy, a chicken market is to be created by unregulated farmers growing chickens at the lowest possible cost, according to the best food, land, labour, and overhead prices offered by goods moving freely among a variety of countries. Automobiles are produced by the assembly of parts obtained from all over the world from the highest-quality and lowest-price producers. Place of production becomes nearly irrelevant to the actual nationality of the product, since most of the parts for the automobile, or the food and breeding stock of the chickens, may have come from other countries. On the usenet, the place where knowledge is created may in fact be impossible to determine. It may be a place somewhere in the intersecting wires and microwave flows between computers—one that in computerese is a "virtual" place, somewhere in "cyberspace."

Again, the *alt.fan.karla-homolka* newsgroup acted for the public as a high-profile symbol of these processes. It was mysterious—produced by ostensibly global forces as new and strange as those that threaten milk marketing boards and move Canadian jobs to the U.S., Malaysia, and Mexico. It was uncontrollable—it defied the jurisdiction of Canadian law as surely as the GATT subverted the power of Canadian and U.S. law. To the populist, it was delightfully rebellious, showing ordinary individuals thumbing their nose at judges and cabinet ministers. To the general public, however, it also offered the same sense of anonymity and impersonality as that offered by a multinational corporation. "Neal the Trial Ban Breaker" could as easily be two or ten people as one. It offered also the same kind of collective creativity—trial details contributed, critiqued, and elaborated on by a variety of people and assembled into a coherent, if rumour-laden, narrative—as that offered by the assembly of Volvo automobiles in Nova Scotia or of Hondas in Ontario.

In its actual content, however, *alt.fan.karla-homolka* appeared to be much more voyeuristic than political. While its organizers claimed to have had noble aims to protect freedom of information, most of the participants seemed more interested in savouring grisly details and anecdotes. Even the account of the "story behind the newsgroup" offered on the Internet by "Abdul, the electronic Gordon Domm" tended to emphasize its shocking and fame-creating aspects over its idealistic ones.

> At first there was a trickle, then there a torrent [sic]. "Alt.fan.karla-homolka" became a home for resident ban-breakers, as new rumors were posted regularly in the group. The most famous of these

early ban-busters was "Neal the Trial ban breaker." His rumors provided shocking insights into the trial that nobody was supposed to know anthing [sic] about, and made him a celebrity in Canadian newspapers such as the *Toronto Star* and the *Calgary Herald*.

"Abdul" went on to describe the newsgroup's activities not as social protest but as "ban-breaking and rumor-mongering." Overall, the tone and content of the newsgroup interaction implied less a general desire to change society than the pleasure of a small technology-linked group at being able to cock a snoot at authority.

The major contributions of detail were made by "Neal the Trial Ban Breaker," who claimed to be at best "sixth removed" from reliable information. His accounts were punctuated with comments of disgust, particularly toward Bernardo, and overtly declared Bernardo guilty. "Paul the pervert," he called him in reporting his first rumour, ██████ ██ ████████████████████████████████. These accounts tended to focus on macabre aspects of the murder, and make frequent reference to body fluids. They included the story about ████████████████████ ██████████████████████████████████████ ██████████████████████████████████████ ██████████████████████████████████████ ██████████████████████████████████████ ██████████████████████████████████████ ██████████████████████████████████████ ██████████████████████████████████████ ██████████████████████████████████████

███████████████████████████████████
███████████████████████████████████
███████████████████████████████████

████████████████████████. "Neal" was particularly
interested in the ████████████ of the case, several times
asserting██████████████████████████████████████
███████████████████████████████████
███████████████████████████████████
███████████████████████████████████
███████████████████████████████████
██████████████████████████████████.

   "Abdul the electronic Gordon Domm" had in contrast
much more interest in corpses and dismemberment. He
began his reports with a story that a shop technician from
Black and Decker had been brought in by police,███████
████. He followed with reports that████████████████.
███████████████████████████████████
███████████████████████████████████
███████████████████████████████████
███████████████████████████████████
███████████████████████████████████
██████████████████████████████████." He
reported that "████████████████████████████
███████████████████████." He too
appeared fascinated with the████████████████ of the murders,████████████████████████████████
████████but also that he believed Bernardo "had logged
hundreds of hours with his video camera" in stalking

298

various potential victims. Both he and "Neal" seem to have been engaged visually by the crimes, as if they were ███████████████████████████████████ ███████████████████████████████████ ██████████████████████████████

The most salacious detail "Lt. Starbuck" offered was a rumour that the flashlight with which Bernardo had been said to have beaten Homolka had been ██████████████ ███████████████████. He was interested much more in the general and dramatic aspects of the crime. Whereas the killers imagined by "Abdul" and "Neal" were█████ ████████████████████ who hide in a darkened house, those of "Starbuck" preyed throughout southern Ontario, possibly being responsible for disappearances and deaths of young women in Toronto and near Lake Huron.

Other contributors offered a variety of rumours. One, claiming to have a friend who knew the sister of someone who was in the courtroom, suggested that the police had seized██████████████████████ and that the Bernardo house had a soundproof room. The person added a story that the killers had ██████████████ ██████shortly after abducting her, so that evidence████ ████████████████. Another, claiming to know a friend who had a friend who knew a lawyer who had a colleague working on the case, alleged that Bernardo and Homolka had made "████████████████████████ ███████████. Two contributors said they had heard that the killers had███████████████████████████ ████████████████████████████████ █████████ One of these reported hearing this from a friend's wife who in turn had learned it from the police.

Another added that the veterinary clinic Homolka worked in had been burglarized, ███████████████ ███████████, around the time of the abductions, and had later "mysteriously burned down." Yet another contributor claimed to have heard that ███████████████ ███████████████████████ one of the victims. Another said that Mahaffy had died accidentally—"probably due to malnutrition."

None of the material on the newsgroup appears to have been contributed directly by people who were in the courtroom. Most seems to have been at least third-hand, and to have had alleged sources in police stations and law offices. Some of the stories—like ones that ███████ ████████████████████████████████████ ███████████████ "—seemed transparently fanciful. Others were at best consistent with publicly acknowledged facts, such as the one that alleged that Bernardo had "████████████████████████████████ ███████████████████████████████ "; Judge Kovacs had observed when sentencing Homolka that "extraordinary steps [had been] taken in an attempt to conceal evidence in the crime with respect to another offender" (*The Toronto Star*, 7 July 1993). While rumours also circulated, both in the media and in the newsgroup, that the American media had obtained most of its material from *alt.fan.karla-homolka*, the stories in the American media in fact did not often follow newsgroup versions. *The Washington Post* reported that ████████████ ████████████████████████████████ ████████, and had died in hospital. It reported that Bernardo had "████████████████████████████ ████████████████████████████ . It agreed with the newsgroup in reporting that among nine hundred pieces of evidence seized by the police from the Bernardo house, there were "████████████████ ████████████████████████████. It otherwise indicated that the trial had revealed "██████████████ █████████████," but chose not to disclose further detail. *Newsweek* repeated much of this report, adding that the trial details had included that "██████████████ ████████████████████████████████████ ███████." Perhaps from having perused *alt.fan.karla-homolka*, it also wrote that "[another] account said that, ██ ████████████████████████████████████ ████████████████████████████████████ ████████████."

Both Canadians and Americans, then, read accounts of the trial and of the murders that were not demonstrably accurate and in general could not be. Readers of the accounts in the U.K.'s London *Times* found confirmation only of Tammy Homolka's death and ██████████████ ████████████████████████████████████ ████████████████. Readers of the *Sunday Mirror* were told that ██████████████████████████████████ ████████████" and that she and Bernardo had been "[i]mplicated in the disappearance of several other young girls" (Miles, *Sunday Mirror*, 19 September 1993). Overall, the stories about the case offered by *alt.fan.karla-homolka* or by smuggled newspapers and magazines tended both to increase the range of what was suspected about Homolka and Bernardo and to destabilize the reliability of particular circulating facts. Not all the alleged and often contradictory "facts" could be true. Some seem to have been deliberately ignored by ostensibly reliable media. Some of the media's "facts" had at best been rumours on *alt.fan.karla-homolka*.

In the "FAQ"—an Internet "frequently asked questions" summary—written by "Abdul the electronic Gordon Domm" for new participants in *alt.fan.karla-homolka*, only on the ninth page did he offer any cultural or legal arguments about the ban. These he wrote under the heading "There are several reasons to oppose the publication ban." His first of three reasons was that the ban was "unenforceable": "Internet's electronic superhighway has irrevocably broken the ban, and that is reason enough to justify lifting it." This argument was tantamount to a Jack the Ripper arguing that criminal sanctions against murder should be lifted because the police had been unable to catch him, or to a wife-batterer arguing that a judge should not issue a restraining order against him because he would be unable to restrain himself from breaking it. His second reason was that the ban had "sensationalized this case beyond reasonable proportions" and caused "fact and rumor to become inseparable," and he pointed out that some of the information on the newsgroup was based "solely on rumor and hence unreliable." But again the argument was disingenuous—again he was using his own activities to justify lifting the ban. If he had not wished "fact and rumor" to have become confused, he could have helped achieve this by not contributing either fact or rumour to the newsgroup, and by not gathering them into his FAQ. Abdul's third reason was that the ban wrongly assumed "that people who know anything about this case are going to be unreliable jurors." "This is an insulting proposition," he asserted, echoing remarks that had been made by several journalists. This was the best of his arguments, but it was subverted by the general tone of disgust toward Paul Bernardo that had permeated the FAQ and much of the newsgroup. The newsgroup participants, who had come to know "something" about the case, seemed to detest "Paul the pervert." "Neal the Trial Ban Breaker" predicted that Bernardo would soon be "safely ensconced for the rest of his unnatural life behind bars." It is difficult to imagine that any of these people might make impartial jurors.

Alt.fan.karla-homolka was at best a symptom of populist unrest, and of its new joining with computer media, but not quite a sign of new populist power. Power was certainly available to its participants. Indeed, the Internet had proved that its global web of communications was virtually impossible for a single national judicial system to block. *Alt.fan.karla-homolka* could be blocked or deleted on particular university, government, or commercial computers, but its users could also employ a variety of electronic means to access directly the computer-news services of computers in other cities or countries. On many computer systems, each time *alt.fan.karla-homolka* was blocked, it reappeared like a new word on Charlotte's web: as *alt.pub-ban.homolka* or *alt.pub-ban*. Blocked from these, users could arrange to have "Abdul" set up an automatic mail feed from Finland, so that new information in *alt.fan.karla-homolka* was anonymously sent to them as private electronic mail as soon as it was posted.

But the power of *alt.fan.karla-homolka* was wasted, much like the power of many of the media, in voyeurism and self-congratulatory vanity. Rather than marshalling a philosophical challenge against the assumptions of Judge

303

Kovacs and of the judicial system of which he was a part, the participants revelled in the supposed possession of forbidden facts, and imagined themselves undertaking a more exciting and important mission than they were. While they apologized for many of the stories being hearsay (often hearsay at fourth or fifth hand), and prefaced many of their remarks with intriguing tags like "this is almost certainly true," "don't know how accurate these are," or "this is unsubstantiated rumor," they also applied little critical intelligence or skepticism to them. Their reservations that what they were saying was rumour served mainly to make them feel free to report more elaborately grisly narratives. Despite the protestations that they were serving a noble social function by challenging the ban, the result of the challenge was little different in quality than tabloid coverage of the Bobbitt and Simpson cases. From *The Toronto Sun*, with Michele Mandel's bodice-ripping account of the murderer's delight in having seized "Kristen," and Scott Burnside's protestations that he had been "muzzled," *alt.fan.karla-homolka* took a reader to ███████████████████████████ ███████████████████████████████ ██████████████████████. The former accounts, appearing in an unrestrictedly public space and open to public challenge and scrutiny, were arguably preferable.

Surprisingly, the populist belief that computer users are too wise to need administrative supervision is visible in *alt.fan.karla-homolka* only in its effect and not at all as an articulated philosophy. There have been few railings against the arrogant assumptions of an élitist and cloistered judiciary, and few exhortations to participants to act responsibly or with "correct manners" or "proper netiquette." But

the effects of this populism were significant. The participants felt unrestricted by Judge Kovacs's ban. They felt
free to act out of their own separate wisdoms. They took
pride in being "ban-breakers" and "ban-busters" and "trial
ban-breakers." In this they echoed the certainty of the
more traditionally populist non-electronic Gordon
Domm, sentenced to a $4,000 fine for having made a
public spectacle of his ban defiance, and still proclaiming
that there should be "no place for secrecy" in the
Canadian court system. In some ways their pride resembled that of Alberta Christian fundamentalist broadcasters
who have defied the CRTC. It was reminiscent also of the
pride of Sons of Freedom Doukhobours, in British
Columbia during the 1960s, being led to jail naked and
singing hymns for their protests against Canadian laws, or
the pride of some Canadian politicians in defying conventional Canadian social wisdoms and cutting back on
health and educational funding.

Yet symbolically the defiance of *alt.fan.karla-homolka*
was extraordinarily powerful, and suggested both a new
technological empowerment for traditional Canadian
populism and an evolution if not transformation in
Internet culture. For the disdain for political and administrative authority that had marked usenet and Internet in
earlier years had been that of a large, well-educated
minority, secure about its position in society but cynically
aware of its relative powerlessness in relationship to its
academic and corporate employers. The discontent of
Canadian populism had been that of farmers and workers
and small-business people who felt themselves to be out-
siders to the political system. Only recently had its causes
been joined by briefcase carriers of *Alberta Report* and

Saturday Night and their hopes for a reduction in state regulation. *Alt.fan.karla-homolka* revealed a new convergence of these various kinds of outsidership. The opening of Internet to a much larger range of users had provided an unexpected and relatively spectacular new place for stubborn resistance to state power.

> A general tax revolt. If everyone stopped paying at the same time, while initiating a constant harassment of politicians, some change might result. In other words, our very own Boston Tea Party. I have been told by an economist friend that throughout history tax revolts have started when taxation has exceeded 33 per cent. This level has been exceeded. So, who is going to head this revolt? Are you? (Douglas Davis, president of D.A.C. Davis Investment Counsel Inc., "Don't trust politicians with the business of government," *The Globe and Mail*, 14 July 1994.)

In the upstairs study of the Port Dalhousie "fairy-tale" bungalow, perhaps only feet from where Mahaffy and French were kept prisoner, sat a desk with a computer and printer. In 1993 only 30 per cent of Canadian households possessed computers—the primary requirement for participation on the Internet. Paul Bernardo, Neal the Trial Ban Breaker, and Abdul the electronic Gordon Domm were all part of that 30 per cent. For Bernardo, the computer went with his Nissan 240SX, his University of Toronto Bachelor of Commerce degree, and his Generation X lifestyle of rented affluence and part-time self-employment. It had at best a marginal connection to his alleged smuggling activities which marked him as an independent and rebellious thinker, and possibly no connection to the anti-authoritarianism of *alt.fan.karla-homolka*, or to populist urgers of tax revolts like Douglas Davis—who often cloak their potentially anti-democratic activities in pretences of democracy and civic service.

There is little doubt that the person who took Leslie Mahaffy and Kristen French for his idiosyncratic pleasures was also a kind of self-administering entrepreneur, acting if not outside the rules of Canada Customs at least far outside democratically legislated Canadian criminal law. The legal system that Canadians hoped would catch and punish Mahaffy and French's killer is also the legal system that both killer and *alt.fan.karla-homolka* defied.

The home of Karla Homolka's parents in St. Catharines.

LIFE AFTER
KARLA

The abduction and sex-slaying of two young women, each of whom had barely emerged from childhood, not only provoked the outrage such crimes deserve but, as its media and legal narratives unfolded, touched raw nerves across an already unsettled Canadian nation. The two victims were not only the daughters of two southern Ontario communities but were also everyone's imaginary daughters—in their separate ways hopeful, attractive, idealistic, adventurous, trusting. Between the two they encompassed a range of adolescent testing of limits familiar to most parents, from academic success and athleticism to rebellion and defiant attempts to define a separate teenage community. But the people accused of their murders appeared also familiar to us. They were the yuppie couple of the nineties, Generation Xers, renting and imitating a lifestyle which the "real" yuppies of the eighties had come to believe was their due. Educated but not well-employed, ambitious but without clear opportunities on which to focus their ambitions, fascinated with the material symbols of success, Paul and Karla Bernardo were in many outward ways like numerous couples our families and our society had produced in a time when technological change redefined both industrial patterns and employment categories. Like hundreds of thousands of other young couples, the Bernardos were a childless, one-dog, one-computer, two-car, two-income middle-class family. Bernardo himself was, like many of his generation, underemployed, and like many office workers of the nineties, enabled to work at home by the computer revolution. Like a million or more Canadians, they were part of the general tax revolt and cross-border shopping phenomenon that had swept southern Canada in 1989–93. Like millions of Canadians also, they were part of the video revolution which saw people abandon the theatres and other public spaces for the seclusion of their living rooms and the palm-size entertainment of the video cassette.

Victims and accused were not only part of the same physical community, they were part of the same psychic and cultural community. Had Mahaffy or French lived long enough to marry, they might have had or wished for "fairy-tale" weddings similar to that of the Bernardos, and similar to weddings we and our parents and brothers and sisters have had or wished for. In news stories almost a year apart, reporters wrote that Kristen French had loved animals and wanted to be a veterinarian, and that Karla Homolka had loved animals and had gone to work for a veterinarian. Kristen French's dog waited in vain on that rainy 16 April 1992 for his mistress to return. The next year Karla Homolka's Rottweiler appeared in news photos "forlornly" at the Homolka front window watching his mistress leave for sentencing and jail. The parents of Mahaffy and French suffered pain in the courthouse for their lost daughters not all that differently from Homolka's parents a few benches away, with one of their three daughters also dead, and a second who would be forever a killer, a betrayer of her own gender and of the trust of her little sister. Overall, the crimes were in-family crimes, involving a general sense of white lower-middle-class family close to the Canadian imagined norm of what a family and its hopes and tensions consist of.

Even the discordant parts of this general family picture acted more to generalize the emerging portrait, and make it belong to most people. The fact that the "storybook" blond couple, with their Generation X fondness for technology and consumer goods, were the offspring of European immigrants—Bernardo a third-generation descendant of Portuguese immigrants, Homolka a second-generation descendant of Czech immigrants—broadened rather than differentiated their images. These were families that had struggled and succeeded, coming to own modern homes and swimming pools that most Canadians could admire. Leslie Mahaffy's teenage rebellions, and the family counselling that had ensued, were a part of the experiences of many families. The alleged dysfunctionality of the Bernardo family, even with the conviction of Paul's father for sexual offences, did not seem astonishingly unusual in a period in which crimes of incest, pedophilia, child abuse, and spousal abuse are routinely recounted in the media, and in which experts tell us that unreported similar crimes are up to ten times as numerous as the reported offences. Most Canadians now not only know people who have done such things but also can identify moments in their own lives when they were threatened with family crime, or experienced themselves at least some weak feelings of temptation to commit it. They know that human beings like "us" are susceptible to inflicting and enduring such abuse—that it is, like it or not, in our families.

But although these family aspects of the case allowed ample openings for Canadians in general to identify with its actors and events, these opportunities were almost universally ignored. Instead, it is the way in which the case's treatment and legal aspects engage the national situation of Canada and similar nation-states in the 1990s that gives it its most powerful symbolic importance. For although the victims and the accused look astonishingly like ordinary citizens, this very ordinariness was quickly used against itself—used to reinvent them as mythological and media figures. Especially transformative was the media's treatment of two social tragedies as provocative and continuing entertainments. Here the young women were changed into exploited sexual bodies as surely by journalists as they had in more horrifying ways by their killers. At an extreme, salacious media evocations of exquisite pain, ruptured taboos, and violently broken bodies offered readers seductively pornographic pleasures. Yet these extremes also lead back to the unfortunately familiar—to the mediatization of the news into the kinds of infotainment that have become increasingly a norm on North American television, and to the mediatization of our own lives where we are no longer certain whether we are acting or experiencing life. The accused killers became darkly romantic figures, and merged with transgressive celebrities—Madonna, Ted Bundy, Roseanne, Jeffrey Dahmer, Michael Jackson, O.J. Simpson—whose perceived "badness" leads millions in the 1990s to watch television and consume "instant" paperbacks and tabloid news sheets. Whether for celebrities, criminals, psychopaths, or fans, transgression and violence become quick and addictive antidotes for anxiety and boredom.

The concurrent investigation of the murders by the media and by the police, the media's mythologizing of both victims and accused killers, the media's perverse eroticization of the crimes, and the extraordinary ineffectiveness of the publication ban all announced to Canadians that something fundamental had changed in our culture. Some new multinational, private-enterprise system of interpretation seemed to be about to take over aspects of their lives that had previously been interpreted by our national and provincial governments, by our laws, and by historic cultural traditions. In a sense, if it could transform the lives and deaths of Mahaffy and French and the lives of Bernardo and Homolka into what the *Sunday Mirror* called "████████████████████████," it could take over the lives of anyone. This new system of interpretation, primarily a commercial one of fantasy entertainment, was welcomed by some Canadians as a kind of carnival de-throning of old and arrogant rulers— of black-cloaked judges and bureaucratic governments. But it was also feared by many others who recognized that individual Canadians had no political rights within this new system. There was no supranational parliament to which Canadians could elect representatives to help pass laws to control American media that broadcast into Canadian space, or to regulate an emerging "information highway" that appeared to operate without boundaries, formal rules, or ethical guidelines.

In the business world, the lowering of trade barriers through GATT and various multilateral and bilateral agreements had created a global environment in which investors and corporations could pick and choose which set of government regulations they wished to be governed by—often choosing the most minimal. If banking regulations and taxation policies were too restrictive in Britain or Canada, they could move to the Channel Islands or to

the Turks and Caicos Islands. If pressure on the illicit nar-
cotics trade was too great in Panama, the merchants could
move to Haiti or the Bahamas. If environmental requirements were too expensive to meet in Canada or the
United States, a manufacturer could relocate in Mexico. If
labour-code and social-welfare provisions in Canada
required higher rates in compensation than in the United
States, entire factories could be moved south of the
border. If safety and labour regulations governing fishing
or merchant ships were onerous in Canada, the United
States, or western Europe, a ship could be reregistered in
Liberia or Panama, or could be sold to an eastern
European buyer and leased back to work in North
American waters. The effect of these possibilities was not
only to erode the legislative power of national states, but
also to create a de facto or "virtual" non-national space in
which multinational companies could operate without
being subject to any regulation. In effect, the multinational companies were reaching a space beyond politics—
a space beyond which individual citizens could exercise
regulatory control through their elected national representatives. There was an overwhelming need developing
around the world for some kind of supranational democratic form of government, but as yet no popular sentiment
developing for such government. Popular sentiment, in
fact, was against supranational government, such as that
of the European Community, and against large federa-
tions such as the Soviet Union, and in parts of Canada
against even the concept of a strong federal state.

While most Canadians had difficulty understanding
how this might be happening to them—how their furni-
ture-manufacturing jobs might be moving to Tennessee,

or their fish might be caught by Liberian-flag fishing ships not governed by any international agreement, or their auto-plant jobs might be moved to Mexico where workers had no health-care benefits and where factories faced few pollution controls—they could understand the lack of control anyone seemed to have over Internet publication of *The Washington Post* or over the speculations of *alt.fan.karla-homolka*. When the anonymous woman asked D'Arcy Jenish "Who are you?" the hidden question was about an apparently new class of citizen, one for whom national rules no longer applied, and international rules were non-existent. The virtual unregulated space which multinational corporations had found was now also a space available to individual Canadians. This space was cyberspace, and it was soon, the nation's media proclaimed, to be a space occupied not merely by corporations using CompuServe or amateur criminologists on Internet, but by multinational "information providers" who were about to combine it with telephone and cable-vision to create an "information superhighway."

Although journalists like Jenish could apparently already import and export information with as much impunity as Paul Bernardo had allegedly been able to move tobacco and liquor across the Niagara border, or Kristen French into his home, and individuals on the Internet could spread their rumours, leaks, and insinuations of Bernardo's guilt from Canada to Finland and back again, in the future loomed even greater incursions beyond Canadian national control. *Alt.fan.karla-homolka* signals not only the growing inability of Canada's courts to enforce their own orders, but also the Canadian government's inability to enforce its own sovereignty, thus signalling the growing impossibility for Canadians to define their own nation. Whether Canadians approved or disapproved of the publication ban, the fact that there could be one was visibly outside their own determinations.

Such is the social crisis represented by the Homolka case and the media treatment it has received. In almost every stage of the case, Canadians have been made to feel as if the events were out of their control, and even beyond the control of the police forces and lawmakers whom they employ. In the early stages the media presented a portrait of the police as inefficient and inept, and of themselves— employees of private publishing corporations—as more knowledgeable and intelligent. For almost two years southern Ontario young women seemed to be at open risk. Here and in the arrest and trial stages, the media transformed both the victims and the alleged killers, whom Canadians might otherwise have identified with as individuals, and whom to some extent they continued to identify with in terms of class and generation, into saints and fairy-tale monsters beyond social understanding or influence. The victims and the accused were not products of Canadian society, the media implied, nor people who reflected back our own beliefs and aspirations. These were people, particularly the alleged killers, who seemed ordinary, the media implied, only because they were extraordinary. Bernardo and Homolka's resemblance to ourselves was especially to be dismissed, a diabolical contrivance. Their fairy-tale house concealed a witch and a monster. Their evil, the media argued, was sensational because it was inhuman. It was alien, and would have occurred no matter what Canadians had done, or what kind of culture they had constructed. Canadians were therefore free of responsibility for any part of what had happened.

Canadians' own cultural history offered few socially useful understandings of such cruel killings, and tended itself to attribute them to outside powers or people from other cultures. Meanwhile, a subtly Americanized Canadian media, together with intrusions from the United States itself, offered further portrayals of the killers as monsterized versions of Mattel Corporation's Barbie and Ken dolls, as if they had been toys-gone-bad rather than individuals whom Canadian society had helped shape and educate. In the latter stages, with a publication ban flouted by two small Canadian publications, microfilm copies of ban-breaking foreign newspapers and magazines in most major Canadian libraries, American newspaper accounts of Homolka's trial available on CompuServe and other Internet databases—accessible even through the Ontario government's own civil service computers—and with potentially hundreds of thousands of Canadians able to "enjoy" the earnest pornographies of *alt.fan.karla-homolka*, Canadians visibly had no control over their own story or ability to enforce an order of their own legal system.

While negotiators from the United States Department of Commerce have argued repeatedly that Canada's attempts to protect its cultural resources constitute an impediment to trade, and that what Canadian negotiators call "culture" is simply a collection of exportable commodities like films, television shows, magazines, and recordings, the Bernardo–Homolka case has demonstrated that this is definitely not so. The virtually uncontrolled export of culture into a distinct national space has handicapped here the ability of Canadians both to respond socially to the crimes and to administer their own understandings of justice.

The increasing globalization of trade, manufacturing, banking, and information exchange promises even further incursions into national sovereignty. While national sovereignty is not necessarily a good in itself, it is at present the only route through which individuals can exercise democratic rights to elect their legislators, decide social policy, administer a judiciary, and in general construct the social space in which they live. Increased globalization at present brings only an increase in the extent to which individual lives are controlled by de facto governments they have not elected and over whose policies they have little if any control. It is one thing for nation-states to lose sovereignty to elected bodies like the European parliament, or even to the United Nations with its fiction of justly constructed representation of national governments; it is quite another to lose it to vast commercial enterprises or to utopian anarchies like the present Internet. The challenge which the Homolka case raises to countries like Canada is how to re-establish democracy in an age of globalization. If economies, cultures, and information are no longer to be nationally defined, can political representation afford to remain merely national? Or are Canadians, like much of the world already, destined to become merely citizens of an amoral web of global corporations—additional actors in "████████████████ ███████████"? The answers can mean little now for Leslie Mahaffy or Kristen French, but a great deal for people still trying to shape their own lives in places like Burlington, Niagara Falls, and St. Catharines.

318

ENDNOTES

THE MARTYRDOM OF VIRGINS

1. Julia Kristeva, *Powers of Horror: An Essay on Abjection*, tr. Leon S. Roudiez (New York: Columbia University Press, 1982 [1980]), 3.

2. Kristeva, *Powers of Horror*, 155.

THE FANS OF KEN AND BARBIE

1. John Fiske, "The Cultural Economy of Fandom," in *The Adoring Audience: Fan Culture and Popular Media*, ed. Lisa A. Lewis (London: Routledge, 1992), 30.

2. Stephen Leacock, *Sunshine Sketches of a Little Town* (Toronto: McClelland and Stewart, 1960 [1931]), 123.

3. Glen O. Gabbard, *Psychodynamic Psychiatry in Clinical Practice: The DSN-IV Edition* (Washington, D.C.: American Psychiatric Press, 1994), 533–34.

4. Gabbard, *Psychodynamic Psychiatry*, 540–43.

5. James Chatto, "The Bernardo Industry," *Toronto Life*, May 1994, 58.

THE MURDERER IN THE MIRROR

1. Samuel Hearne, *A Journey from Prince of Wales's Fort in Hudson's Bay, to the Northern Ocean...in the Years 1769, 1770, 1771 and 1772* (London: Strahan and Cadell, 1795), 143–44.

2. Hearne, *A Journey from Prince of Wales's Fort*, 152.

3. Hearne, *A Journey from Prince of Wales's Fort*, 153–54.

4. Hearne, *A Journey from Prince of Wales's Fort*, 154.

5. Hearne, *A Journey from Prince of Wales's Fort*, 154–55.

6. Hearne, *A Journey from Prince of Wales's Fort*, 156.

7. John Richardson, *Wacousta* (Toronto: McClelland and Stewart, 1967 [1831]), 248.

8. Richardson, *Wacousta*, 134.

9. Richardson, *Wacousta*, 274.

10. Robin Mathews, "The Wacousta Factor," in *Figures in a Ground*, eds., Diane Bessai and David Jackel (Saskatoon: Western Producer Prairie Books, 1978), 296.

11. Mathews, "The Wacousta Factor," 297.

12. George Bowering, *Caprice* (Toronto: Viking, 1987), 17.

13. Bowering, *Caprice*, 17–18.

14. Bowering, *Caprice*, 18.

15. Morley Callaghan, *The Loved and the Lost* (Toronto: Macmillan, 1951), 93–94.

16. Frederick Philip Grove, *Settlers of the Marsh* (Toronto: McClelland and Stewart, 1966 [1925]), 37.

17. Grove, *Settlers of the Marsh*, 220.

18. Grove, *Settlers of the Marsh*, 224.

19. Grove, *Settlers of the Marsh*, 225.

20. Grove, *Settlers of the Marsh*, 225.

21. Hugh MacLennan, *Each Man's Son* (Boston: Little, Brown, 1951), 232.

22. MacLennan, *Each Man's Son*, 233.

23. Adele Wiseman, *The Sacrifice* (Toronto: Macmillan, 1956), 302.

24. Wiseman, *The Sacrifice*, 303.

25. Sheila Watson, *The Double Hook* (Toronto: McClelland and Stewart, 1959), 100.

26. Watson, *The Double Hook*, 115.

27. MacLennan, *Each Man's Son*, 232.

28. Neil Boyd, *The Last Dance: Murder in Canada* (Toronto: Seal Books, 1990), x.

29. Margaret Atwood, *Bodily Harm* (Toronto: McClelland and Stewart, 1981), 15.

30. Atwood, *Bodily Harm*, 14.

31. Atwood, *Bodily Harm*, 117.

32. Atwood, *Bodily Harm*, 210.

33. Atwood, *Bodily Harm*, 211.

34. Atwood, *Bodily Harm*, 211.

35. Atwood, *Bodily Harm*, 289.

36. Atwood, *Bodily Harm*, 293.

37. Atwood, *Bodily Harm*, 290.

38. Atwood, *Bodily Harm*, 29.

39. Margaret Atwood, *The Handmaid's Tale* (Toronto: McClelland and Stewart, 1985), 42.

40. Atwood, *The Handmaid's Tale*, 43.

41. Atwood, *The Handmaid's Tale*, 289–90.

42. Atwood, *The Handmaid's Tale*, 291–92.

43. Atwood, *The Handmaid's Tale*, 38.

44. Bowering, *Caprice*, 126.

AT WAR WITH THE U.S.

1. George Bowering, *At War with the U.S.* (Vancouver: Talonbooks, 1974), 5.

2. Susanna Moodie, *Roughing It in the Bush* (Toronto: McClelland and Stewart, 1989 [1852]), 137.

3. Moodie, *Roughing It in the Bush*, 137.

4. Moodie, *Roughing It in the Bush*, 411.

5. Moodie, *Roughing It in the Bush*, 501.

6. Thomas Chandler Haliburton, *The Clockmaker* (Toronto: McClelland and Stewart, 1958 [1836]), 48.

7. Haliburton, *The Clockmaker*, 51.

8. Haliburton, *The Clockmaker*, 48.

9. Haliburton, *The Clockmaker*, 73.

ALT.FAN.KARLA-HOMOLKA

1. Eric Braun, *The Internet Directory* (New York: Fawcett, 1994), ix.

2. Braun, *The Internet Directory*, xxi–xxii.

3. Braun, *The Internet Directory*.

BIBLIOGRAPHY

American Psychiatric Association. *Diagnostic and Statistical Manual of Mental Disorders*. Fourth Edition. Washington, D.C., 1994.

Alaton, Salem. "Why does the Homolka case thrill us so?" *The Globe and Mail*, 17 July 1993: D3.

Atwood, Margaret. *Bodily Harm*. Toronto: McClelland and Stewart, 1981.

_____. *The Handmaid's Tale*. Toronto: McClelland and Stewart, 1985.

_____. *Lady Oracle*. Toronto: McClelland and Stewart, 1976.

_____. *Surfacing*. Toronto: McClelland and Stewart, 1972.

_____. *Survival*. Toronto: Anansi, 1972.

Benjamin, Walter. *Illuminations*. New York: Harcourt Brace Jovanovich, 1972 [1958].

Bowering, George. *At War with the U.S.* Vancouver: Talonbooks, 1974.

_____. *Caprice*. Toronto: Viking, 1987.

Boyd, Neil. *The Last Dance: Murder in Canada*. Toronto: Seal Books, 1990.

Braun, Eric. *The Internet Directory*. New York: Fawcett, 1994.

Callaghan, Morley. *The Loved and the Lost*. Toronto: Macmillan, 1951.

Canetti, Elias. *Crowds and Power*. Translated by Carol Stewart. New York: Viking, 1962.

Chatto, James. "The Bernardo Industry." *Toronto Life*, May 1994: 50-58.

Cohen, Leonard. *Beautiful Losers*. Toronto: McClelland and Stewart, 1966.

Cooley, Dennis. *Bloody Jack*. Winnipeg: Turnstone Press, 1984.

Desbarats, Peter. "Publicity ban ignores modern realities." *The London Free Press*. 11 December 1993: E2.

Erwin, Campbell. "██████████." *The Daily Victorian.* ████ ████ .

Finkle, Derek. "The *Current Affair* Affair." *The Globe and Mail*. 4 December 1993: D1, D5.

_____. "Six Pack." *Quill and Quire*. May 1994:

Fiske, John. "The Cultural Economy of Fandom." In *The Adoring Audience: Fan Culture and Popular Media*. Edited by Lisa A. Lewis. London: Routledge, 1992: 30-49.

Fotheringham, Allan. "A democratic society can't tolerate Homolka ban." *The Financial Post*, 18 December 1992: 15.

_____. "In the case of Homolka ban, the law is a farce." *The Financial Post*, 18 December 1992: S3.

_____. "Judge's ruling on Homolka trial an exercise in naiveté." *The Financial Post*, 10 July 1993: S3.

Frye, Northrop. *The Bush Garden*. Toronto: Anansi, 1971.

Gabbard, Glen O. *Psychodynamic Psychiatry in Clinical Practice: The DSM-IV Edition*. Washington, D.C.: American Psychiatric Press, 1994.

Gleick, Elizabeth, Fannie Weinstein, Scott Burnside, and Alan Cairns. "Bloody Wedding." *People*, 22 November 1993: 118.

The Globe and Mail. "Of feeding frenzies and fair trials" (editorial). 6 December 1993: A14.

_____. "A weak excuse to close a courtroom" (editorial). 7 July 1993: A18.

Goldie, Terry. *Fear and Temptation: The Image of the Indigene in Canadian, Australian, and New Zealand Literatures*. Montreal: McGill-Queen's University Press, 1989.

Greenspan, Edward. "The media on trial: guilty or not guilty." *The Globe and Mail*, 26 May 1994: A21.

Grove, Frederick Philip. *Settlers of the Marsh*. Toronto: McClelland and Stewart, 1966 [1925].

Haliburton, Thomas Chandler. *The Clockmaker*. Toronto: McClelland and Stewart, 1958 [1836].

Hearne, Samuel. *A Journey from Prince of Wales's Fort in Hudson's Bay to the northern ocean...in the years 1769, 1770, 1771 and 1772*. London: Strahan and Cadell, 1795.

Jenish, D'Arcy. "Cashing in on tragedy." *Maclean's*, 8 November 1993: 48.

_____. "Leaks in a gag order." *Maclean's*, 13 December 1993: 16-18.

Kristeva, Julia. *Powers of Horror: An Essay on Abjection.* Translated by Leon S. Roudiez. New York: Columbia University Press, 1982 [1980].

Laframboise, Donna. "Tobacco teaches a lesson." *The Toronto Star*, 2 May 1994: A21.

Leacock, Stephen. *Sunshine Sketches of a Little Town.* Toronto: McClelland and Stewart, 1960 [1931].

Lynde, Adam. "Money motivates the media." *The London Free Press*, 12 January 1994: B7.

Macintyre, Ben. "Murder that dare not speak its name." *The Times*, 6 December 1993.

Mackie, Richard. "High taxes feed defiance of law." *The Globe and Mail*, 26 January 1994: A4.

MacLennan, Hugh. *Each Man's Son.* Boston: Little, Brown, 1951.

Mandel, Michele. "To catch her killers." *The Toronto Sun*, 26 July 1992: 35-38.

Mathews, Robin. "The Wacousta Factor." In *Figures in a Ground.* Edited by Diane Bessai and David Jackel. Saskatoon: Western Prairie Producer Books, 1978: 295-316.

Mathias, Philip. "In Canadians' eyes, Homolka has yet to be tried." *The Financial Post*, 10 July 1993: S2.

McFadden David. "U.S. Tourists." *A Knight in Dried Plums.* Toronto: McClelland and Stewart, 1975: 54-55.

Miles, Tim. "███████." *Sunday Mirror.* ███████.

Moodie, Susanna. *Roughing It in the Bush.* Toronto: McClelland and Stewart, 1989 [1852].

Moss, John. *Sex and Violence in the Canadian Novel.* Toronto: McClelland and Stewart, 1974.

The New York Times. "A Bad Gag Order in Canada" (editorial). 4 December 1993: 20.

Northey, Margot. *The Haunted Wilderness: The Gothic and Grotesque in Canadian Fiction.* Toronto: University of Toronto Press, 1976.

Nowell, Iris. "Don't shoot the panelist: reflections on an angry audience." *The Globe and Mail*, 3 April 1994: A13.

Posner, Michael. "A Town in Limbo." *Chatelaine*, February 1994: 29-33.

Pron, Nick, and Kevin Donovan. *Crime Story*. Toronto: Seal Books, 1992.

Reaney, James. *The Donnellys*. Victoria: Press Porcépic, 1983.

Richardson, John. *Wacousta*. Toronto: McClelland and Stewart, 1967 [1832].

Sheppard, Robert. "Homolka ban isn't about free speech." *The Globe and Mail*, 6 December 1993: A15.

Sherizen, Sanford. "Social Creaton of Crime News." In *Deviance and Mass Media*. Edited by Charles Winick. Beverly Hills: Sage Publications, 1978: 203-224.

Smith, Jacqueline. "███████████████████████ ████████." *The Sunday Times*, ███████████████.

The St. Catharines Standard. "A disappointing ruling" (editorial). 6 July 1993: C6.

————. "Listen to the people" (editorial). 8 July 1993: C8.

————. "Righteous Outrage" (editorial). 7 July 1993: C6.

Swardson, Anne. "████████████████." *The Washington Post*, ███████████.

Tordorov, Tzvetan. *The Fantastic*. Translated by Richard Howard. Ithaca, N.Y.: Cornell University Press, 1975 [1970].

The Toronto Star. "Unshackle the media in the Homolka case" (editorial). 1 December 1993: A20.

The Toronto Sun. "Contemptible" (editorial). 7 July 1993: 43.

Valpy, Michael. "When is a ban not necessarily a ban?" *The Globe and Mail*, 30 December 1993: A2.

The Washington Post. "Canada: Crime and Censorship" (editorial). 4 December 1993: A18.

Watson, Russell. "████████████████." *Newsweek*, ██████ ██████.

Watson, Sheila. *The Double Hook*. Toronto: McClelland and Stewart, 1959.

White, E.B. *Charlotte's Web*. New York: Harper and Row, 1980 [1952].

Wiseman, Adele. *The Sacrifice*. Toronto: Macmillan, 1956.

INDEX